THE ONE-PAGE INVESTING PLAN

THE ONE-PAGE INVESTING PLAN

START SIMPLE, STAY PATIENT, BUILD SERIOUS WEALTH

SCOTT PHILLIPS

WILEY

First published in 2026 by John Wiley & Sons Australia, Ltd

ISBN: 978-1-394-44688-9

NATIONAL LIBRARY OF AUSTRALIA

A catalogue record for this book is available from the National Library of Australia

Registered Office
John Wiley & Sons Australia, Ltd. Level 4, 600 Bourke Street, Melbourne, VIC 3000, Australia

For details of our global editorial offices, customer services, and more information about Wiley products visit us at www.wiley.com.

Wiley also publishes its books in a variety of electronic formats and by print-on-demand. Some content that appears in standard print versions of this book may not be available in other formats.

Cover design by Wiley
Cover art: © Max Blain/Adobe Stock Photos

Set in 11/16pt and Utopia Std by Straive, Chennai, India.

SKY10164910_080726

For Peter and Ian. You were my inspiration in writing this book.
And for Ruth. Thank you for believing in me.

CONTENTS

About Scott Phillips		*ix*
Introduction		*xi*
1	Why invest? And why investing works	1
2	Money myths and the stories we tell ourselves	15
3	The real enemy: You(r brain)	29
4	The magic of compounding	43
5	Why 'investing' eats 'trading' for breakfast	59
6	Risk (the scary chapter)	77
7	The building blocks of wealth	99
8	Getting started, where you are, with what you have	117
9	Keep investing simple, stupid	141
10	The WTF of ETFs	157
11	You're buying a business, not a stock	169
12	Buying, holding and ... selling?	185
13	The next crash is coming	207
14	Understanding fees and taxes (without being bored to death)	243

15 Control your money, don't let it control you 263

16 Retirement is the end...of the beginning 281

17 What future 'you' looks like 301

18 The secret of investing well 317

Acknowledgements *335*

References *337*

Index *341*

ABOUT SCOTT PHILLIPS

Scott Phillips is an investor, writer and commentator on business, markets and money. He is the chief investment officer of The Motley Fool Australia, where he has spent more than 15 years helping everyday Australians make the most of their money.

He has been a regular presence across television, radio and print media, and hosts the *Motley Fool Money* podcast.

Scott doesn't believe investing should be complicated. In fact, he thinks most of the difficulty comes not from the markets, but from our own behaviour: fear when prices fall, overconfidence when they rise and the constant temptation to do something when doing nothing would be better.

He is a strong advocate for financial literacy and believes that investing should be accessible to everyone — not just professionals or insiders. Much of his work is aimed at demystifying markets, explaining key concepts in plain English and helping people feel more confident about taking control of their financial future.

Through his writing, podcasting and media appearances, Scott tries to cut through the noise and offer something simpler, calmer and more useful: a way to think about money that actually works over time.

At the heart of Scott's philosophy is a simple belief: Investing isn't about being the smartest person in the room. It's about having the discipline to stick with a sensible plan, even when it feels uncomfortable.

He lives in the Southern Highlands of New South Wales with his family, and when he's not thinking about investing, he's probably planning his next road trip and spending as much time as possible away from screens, ideally somewhere outdoors.

scottphillips.com.au
X: @TMFScottP
Facebook: /scottphillipsmoney
Instagram: @tmfscottp

INTRODUCTION

Investing.

The word may excite or scare you.

Maybe you associate it with money, wealth, freedom and time.

Or maybe you're thinking about traders with six computer screens, the movie *Wall Street*, the 'smart money' having an edge, or those ads that promise an easy life if only you'll cough up a small fortune to buy their 'trading package'.

Me? I grew up in a house where we didn't talk about investing at all. I'm so old, I remember when Telstra was still called Telecom, and it and the Commonwealth Bank were still owned by the government, compulsory super was still years away and most people didn't own shares.

I vividly remember one time the share market was mentioned around the dinner table, and my dad told me it was a casino.

Fair enough, too. That's how it seemed to almost everyone. Still does to many. Each night, on the news, some talking head (that's me sometimes... how times have changed!) would tell viewers that the share market was up, then down, then up again.

And, every so often, the whole thing would keel over and have an almighty crash.

I wouldn't blame anyone whose instinctive reaction was 'No thanks... whatever investing is, I don't want any of it.'

But I got lucky.

I had a maths teacher in Year 8, Mr Moir, who taught us about compound interest.

I had an economics teacher in Year 11 and 12, Mr Barnett, who showed us the tables that contained the names, prices and other statistics of all of the companies whose shares traded on the Australian Securities Exchange (ASX). (Yes, kids, it was in the newspaper. I was in high school before the internet was a thing!)

And, you know all of that dodgy stuff I mentioned above? It's all true ... for some people.

If you want to treat the stock market like a casino, you'll probably get the same returns you get in a casino.

Not good.

If you want to be a Masters of the Universe day trader, and try to out-trade the super computers, be my guest. But I'm betting on the computers.

If you want to buy some fancy 'trading package' with dreams of living the high life, I wish you all the best ... but get ready to replace your full-time job with another full-time job — trading — with all of the stress and uncertainty that brings.

And I wouldn't bet on replacing your income.

But, here's the other thing: it doesn't have to be like any of that.

No, I'm not going to give you a better way to day trade or some way to outsmart the casino.

The no-shortcut shortcut

I'm going to offer you a very simple way to build long-term wealth.

No secret formula. No bells and whistles. No shortcuts. And almost no maths. (The maths I will tell you about is bloody simple!)

Bottom line: You already have enough knowledge to invest well, and to build a sizeable nest egg. My job — literally, my day job but also, in this case, in this book — is to put it all together in a simple and easy-to-follow way.

What follows, then, is the answer to the question I get all the time: 'How should I invest?'

It's the book I wish I'd read when I was 17.

It's the book I wished I could have given the tradies who asked me 'Is it possible?' and 'Can I really do it?'

It's the book I want my sons to read. (Maybe now I'm a published author, my 13-year-old will realise I might know what I'm talking about? Okay, probably not ...)

This is the knowledge I wish every Australian (and non-Australian, for that matter!) had so they could set themselves up financially.

Is that too lofty a goal? Probably. Is it too egotistical? Probably. But I'm giving it my best shot.

I really want you to set a course for financial freedom, and I hope what follows will give you both the map and a compass to steer by.

What I hope you will get out of this book

At its core, this book revolves around the One-Page Investing Plan. Everything you're about to read is designed to help you actually follow that plan when it matters most.

Because, at its core, investing well is really simple.

It is simply a case of understanding a few things, doing a few things properly and repeatedly, and being emotionally and mentally prepared for the journey.

That's literally it.

Everything else is just noise.

So why isn't this book just one page? Well, you wouldn't buy it, would you? I'm kidding, of course (though my publisher says that's still right!).

This is a book because there's a difference between giving an idea lip service and really committing to it.

There's a difference between *knowing* something and *understanding* it.

I can say 'Just do this', and you'll nod along. You might even do it.

But when it gets hard? When you don't want to? When your spouse/kid/neighbour tells you you're wrong, and you wonder if they're right?

Your conviction will waver. You'll doubt yourself. You'll wonder if you really should have listened to that Phillips bloke after all.

The answer is, I hope, this book. I hope by the time you've read it, you'll not just have a plan, but you'll have the conviction to stick with it, whichever way the wind blows, and you'll understand 'why'.

In my experience, that's the best way to make sure you follow through on what you're aiming to achieve.

If you just grab the One-Page Investing Plan, how do you know it's not just nonsense? You don't. You owe it to yourself to take responsibility for what you're setting out to achieve.

How not to use this book

Finances are personal. Guides like this book are very general. It's possible that you might be able to use fancy trading tricks and complex tax strategies. They might even work. Or, you know, not.

You could do better using huge leverage, or that leverage could turn your portfolio into a smouldering wreck.

My point? I have two.

First, this book isn't going to give you personal advice (or advice at all). It's going to help you, I hope, build a financial future based on solid principles. Sure, you could drive at risky speeds and get to your destination sooner. Other people have done it, and they were fine.

But is it worth the risk of not getting there at all if things go badly? No.

My aim is to get you there safely.

Second, someone else is going to point out that I didn't use this tax strategy or allow for that particular circumstance. Absolutely true. If your circumstances are such that you think you could benefit from personal financial advice, go for it. If the extra value is greater than the fees, you'd be mad not to get that advice. But this book isn't that. It's 'investing for the rest of us'—a guide to get you started, not a sharpening stone to give you a millimetre-perfect edge.

This book isn't about beating the market.

It's about behaving in a way that lets the market work for you.

Let's go

One of my favourite quotes, stolen from my wife's quote list, is:

> *If you want to build a ship, don't drum up people to collect wood and don't assign them tasks and work, but rather teach them to long for the endless immensity of the sea.*
>
> *Antoine de Saint Exupéry*[1]

It is my hope that this book will do both. I hope you'll see the potential power of investing, and be seized by the desire to see it fulfilled. When that does happen for you, I hope that this book is a touchstone for how to do it.

My aim, then, is to give you a really good map *and* a top-quality compass, but you're the skipper. Once you sail your portfolio over the horizon and can't see land any more, you need to take charge.

The map and compass will get you there, but only if (when!) you follow through.

It's my fervent hope that you will.

When you reach that distant shore, I hope you'll look back on today as the first leg of a long, occasionally scary, but wholly worthwhile journey with pride and a sense of accomplishment. I suspect *future you* will thank *current you* for embarking on it.

And I hope you'll pass the map and compass on to someone else who can use it, because the journey is best shared, and you'll want others to enjoy the same experience.

Thanks for reading. I can't wait to hear about your (long-term) success.

Now, before we talk about how to invest, we need to be clear about why you're doing it in the first place.

What really matters

- Investing isn't about finding a secret or beating everyone else, it's about following a sensible approach long enough for it to work.
- The biggest advantages most investors have are patience, discipline and time.
- You don't need brilliance or complexity to build wealth, but you do need a plan you're willing to stick with.

On the following page is the entire One-Page Investing Plan. That's it. You could stop reading now.

Except… there's a difference between 'knowing' something and really internalising it.

And that's why this is a book, not just a pamphlet.

Humans connect ideas to people, places and things. We learn not from bullet points, but from context.

I can say 'You should do this', and you might even think 'yeah, good idea'.

But, as they say, no plan survives contact with the enemy.

In investing, the enemy is the market, the economy… and ourselves.

The aim of this book is to give you the touchstones to help you stay the course, to help you understand and internalise, not just 'know'.

So, by all means, stop reading now, if you want. But I hope you'll find that by the time you see the plan, you'll have more conviction in the reason to follow it, and your ability to do so.

And by the time you see it the third time, I hope it confirms everything you've read, and cements both your ability and conviction to become a lifetime investor, with all of the knowledge and tools you'll need to succeed.

Here's to that success.

THE
ONE-PAGE INVESTING PLAN

INVEST. ADD. WAIT.

Know your why
Be clear about what you're investing for — security, freedom, generosity — and write it down so you have a north star when markets wobble.

Earn more over time
Grow your income through skills, effort and opportunity — you can only invest what you don't spend.

Pay yourself first
Automatically invest around 10 per cent of your take-home pay every single payday, before your lifestyle expands to consume it.

Spend intentionally
Focus on what truly matters, avoid lifestyle creep and protect the surplus that funds your future.

Build your 'oh, shit' fund
Hold three to six months of expenses in cash so emergencies never force you to sell.

Invest regularly
Add money on a schedule — no matter what.

Own diversified, productive assets
Buy diversified, broad, low-cost ETFs and/or quality shares representing real businesses earning real profits.

Reinvest and minimise costs
Reinvest dividends, avoid unnecessary trading, and keep fees and taxes as low as possible.

Stay the course — even in retirement
Expect volatility, shift gradually from growth to income when needed, but let compounding start (and keep) working for decades.

That's it. That's the whole thing. Everything else is details.

1

WHY INVEST? AND WHY INVESTING WORKS

> *Investing isn't about* getting *rich, it's about being free.*

Why invest? What a strange question. I mean, the answer is obvious, right?

Except, is it? Really?

For most of us, the instinctive answer will be 'to have more money'.

But why?

Sure, more money is better than less, all things considered. But the thing about investing is that to have more money later, you need to spend less now.

Yep, you want more money, but you have to spend less to get it.

And then there's the question of how much more.

Maybe just 'as much as possible' or $1 million or 'enough to buy that car/house/boat'.

Now, it's true that you don't need to be able to answer that question to make full use of this book. You can just follow the steps in the One-Page Investing Plan with as little as $1 or with a portfolio of $10 million.

So, why am I starting here?

Because, as you'll find out, investing well isn't about what you know. It's about your ability to do the simple things well, and continue to do them for months, years and decades.

It's not a test of intellect, but a test of temperament, with just a little maths thrown in.

As Warren Buffett, the brilliant investor and former CEO of investment company Berkshire Hathaway said: 'Once you have ordinary intelligence, what you need is the temperament to control the urges that get other people into trouble in investing.'[2]

We'll cover some of those urges (and their treatments) later on, but the first temperamental challenge is foundational.

As author Morgan Housel wrote, 'When most people say they want to be a millionaire, what they might actually mean is "I'd like to spend a million dollars." And that is literally the opposite of being a millionaire.'[3]

Here's my 'why'

Let me share my 'why' with you. I invest for these reasons, in rough order of both importance and chronology:

1. As a financial cushion, if life throws me a curveball
2. To give me choice of whether, when and how to work
3. To be able to enjoy my current standard of living in retirement
4. To be able to help my kids, if and when they need it
5. To use my accumulated wealth to give charitably and leave an inheritance for my kids.

(In case you're wondering, I've sorted number one and working on number two!)

They don't need to be sequential, and yours will be different to mine, but that's my investing 'why'.

As to why it's important to me to have that list, it comes down to a few things.

First, it helps me visualise the outcome, even though it's decades away, which keeps me motivated when the market falls, my portfolio is volatile or when I'd really rather buy that new gadget than invest the money.

(What's 'the market'? It's just another way of saying 'all of the companies listed on the ASX as a group'.)

Second, it lets me sense check my progress. Or, more simply, I can work out whether my current savings rate will get me to where I want to go, and I can adjust accordingly.

Last, and this might sound strange, particularly if you're young, but it helps me know when to stop. Many Australians will die with more money than they had when they retired! Now, that's a pretty good problem to have, but how many of those people could have had a better standard of living in retirement (or could have retired earlier) if they'd been confident that their money would last?

As it happens, I love my job, and I work for a company that values flexibility and work-life balance. But what if that wasn't the case? What if my needs and desires change?

I might want to work part-time. Or retire early. I might wake up one day gripped by the desire to spend a year travelling around the country, or to become a llama farmer.

Okay, I'd be the worst llama farmer (I see more than just a little of myself in Jeremy Clarkson in *Clarkson's Farm*!), but my point is that, for me, investing is about security, freedom and generosity.

Like everyone, I can tend to default to 'more' when I think about how much money I'd need to fulfil those goals. And the idea of just stopping and letting go is still a bit scary but I'm getting there.

My wife and I have worked out roughly what our 'number' is. Not that we intend to do anything drastic when we get there, but that'll be the point at which we can exhale, knowing we have enough.

That'll be the point at which we can move through numbers two and three, and put more time and effort into four and five (though we hope the inheritance is more than a few years away from being bestowed!).

We know that, should the worst happen, or even just something bad, we'll be okay.

We're looking forward to the extra freedom and option of knowing we can pay the bills using the cash coming from our investments. And to being a force for good for our kids and others when the opportunity arises.

Investing isn't about getting rich.

It's about being free.

Your 'why' is what will keep you following the plan when markets fall and headlines scream.

So that's my 'why'.

What's your 'why'?

Before you answer, let me share a little something that car maker Toyota learned years ago that might help.

Toyota's founder, Sakichi Toyoda, instituted an idea that came to be known as the 5 Whys. The man who created the company's famous 'just in time' production system described the 5 Whys this way:

> *The basis of Toyota's scientific approach is to ask 'why' five times whenever we find a problem. By repeating 'why' five* times, *the nature of the problem as well as its solution becomes clear.*[4]

Though simple (and some criticise it as simplistic) in its approach, the benefit is that it stops us from stopping at the first, sometimes superficial, answer. Let me share an only slightly fictional example:

1. Why am I not at an ideal weight? Because I ate the chocolate.
2. Why did you eat the chocolate? Because it was in the cupboard when I was hungry.
3. Why was it in the cupboard? Because I was tempted when I was at the supermarket.
4. Why were you tempted? Because I went shopping when I was hungry.
5. Why did you go shopping hungry? Because I hadn't planned ahead.

Now, it doesn't mean that the only reason I'm not at an ideal weight is because I didn't plan ahead, or that planning ahead would have been a guarantee... but it helps me understand the chain of events and identify some sort of root cause.

And, in my case at least, it stops me justifying myself with a convenient excuse!

Whether in business or in front of a pantry when you're hungry, the 5 Whys is a useful tool to bring out whenever you really want to understand why something happens.

What's that got to do with investing? Well, I hope it'll help you really bear down on your underpinning 'why'.

I hope it might help you work out what you *really* want so you can set your own goals.

Maybe your 'why' isn't five questions deep, but I hope it'll help you get past the instinctive answer of 'to have more money' or 'to stop work'.

With any luck, it'll prompt you to think about what you really want, deep down, that underpins those initial answers.

And once you find it, I hope it'll help you crystallise your investing goals.

Now, let's turn our attention to why and how investing can get you there.

Why investing works

'Whoa there, big fella. You can't just tell me why it works. You have to show me that it works in the first place!'

You're right, dear reader. And both of those things — that it works and why it works — are intertwined.

So let's put the horses back in front of the cart, shall we.

In fact, before we let the horses out of the stable, can we be *sure* investing will work?

I hope you're ready for an uncomfortable truth, because the answer is 'no'. Other than death, nothing can be predicted with absolute certainty. No, not even taxes.

There's a pretty good chance the sun will rise tomorrow. But we could be hit by an almighty asteroid tonight.

There are no guarantees in investing.

History suggests that productive businesses, over time, have created extraordinary wealth.

That's good enough for me.

So I invest. And I expect investing will deliver very good long-term returns.

I could choose not to, of course. I could spend everything, and hope that I die early or discover I'm a beneficiary of the will of a hitherto unknown elderly relative. The former isn't something we should wish for, and the latter is remarkably unlikely.

I could just save in cash... and let inflation destroy my purchasing power over time.

Or I could look at history, and ask myself if I think it's likely that the forces that shaped more than a decade of stock market returns are likely still in force.

Let's take each in turn: the returns and then the 'why' (there's that word again).

My single favourite picture in all of investing isn't a photo of a $100 note, or that golden charging bull that seems to be in every second investing story online. It's a chart, updated once a year, by fund manager Vanguard, showing the journey of a hypothetical $10 000 investment over the preceding 30 years (see figure 1.1, overleaf).

When you zoom right in, you see volatility. Ups and downs. Recessions. Wars. Pandemics. Terrorism. Fear. Euphoria.

When you zoom right out? You see a market that, despite all of that volatility, creates extraordinary wealth.

The most recent one, at the time of writing, finished in June 2025. It showed that in the prior 30 years, that hypothetical $10 000 gained 9.3 per cent per annum.

And what does ten grand become over that time, at that rate of return?

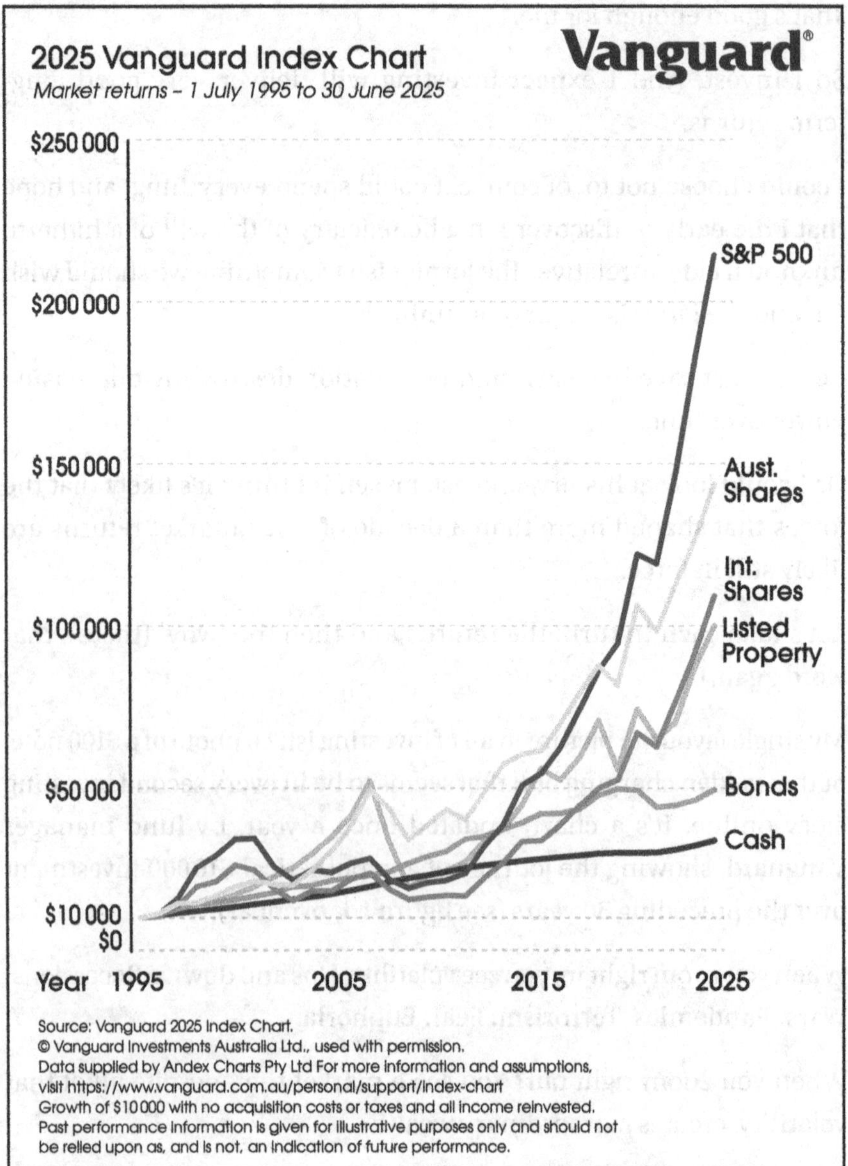

Figure 1.1 2025 Vanguard Index chart,[5] 1 July 1995–30 June 2025

A cool $143 786.

That's a 14-fold gain. Or, if you prefer, a pre-tax profit of $133 786.

For doing what?

Nothing.

Literally, precisely and only ... nothing.

Maybe that's a rogue 30 years, right?

No.

I've been doing this for a while, and the 30-year return has always been around that order of magnitude (with obvious variation) for as long as I can recall.

But what about before that? I'm glad you asked.

Different analysis, this time from UBS, shows that Australian shares have returned a real (that is, adjusted for inflation) return of 6.4 per cent per annum since 1900. Inflation has been around 3.9 per cent per annum (on average) since 1923 (official data doesn't go back further than that), adding the two together, we get a *rough* 10.3 per cent per annum before inflation.

(A 'share', by the way, is just a tiny slice of a real business. If you own shares in Woolies, you own a tiny slice of it — its assets, revenues and profits.)

In other words, over a century-and-a-quarter, the Australian share market has probably compounded at around 10 per cent per year.

Now, few of us will have investing horizons that long, but imagine your great, great, great grandfather had invested the equivalent of $100 in the ASX's predecessor back then.

Are you ready?

You'd have a portfolio worth $14.9 million.

And remember, in both of those examples, that's an initial investment and not a single dollar more. In the vast, vast bulk of cases, the investor (and their kids and grandkids in the latter example) would have continued to add to their portfolios, creating extraordinary wealth in the process.

Now we get to the 'why' — and also why I can't promise it'll continue, but I'm investing on the expectation that it will.

First: time.

Well, duh. But, seriously, time did almost all of the heavy lifting. Not 'stock picking', not buying and selling. Just buying and ... waiting.

Second, the stock market tends to be the place you find almost all of the biggest and best companies in the country. (What do we mean by 'biggest'? You can look at it a few ways: by sales, by profit or by the combined value of all of the shares of the company. The latter is the one usually used.) Now there are some great private businesses, and not all companies on the stock market are 'best' ... some are downright awful. But, as a group, they tend to be the companies that survive and thrive, and that grow faster than their peers, delivering above-average returns.

And third (and most importantly for our long-term objective here), humans are pretty cool. No, not 'hipster cool'. No, not even 'dad cool' (my youngest reckons there's no such thing and I suspect he's right). We're cool in the sense that we're really good at finding new solutions to new and old problems.

We've come a long way, and we're not done yet

Humans have a history of innovation, which is nothing short of incredible. I don't know if we were already using tools before or after we took a new evolutionary branch away from the monkeys, but tools have been with us pretty much since the beginning. Then to the wheel, mastery of fire and right up to the internet and AI — we are inquisitive, clever and pretty dogged as a species.

Look around you right now. Unless you're in the middle of virgin bush with no signs of human existence, you're looking at the result of innovation. And not just a single innovation, but the result of many, many, many innovations stacked one on top of the other.

And, to return to our previous point, we tend to create extraordinary value for society and for the companies that provide those innovations.

Now, you can take the view that we've arrived at peak human ingenuity. In that worldview, the middle of the 2020s turns out to be as good as it gets, and it's all downhill from there. But if you have that view, can I suggest, gently, that you're probably misunderstanding both history and human nature.

No, I don't think humanity is done — not by a long shot. I mean, just think of the biggest seven companies on the US stock market at the time of writing. Alphabetically (no pun intended):

- Alphabet: Google's parent company, owns YouTube, only exists because of the internet
- Amazon: Retail behemoth, originally a bookshop, out Walmarted Walmart
- Apple: Born in the 1970s, almost died in the 1980s, redefined smartphones
- Meta: The holding company for Facebook … and Instagram … and WhatsApp
- Microsoft: Like Apple, born in the 1970s, smashed by the dot.com crash, now a cloud computing giant
- Nvidia: Invented the chips that ran games, then Bitcoin miners, now powers AI
- Tesla: Single-handedly drove the uptake of electric vehicles (EVs).

Of those, only Microsoft was even close to the rarified air of the biggest companies in the world 20 years ago.

And 20 years ago, people might have said that innovation was dead and human ingenuity was at its peak. The lesson? Humans are impressive. We've got a long way to go, I reckon.

And the lesson I take as an investor?

If the future remains bright, and stock markets remain the place some of the biggest and best companies can be found, I reckon the future for long-term investment returns is pretty bright.

That, in my opinion, is why investing works.

And why putting a little bit of money away now for the potential of a lot more in the future is well worth the sacrifice.

But before you can build wealth, you have to dismantle the beliefs that quietly stop you from even starting.

What really matters

- Investing isn't about 'having more money', it's about what that money allows you to do: security, choice, generosity and freedom.
- Knowing your personal 'why' helps you stay invested when markets fall or life tempts you to spend instead of save.
- Over long periods, productive businesses have historically created extraordinary wealth, even through crises and uncertainty.

2

MONEY MYTHS AND THE STORIES WE TELL OURSELVES

> *Before you build wealth, you often have to unlearn the stories that stopped you from trying.*

People once believed that the sun orbited around the Earth.

The Earth is flat, and 'here be dragons'... except it isn't, and the dragons were supposed to be in places that were, at the time, unmapped by Europeans. (That place? Pretty much Australia... and we do have bearded dragon lizards, so perhaps they weren't entirely wrong.)

That's the problem with things that everyone believes to be true. That very communal view tends to stop people thinking and, at worse, props up deliberate deception.

One such view, that 'the share market is a casino' is an example, at least among some people. And it stops them investing.

Other views about the way investors should go about building a portfolio and saving for retirement abound. So, before we go any further, I want to spend a little bit of time breaking down common preconceptions, and setting the record straight.

See, I reckon many people don't fail at investing because they pick the wrong shares.

They fail because they never really start.

And when you scratch beneath the surface, the reason is almost never a lack of intelligence, education or opportunity. It's a story. A story they've been telling themselves for years … about money, risk, markets and who investing is 'for'.

We all carry these stories around. We repeat them casually, sometimes without even noticing. They sound like common sense. They feel protective.

And they're often wrong.

This chapter isn't about numbers or strategies or portfolios. It's about uncovering the quiet beliefs that shape your financial decisions long before a single dollar is invested. Because until you understand those stories — where they came from, why they stick and whether they still deserve a place in your life — everything else you learn about investing will sit on dodgy foundations.

Let me tell you why we *instinctively* shy away from investing: Because investing well might be simply defined as 'the ability to subdue our evolutionary impulses'. Here's why.

We don't choose our money beliefs: We absorb them

Very few people sit down and consciously decide (or examine) what they believe about money.

Instead, those beliefs seep in gradually. From parents and grandparents. From dinner-table conversations. From overheard comments, throwaway remarks and one-off anecdotes that somehow lodge themselves deep in the brain.

- Shares are risky.
- Property is safe.
- You can't go wrong with bricks and mortar.
- Property always goes up.
- Money changes people.
- Rich people are greedy.
- I'm just not good with money.

None of these statements arrive with footnotes or data attached. They're passed on socially, emotionally and often unconsciously.

If you grew up in a household where money was tight, investing may have felt like a luxury reserved for other people. If you watched a parent lose money — or even just stress about it — you may have learned, very early, that investing equals anxiety. If your family prized property ownership above all else, shares may have seemed abstract, suspicious or vaguely irresponsible by comparison.

Here's the important thing to recognise: Most of these beliefs made sense at the time you learned them. They helped you interpret the world with the information you had. But that doesn't mean they still deserve to run your financial life today.

Your money story isn't dumb. It might just be outdated.

Common money myths

Some money stories are so widespread they almost feel like laws of nature. Let's look at a few of the most common ones — not to ridicule them, but to understand why they're so persuasive.

Myth #1: Shares are gambling

This is one of the most damaging beliefs around, and one of the hardest to dislodge.

To many people, shares feel intangible. You can't live in them. You can't touch them. Their prices move constantly, sometimes violently. And every night, the news tells you which ones 'soared' and which ones 'crashed', as if the market was some particularly dangerous air expo.

It's no wonder shares feel like a casino. Indeed, as I've already told you, that's the very word my father used to describe them when I was a teenager. And it wasn't his fault — he didn't know any differently.

But, here's the missing piece: shares aren't bets on prices. They're ownership stakes in real businesses. Businesses that sell products, employ people, earn profits, pay taxes and (over time) grow.

What looks like gambling is often just people *treating* shares as gambling. Buying hot tips. Chasing trends. Selling in panic. Watching prices instead of businesses.

The danger of the 'gambling' myth isn't just that it scares people away from shares, it's that it encourages them to avoid learning how investing actually works.

Long-term ownership of productive assets is not gambling; obsessing over price movements is.

Myth #2: Property is safe, shares are dangerous (property always goes up)

Man, this one runs deep in Australia.

Property feels solid. It's physical. You can walk through it. Renovate it. Point to it proudly at family barbecues. And because house prices aren't updated every minute, they feel stable, even when they're not.

Shares, by contrast, confront you with volatility. Prices flash red and green. Losses feel immediate and personal. Gains feel fragile.

But here's the uncomfortable truth: Property isn't inherently safer than shares. It just hides its volatility better.

Property prices move in cycles, too. They fall. They stagnate. They can wipe out equity when purchased with too much debt. But because those movements are slower, less visible and less frequently reported, they don't trigger the same emotional response.

If your house were repriced every minute like a share portfolio, you'd probably find owning a property every bit as stressful as owning shares.

Safety isn't about how calm something feels, it's about the underlying risks you're taking—and whether you understand them.

Myth #3: You need to be smart, rich or early to invest

This myth keeps a lot of perfectly capable people on the sidelines.

Some people believe investing is only for finance types and maths nerds. Others assume you need a large lump sum to get started. Many think they've 'missed the boat'—that all the good opportunities belong to earlier generations.

It's just not true.

Investing doesn't reward genius, it rewards consistency. It doesn't require large sums, it requires habits. And the idea that there was once a magical golden era when investing was easy (and that it's now too late) is just not true.

Every generation feels this way. And every generation that stays invested long enough discovers that time, not timing, does the heavy lifting.

If investing required brilliance, very few people would succeed. The uncomfortable truth is that it mostly requires the ability to do boring things, repeatedly, while ignoring noise.

Got a $2 coin in your purse, a top drawer or behind the couch cushion? You've got enough to start.

Yes, really.

(Kids, ask your parents about coins. No, not Bitcoin, actual coins. They're the numbers you see on the screen, but stamped on pieces of metal... Actually, never mind.)

These days, there are investing apps that let you start with as little as $2 and add similar amounts regularly. Now, adding only $2 a go is probably not going to set you up for retirement, but if that's all you've got handy, it's a bloody good start.

Because the power is, as they say, in beginning. Once you start, it's amazing how much easier the second step is. And then the third.

Eventually, I want you to do whatever you have to do (keep it legal!) to work up to saving 10 per cent of your pay. But for now, just start. With $2 or whatever you've got.

Myth #4: I'll start when things are more certain

This is the most seductive myth of all.

It feels responsible. Sensible. Patient.

It's also a trap.

Markets are never certain. When things are going well, prices feel too high. When things are going badly, the future feels too scary. Waiting for clarity often just means waiting forever.

The decision to delay feels passive, but it isn't. It's an active choice — one that quietly trades time for comfort.

Certainty never arrives with an announcement. It rarely arrives at all. Meanwhile, opportunity sneaks past while you're waiting.

Myth #5: I don't know where to start

Nice try! That *might* have been true before you picked up this book, but now you do know where to start (or you will, once you've finished reading).

But, in all seriousness, I get it. The whole thing just seems so… overwhelming, right? Brokers, apps, shares, saving, compounding… and that's before shares fall, sometimes quickly and steeply.

Let's take a sec to just touch on compounding: It's the idea that you make money, then that money makes even more money. So you invest $100 and it grows 10 per cent to $110. When things go up *another* 10 per cent, the extra $10 you made last year *also* gains 10 per cent, or another $1. That's how your money makes money, and that money makes even more money. And it's one of the most powerful forces in the universe.

I can still vividly remember the first time I set up a brokerage account. It all looked very foreign and confusing. The good news is that what the web designers call 'user experience' has come a long way since then.

I want you to try to think about when you first started using internet banking. It was confusing and a bit daunting, right? And now? You click, swipe and tap like a banshee. You'll look back on your investing app or website exactly the same way.

You're just going to have to give it a go. And the good thing? If you're really worried, just start with a few bucks. It's pretty low risk, and soon you'll be flying.

When one bad experience becomes a lifetime rule

Humans are brilliant pattern-makers—sometimes too brilliant for our own good.

If someone invests once, loses money and vows never to invest again, that decision makes emotional sense. Psychologists tell us that loss hurts far more than a similar-sized gain feels good. A single bad outcome can overshadow years of potential future success.

But this is where our instincts mislead us.

One experience doesn't define an entire strategy. Buying near a market peak doesn't mean investing is flawed. Following a tip that goes wrong doesn't mean the markets are rigged. It means something didn't work once—under specific circumstances—at a specific point in time.

Yet, our brains are wired to treat vivid, emotional experiences as universal truths. We remember the pain, not the probabilities. We generalise from the specific to the absolute.

This is why so many people say: 'I tried shares once. Never again.'

They didn't fail at investing. They learned the wrong lesson.

The media's role in shaping our money stories

If an alien arrived on Earth tomorrow, they might reasonably assume markets exist solely to surprise, frighten and enrage people.

Headlines scream. Experts argue. Predictions are made with great confidence and are forgotten just as quickly. Calm, long-term progress rarely makes the cut.

That's not a conspiracy. It's an incentive problem.

The media is rewarded for attention, not accuracy. Drama beats patience. Urgency beats perspective. And fear is far more clickable than contentment.

The problem isn't that the media lies. It doesn't. But it does magnify the short term and dramatic, and trivialises or ignores the long-term and steady progress. It makes noise feel like information and movement feel like meaning.

If investing were reported the way it actually works — slow, uneven, boring most of the time — hardly anyone would watch or read.

Some headlines you'll never read:

- Woolies sold a few more tins of baked beans today.
- Living standards increased, almost imperceptibly, this week.
- Shares are up strongly over the past three decades.
- Investors received more dividends again today.

Long-term investors must learn a difficult skill: staying informed without becoming consumed. Understanding what matters without reacting to everything.

The comfort of bad stories

Some money stories stick around not because they're true, but because they're comfortable.

- I'm just not a money person.
- The market's rigged anyway.
- It's too late for me.

These beliefs protect us from discomfort. They excuse inaction. They let us avoid confronting uncertainty, learning new skills or risking embarrassment.

That doesn't make them evil. It makes them *human*.

But comfort has a cost. And over time, that cost compounds just as powerfully as returns do.

I'm not trying to shame you for having these beliefs. I'm not going to criticise you. They are 100 per cent normal and natural. The goal, instead, is to help you recognise and address these evolutionary impulses, and to put our rational brains in charge instead.

Property, shares and the Australian psyche

Australians have a complicated relationship with investing.

We distrust shares (except the ones inside our superannuation). We love property (even though it's often the most leveraged investment we will ever make). We speak about housing with confidence and about share markets with suspicion.

This contradiction tells us something important: Our beliefs aren't purely rational. They're cultural.

Most Australians are already investors. They just don't see themselves that way.

Understanding this can be liberating. Investing doesn't require joining a strange new world. You're already part of it. The question is whether you'll engage with it consciously and deliberately or let it run in the background without your involvement.

Rewriting your money story

Here's the good news: Money stories aren't permanent.

They can be rewritten.

Not overnight. Not with affirmations or slogans. But with awareness, curiosity, a little education and better questions.

Try asking yourself:

- Where did this belief come from?
- Was it learned or tested?
- Does it describe reality or emotion?
- What would a calmer, more useful version of this story sound like?

This isn't about becoming reckless. It's about becoming accurately realistic.

Try replacing:

- 'shares are risky' with 'prices fluctuate but businesses endure'
- 'I'm bad with money' with 'I was never taught'
- 'I missed my chance' with 'time still works'.

I hope this book will help you rewrite your stories by giving you the confidence and the tools to start (or continue) building your financial future on strong foundations.

Most people don't fail at investing because of markets. They fail because of the stories they tell themselves about markets, and that they let the markets tell them.

It's not them... it's you

Once you start examining your money stories, something important becomes clear.

The hardest part of investing isn't choosing assets. It isn't forecasting markets. It isn't beating the index.

It's managing yourself.

Before you learn how markets work, you need to understand how you work—especially when things get uncomfortable.

If your money stories are wrong, you won't follow the plan, no matter how simple it is.

Because, once the stories loosen their grip, the real work begins. And the real work isn't understanding markets. It's understanding yourself.

What really matters

- Many people never start investing because of stories they absorbed growing up: myths about risk, wealth and who investing is 'for'.
- Shares aren't gambling, property isn't magically safe and investing doesn't require genius or huge sums.
- Waiting for certainty is one of the most convincing excuses people use to stay on the sidelines forever.

3

THE REAL ENEMY: YOU(R BRAIN)

> *Investing success is less about intelligence than learning to keep your brain from getting in your own way.*

You don't have to look far to see evidence of, if I can be immodest on our species' behalf, human brilliance.

No, not on reality TV. No, not the influencers on social media, or even social media itself.

But, almost everywhere else.

In the blink of a universal eye, in perhaps as little as 400 000 years, humanity mastered our particular branch of the evolutionary tree, and we've never looked back.

We mastered fire. Invented language. Learned to farm.

We invented the wheel. Codified science and created mathematics.

We codified the scientific method. Harnessed the printing press.

And the industrial revolution, a phrase that rolls off the tongue, truly was a ground-shaking revolution that changed everything.

The problem? Our inventions and improvements have outpaced our biology.

We have caveman brains but we're living in the space age.

Or, as EO Wilson so wonderfully put it: 'The real problem of humanity is the following: we have Paleolithic emotions, medieval institutions, and god-like technology.'[6]

Think about investing for a second: It's the idea of sacrificing some consumption today (saving, rather than spending), enduring volatility and fear without acting, and building a portfolio where the payoff will be felt in decades. Most of us will be investors for about 60 to 80 years — that's close to *double* the average total lifespan of only 150 years ago.

At best, our forebears would have stored grain for maybe a season or a year. Now we're investing for decades.

Those who came before us thought they heard a lion's roar, and had to choose between panicking and waiting around to see if it really was a lion. Hint: The latter group likely don't have any modern descendants.

Not that many generations ago, planning for the future was not only a luxury, but largely useless. That's still the case for many people in the developing world, today.

And so, when I said in the last chapter that investing well is 'the ability to subdue our evolutionary impulses', I meant it.

The instincts that kept us alive in the past largely work against what we know to be successful investing practices.

We need to think in decades, not seasons.

When everyone else is panicking, we need to remain calm.

When they are euphoric, we shouldn't get carried away.

We need to sit with discomfort, not cauterise the wound.

The greed that made us fill our bellies with ripe fruit will make us reckless investors.

Just because the volcano erupted last year doesn't mean it'll do it again this year.

In short: Our brains evolved to keep us alive, not to help us compound our wealth.

So we have to consciously take charge of, and subdue, our impulses.

The good news is that there are ways to do that ... but, first, let's look at the ways we can bring ourselves undone.

The urges that get us into trouble

Fear

This one's not a surprise. I'm no evolutionary biologist or social psychologist, but as I've already mentioned, we know from research that we feel the pain of loss much more severely than we enjoy a gain of a similar size.

Similarly, fear is a far greater motivator than greed. Just look at how many times you read breathless stories of market crashes, and how rarely you see a similarly prominent story about long-term gains. (And it's not the media's fault — we wouldn't read stories about the latter, even if they wrote it!)

Humans are programmed to respond to fear. To deal with it, usually, by removing ourselves from the situation.

Worried the market might crash? That we might have a recession? That a company's shares might drop?

The very strong impulse is to get the hell out of Dodge.

But what does a long-term view tell us? That markets go up more than they go down. That they go up, a lot and by a long way, over the long-term. That being invested (and staying invested) is the best way to earn long-term wealth, if we invest sensibly.

As FDR famously said, 'the only thing we have to fear is fear itself'... especially if we're properly diversified and investing for the long-term.[7]

Greed

You can't get a break, can you? First I tell you not to give in to fear, and now I'm telling you not to give in to greed.

This one is just as important. (Sorry.)

When you're fearful, you're likely to sell, and miss out on significant gains.

But when you're greedy, you're likely to pay too much, or hang on too long.

Don't get me wrong, greed (or, more politely, the desire to compound wealth) is a good motivator. But when greed overwhelms us, we only see the upside. The 'get-rich-quick' scheme starts to look good as we paper over our misgivings. The stock tip from the Uber driver that's 'just about to double' becomes a sure thing in our minds.

The corollary to these two? Warren Buffett has it: 'Be fearful when others are greedy, and greedy when others are fearful.'[8]

And isn't that just the opposite of our evolutionary impulse. We usually look for confirmation from our family and peers. We rarely want to zig when they zag, but if you're going to be fearful or greedy, do it when the odds are in your favour!

Envy

It's one of the seven deadly sins for a reason. It clouds judgement with emotion. And, as Buffett's long-time business partner Charlie Munger famously said: 'Envy is a really stupid sin because it's the only one you could never possibly have any fun at. There's a lot of pain and no fun. Why would you want to get on that trolley?'[9]

Enough said.

Boredom and the tendency to action

The parents reading this will know how hard it is for kids to deal with boredom. Usually there's a lot of whinging and carrying on.

And then, if you're lucky, they find something worthwhile to do. The alternative? Well, as they say, idle hands are the devil's workshop!

Except, that's not true only about kids.

Our brains like action. They despise inaction. That's true culturally, too, in the saying 'Don't just sit there ... do something!'

And so, we buy shares and wait. Maybe they go up a bit, then do nothing for a while. Maybe they go down and stay down. Maybe we just refresh the portfolio page on the brokerage website, and the price just blinks back.

'I can't stand it anymore,' our brain screams (sometimes almost audibly). 'Nothing is happening ... maybe we should make a change ...'

So we sell and buy something else. And it doesn't do any good, so we try again.

Or we look at last year's winning stocks and kick ourselves for not buying them (bloody broken crystal ball!), and wonder if it's not too late.

There's an incredible stat out of the US. As investment writer Jason Zweig wrote in 2002:

> Stunningly, while the average fund generated a 5.7 per cent annualized total return over the four years, the average fund investor earned just 1 per cent. In every category except two (equity income and utilities), investors earned less than their funds did.[10]

'It's terrible how much money was destroyed', laments Laurence Siegel of the Ford Foundation. 'If investors earned the rates of return that the funds report, we'd all be rich. And why aren't we all rich? Because people keep shooting themselves in the foot by chasing hot funds that just can't sustain their performance.'[11]

In other words, we just couldn't leave well enough alone. Don't be that person.

If you need action and a hit of adrenaline, go to a football game, the shops or jump out of an aeroplane (with a parachute!).

If your investing isn't like watching grass grow or paint dry, you're doing it wrong.

Under-confidence and overconfidence

Yes, here's another time I want you to be like Goldilocks, and not be too hot or too cold, but instead, aim for being 'just right'.

I vividly remember being 16, and heading out for my first drive on my L plates. I was really nervous, braking unnecessarily before slight curves and taking corners like I was driving a semitrailer. 'You're not driving a truck, mate ... you don't have to swing out before turning right', said my old man at one point.

A short few years later, and it's entirely possible I had a slightly elevated sense of my own driving ability, I may have taken a corner too quickly in wet weather, resulting in the car ending up at a 90-degree angle to the direction it should have been facing.

You'll be as pleased as I was relieved that it was late at night, so there was no other traffic, and I managed to avoid the rocks on one side and the road barrier on the other.

My point, other than to remind my younger readers to drive safely, is to highlight the dangers of under- and overconfidence.

For investors, under-confidence harks back to the last chapter: it's easy to assume that investing 'just isn't for me', or that you don't have the money, skills or ability to invest. That reluctance might just keep you from compounding life-changing wealth.

The flip side, though, is the overconfidence that leads to recklessness. I've heard more than enough stories of investors who've started investing, had a few wins and then quickly increased the size and riskiness of their 'bets'. And yes, you're right, those stories don't end well, especially if (and too often when) investors become gamblers and try to 'win back' their losses with ever-riskier trades.

So here's the thing: You absolutely can become a successful investor, even if the most you ever do is regularly buy a few diversified exchange traded funds (ETFs) — more on that, later ...

But also, remember the words a slave whispered in the ear of the victorious Roman general: *memento mori* (you are mortal). It was a reminder that, no matter the previous victory, future success was far from assured. It was designed to keep those generals humble so they wouldn't get carried away.

Temperament beats IQ… hands down!

Remember this quote from master investor, Warren Buffett, a slightly longer version of the one I featured in Chapter 1:

> Investing is not a game where the guy with the 160 IQ beats the guy with the 130 IQ. Once you have ordinary intelligence, what you need is the temperament to control the urges that get other people into trouble in investing.[2]

Now, I don't want to generalise (much), but I will say that, too often in my experience, two groups tend to stumble when they invest, groups that, at first blush, you'd expect to eat this stuff up: smart people and people who've had success in other areas. And, frankly, it's not *because* they're smart or successful that stops them from being good investors.

It's because they know it.

Because they can't quite bring themselves to either realise that intellect isn't enough, or that success in one area doesn't necessarily translate to success elsewhere.

I'll let you into a little secret: I'm almost never the smartest guy in any room I'm in. Even when I'm by myself!

But I'm serious. I mean, I'm no idiot, but there are some seriously impressive brains out there. I hope I'm above average, but that's as far as I'd push it.

What do I bring to the table? Temperament, I hope.

It's a word that means different things to different people, but I'm talking about some combination of emotional control on one hand and self-awareness on the other.

I'm generally pretty good at keeping my ego in check. I'm mostly successful at not seeing the world as just black or white. I can normally accept when someone has a better idea. I'm often able to play devil's advocate, with my own ideas as well as others'.

Also, I'm pretty humble. And very proud of it. (Yes, that's a joke!)

I've seen some really smart people who are really poor investors because they have the IQ, but are missing Buffett's 'temperament' bit. They're so used to knowing the answers in other domains that they assume they know them in investing. And when they come up with an idea, they're too often blind to the ways in which they can go wrong.

Intelligence is helpful. But temperament is decisive.

So what is the right temperament?

Before I answer that, let me reassure you that no-one ever starts with all of their ducks in a row — and you never really get there, either. The job is to understand and then work on yourself, improving over time.

But the things you're looking to cultivate include:

- *independent thought:* the ability to draw your own conclusions without being swayed by the crowd
- *emotional control:* not giving way to fear or greed ... or the ever-present discomfort of uncertainty

- *self-discipline:* doing the right things, at the right time, even when you don't feel like it
- *continuous learning:* curiosity, which leads to discovery, which leads to greater understanding
- *humility:* yes, in front of others, but mostly with yourself — there are things you don't know, and things you think you know that end up being wrong.

Here's a little glimpse into what's coming later. Investing well isn't complicated, but it can be hard ... and it comes down to temperament.

Cultivate the right temperament and you'll go far.

Because your biggest investing risk isn't the market.

It's you.

The plan is simple. Following it is the hard part. But that's what this book is all about.

The collapse of LTCM

In the late 1990s, US hedge fund Long-Term Capital Management (LTCM) was riding high and making a fortune. It wasn't run by loud risk-takers, but by some of the brightest minds in finance and academia. Founder John Meriwether had built his reputation at trading firm Salomon Brothers, while Nobel Prize-winning economists Myron Scholes and Robert C. Merton helped shape the firm's sophisticated mathematical models. Their strategy seemed elegant: find tiny pricing gaps between similar bonds, bet that markets would eventually converge, and use leverage to turn small edges into big profits.

For several years, the results looked almost magical. Returns were strong, volatility appeared low and banks were eager to lend. Success reinforced belief in the models, and perhaps a quiet sense of invincibility.

But markets don't always behave like equations. In 1998, Russia defaulted. It couldn't pay its debts and that shook global confidence. Relationships between assets broke down; prices that 'should' have moved together suddenly moved in opposite directions. LTCM's positions, built on historical assumptions, went badly wrong. Because the fund was so heavily leveraged, losses snowballed quickly.

What failed wasn't intelligence, it was overconfidence and leverage. The team assumed history would rhyme closely enough for their models to hold. Instead, extreme events exposed the limits of their theory. LTCM's near-collapse became a cautionary tale: Brilliance can build powerful systems, but hubris can make them fragile when the real world refuses to cooperate.[12]

Patience. Temperament. Time.

Does this all sound vaguely familiar? It should: your mum and dad told you about the tortoise and the hare when you were a kid.

Turns out... Aesop was right.

Investing is simple but it's not easy. That statement is the reason I wrote this book.

The One-Page Investment Plan is a deceptively simple idea. But being able to follow it (and stick with it, especially when things get tough for all of the reasons I've already outlined) that's the key.

You not only have to *know* what's required to invest well. You need to be mentally, financially and emotionally prepared to do it ... no matter what.

Controlling your behaviour is easier when you understand what you're protecting.

And what you're protecting is *compounding*.

And that's where we're going next.

What really matters

- Our evolutionary instincts—fear, greed, envy and the urge to act—are perfectly designed to sabotage good investing behaviour.
- Investors often destroy returns by reacting emotionally, chasing winners or constantly tinkering with portfolios.
- Successful investing requires deliberately overriding instincts that once helped us survive but now hurt our finances.

4

THE MAGIC OF COMPOUNDING

> *The real miracle of* investing *isn't genius—*
> *it's time.*

Compound interest. There are no more powerful words in investing than those two, together.

If I could spend the rest of this page just repeating those words without annoying my editor, I would.

Because unless I really, really land this idea—and it makes its way into your mind as an investing earworm, most of what follows is of little use.

See, long-term compound returns is what investing is about.

But not only that.

Long-term *historical* compound returns are also the strongest argument I have for investing in the first place.

It's true that Einstein probably never uttered the phrase that begins this chapter.

But, if he didn't, he should have.

Just as his theory of relativity is fundamental to much of modern science and technology, compounding is absolutely fundamental to good investing.

It's also poorly understood, and when it is understood, it's often poorly internalised.

When we were at school, we were taught how to calculate what our maths teachers called 'simple interest'.

If I have $100 in a term deposit paying 4 per cent, then we'd work out that $100 times 0.04 equals $4.

That is, $100 in the bank earns us $4 per year in interest. So far, so good.

Right now, some of you are thinking '$4 for nothing is a good deal'. Others of you might be thinking '$4? That's not much for a whole year of not spending $100!'

You're both right, but I'll humbly suggest the first person might be onto something. Especially over time ... which is coming soon.

When I reflect on my career trajectory, and my longer history as someone who was investing well before I moved into the industry as a professional, my interest in investing can be traced back to a few things.

My maths teacher, who taught us about compounding (more on that later), my economics teacher who taught us about the share market (much more on that later), and the fact that, when I was a kid, I was earning 5, 6 and 7 per cent per annum in bank interest!

The Baby Boomers remember that as a time of very high mortgage interest (trust me, just mention interest rates and they'll tell you about it!), but I was a little younger, and remember the high interest on my savings.

I took my paper 'passbook' into the branch, and deposited some paper money. They'd put the little passbook through a printer and it'd update my account balance with the new deposit and, sometimes, the interest I'd received in the meantime.

(Kids, there was a time before the internet. Ask your grandparents, and be prepared to wonder how on earth they managed to live!)

Seeing that money (almost) magically turn up in my account was, even though I wasn't aware of it at the time, a formative experience.

The good thing was that, while I loved seeing that 'money for nothing' (thanks, Dire Straits!),[14] my maths teacher was making sure I was thinking a little more deeply — and a little more long-term.

And that's the phenomenon I want to share with you here.

The simple beauty of compounding

See, simple interest is impressive enough. But what if you don't take that interest out of the bank, and instead let it … compound?

That's where the real magic happens.

(Maybe you already know all about compounding. Awesome. But do me a favour and keep reading because I want to take it from something you *know* to something you learn to *love*. Try to unlock your 13-year-old self and see this again for the first time. Let the awe wash over you. It really is that important!)

That $4 in interest you earned on your $100? You could take it out and spend it. Next year, you'll earn another $4. If you take that out, you'll get another $4 the next year.

That's actually a wonderful way to fund your retirement without eating into your capital—but that's a whole other chapter.

For now, let's assume you're still working your way *to* retirement. And you've committed to let your money compound, untouched. (That's also the topic of a future chapter!)

Instead of spending your $4 in interest, you leave it there.

At the end of year 1, your $100 becomes $104. Same, same, so far.

At the end of year 2? Things start getting a little interesting. Not 'blow your socks off' interesting, but your account is stirring.

Instead of earning $4 in interest on your $100, you earn $4.16.

I told you it wouldn't blow your socks off!

But something *is* happening.

Your money is starting to make money. And that money is making even more money.

Now, my readers are smart people, so I'm going to skip forward a few steps. And I'm going to take us from cash in the bank to the share market.

Over the last century or so, the average Australian share market return is probably around 9 per cent per year.

(Credit Suisse puts the inflation-adjusted return at 6.7 per cent per annum between 1900 and 2023. Add a rough 2.5 per cent annual inflation to that, and we're at 9.2 per cent. So we'll use 9 per cent as a slightly conservative best guess.)

It's important to add the usual boilerplate here: Past performance is no guarantee of future performance. But also, if the ASX can grow at 9 per cent per year despite two world wars, a few handfuls of regional wars and conflicts, the Great Depression, terrorism, oil shocks, two global pandemics, inflation outbreaks and more ... well, it might be reasonable to at least think it likely that we'll get through whatever comes in future, and the return rate might be similar.)

Well that escalated quickly ...

So, let's use that 9 per cent as both an illustration and a reasonable guess of what the future *might* bring.

And let's say you invest $1000, not $100.

After the first year, your portfolio might have grown from $1000 to $1090. A pretty good start.

In year 2, you earn not $90, but $98.10, and you'll have $1188.10.

Skip forward to year 5, and your 9 per cent will earn you $127.04, with your balance swelling to $1538.62.

Year 10? We'll dispense with the cents: You'd earn $195, and would now have a portfolio worth $2367. You've more than doubled your money, and you're not done yet.

Let's skip to some other milestones: In year 13, you hit $3000.

You hit $4000 only four years later.

And $5000 only *two* years after that!

By year 29, you're earning more in compound returns in a single year than you contributed!

(And your balance has swollen to $12 172!)

In year 30, your account is worth $13 268, and you have more than 13 times as much money as you started with!

For doing... nothing.

Literally nothing... you just left your money alone to compound! I hope you can now see why compound interest (more broadly, compound *returns*) are considered the eighth wonder of the world.

Figure 4.1 is a visual representation.

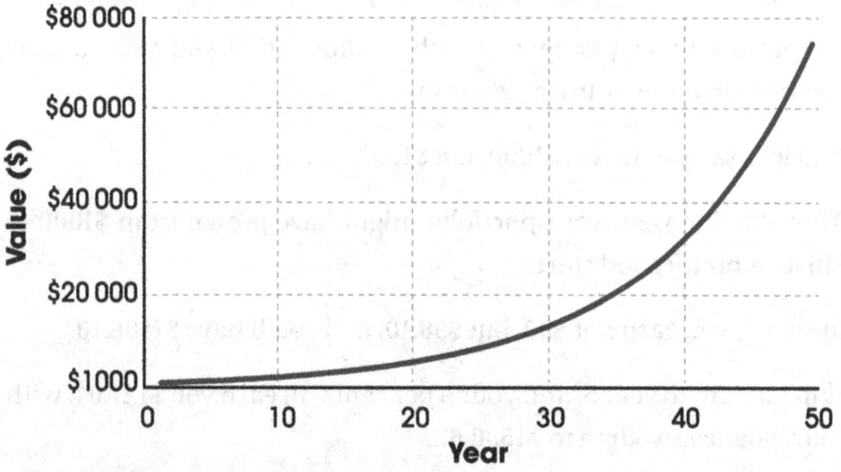

Figure 4.1 Exponential growth for $1000 at 9 per cent annual compounding over 40 years

Time is undefeated.

And compounding is how it keeps score.

The rest of this book is about not interrupting it.

For fun (and profit!), let's just roll forward a little longer:

In year 40, you earn $2593, and your portfolio sits at $31 409 (yes, 30 times your initial investment).

In year 50? Your balance would swell by $6139, to $74 358.

Nice!

Oh, and 50 years may not be feasible for you... but it might be.

If you're 30 now, you'll be very likely to live until 80.

If you're 40, you're a good chance of reaching 90.

And if you're 50, I wouldn't rule out hitting the century.

Alternatively, think about the young people in your life. If you're in a position to put some money aside for a newborn, or a kid or someone who's just turned 18... that could be life-changing for them!

Now, at this point, I do want to mention a couple of things. First, the numbers I've given here are yearly averages. The stock market very rarely, if ever, gives you that return in a given year. Some years it will be 15 per cent. Some will be 4 per cent. Some will be –8 per cent. The average is just that... an average.

And, the numbers in this example don't include brokerage fees or taxes. Now, if you rarely trade and don't sell (the best way to invest!), your fees and taxes will remain pretty low. But not zero. And dividends will carry a tax obligation (but also franking credits... more on those later, too!).

The aim of this section isn't to promise you nirvana. But it *is* to show you the absolutely incredible potential of compounding.

And speaking of things that aren't included, all of those numbers assume one single investment at the beginning, and not a dollar added after that.

What if you added money regularly? Honestly, at this point, the numbers get even more impressive—so much so that they might almost seem made up. They're not... did I mention that compounding is a miracle?

Turbocharging a miracle

Let's quickly compare the account balance assuming the same 9 per cent return, and compare $1000 added at the beginning, then adding the same amount every year (see table 4.1).

Table 4.1 Compound interest comparison

Year	Total contribution ($1000 paid in year 1 only)	Balance	Total contribution ($1000 per year)	Balance
1	$1000	$1090	$1000	$1090
5	$1000	$1539	$5000	$7523
10	$1000	$2367	$10000	$17560
20	$1000	$5604	$20000	$56765
30	$1000	$13268	$30000	$149575
40	$1000	$31409	$40000	$369292
50	$1000	$74358	$50000	$889441

Note: Numbers have been rounded.

That is the power of time.

Pick your preferred time period. Let's say 30 years. For a $30 000 contribution over 30 years, you end up with almost $150 000. That's a pretty nice result, I reckon.

Now imagine if you were able to up that $1000 a year to, say, $1500 or $2000? More?

Could you save $200 a month if you really tried? What about $400? Gets pretty good pretty quickly, doesn't it?

Remember, these might be hypothetical future values, but the return is based on average past returns.

Recall the Vanguard Index chart from page 8 (the one I said was my favourite image in all investing)? That chart shows that a hypothetical $10 000 invested in the ASX on 1 July 1995 (and not a single dollar afterward) would have compounded to $143 786, for an average annual return of 9.3 per cent (before taxes and fees), just above the 9 per cent used in our earlier examples.

Now, let's think about that 30-year period. In 1999 and 2000, we had the dot.com boom and bust. We had the Asian currency crisis that almost no-one remembers now. Terrorist attacks in the US and Bali. The Global Financial Crisis (GFC). Concerns about the collapse of Europe. Britain's exit from the EU. And, yes, COVID and the war in Ukraine.

And the market *still* managed to deliver 9.3 per cent per annum — roughly what it had done for the century before.

(If you're thinking 'yeah, but Australia didn't suffer as much as some other countries during the GFC', you're right … but the US stock market did even better than ours over that time period!)

Rule of 72

The Rule of 72 is one of those beautifully simple shortcuts that sounds almost too easy to be useful — but it's surprisingly powerful.

In short, it helps you estimate how long it'll take for your money to double. Just divide 72 by your expected annual return (in percentage terms), and you'll get the approximate number of years. Earning 9 per cent a year? Your money doubles roughly every eight years (72 divided by 9). At 6 per cent, it's closer to 12 (72 divided by 6). No calculator required.

Now, it's not perfect. As I've just mentioned, markets don't move in straight lines, returns aren't guaranteed and real life includes fees, taxes and the occasional bout of investor panic. But the Rule of 72 isn't about precision—it's about perspective. It turns abstract percentages into something tangible, and reminds us just how powerful time can be.

Most investors underestimate compounding because the early years feel slow. As we've seen, the real magic happens later, when growth starts building on previous growth. That's why patience matters more than prediction. Use the Rule of 72 not as a promise, but as a gentle reminder and motivator: small, consistent returns over long periods can turn modest beginnings into something genuinely meaningful.

Why time beats brilliance

You know what else the numbers show us? That while earning a higher return would be nice—and very welcome, if we can get it—there's no replacement for time.

Indeed, Warren Buffett started investing at 11 and joked that one of his biggest regrets is not starting earlier! He's kidding... sort of.

Maybe you can earn 10 per cent, 11 per cent or 12 per cent per annum on average. But you probably won't. And before you take offence, remember that the average return for the whole market is 9 per cent—that includes the winners and losers all rolled together. If someone is making 11 per cent, someone else may be making 7 per cent.

Of course, if you can earn a higher return *and* invest for a really long time, you'll do better than someone who earns the average over that same time period.

So, sure, if you're the next Warren Buffett, go for it.

But the point here is that time is the friend of every investor, and should be put to maximum use.

'Thanks, Captain Obvious', you might be saying at this point. If so, great! If I've made the point strongly enough that it's lodged in your brain. Mission accomplished.

Sort of.

You know what worries me now? That you'll be furiously nodding along and then ... do nothing.

Not because you're a bad person or a slacker or anything else. Just because, well, life happens.

There's work to think about. Bills to pay. Maybe kids to look after, or a million other things to do. I get it. No criticism from me — life is busy.

But ... I really, really want you to make it a priority. We'll talk about some ways to do it in a bit, but for now, just please promise yourself you'll get onto it, okay?

There's a second group, too. Maybe you're on the wrong side of 40, 50 or 60, and you're thinking 'Well, that's okay for young people, but it's too late for me'.

Kindly, that's nonsense. And I mean that with love.

You're right that if you're 60, you may not be here to see that 50-year return. I hope you are, but you might not be.

The thing is, you probably still have a good 30 or 40 years left. If you're under 60, more than that.

And you can wish you'd started earlier. Me, too. I started investing properly when I was about 26. Not bad, but like Buffett, I can only rue not starting a little earlier (the Rule of 72 tells me that if I'd started at 18, instead, my portfolio would be *twice* the size it is today!).

But, as they say, if wishes were horses, beggars would ride. So, unless you count Doc Brown and Marty McFly as close personal friends, rewriting the past is impossible.

Instead? Well, as the proverb tells us, the best time to plant a tree was 20 years ago; the second best time is today.

You can't go back in time. But you can improve your future by starting investing—where you are, with what you have. Then you can build from there.

(The alternative, of course, is not starting. In which case ... you'll likely have less in 10, 20 or 30 years than you will if you *do* invest. Don't let perfect be the enemy of good.)

The source of the magic

We've just talked about the magic of compounding. And I've already kinda told you where the magic comes from.

But, to be really explicit, the magic of compounding is in *reinvesting* your dividends, and leaving your capital invested to grow. Rising share prices tend to compound on their own, so that's not too hard to understand. If Woolworths sells more baked beans each year, the company's profits rise. That usually means a higher and higher share price. As long as you don't sell, you'll benefit from that compounding just by hanging on.

That can be hard, and we'll talk about it more in the next chapter, but there's nothing complex about it.

The next bit can be a little harder: reinvesting your dividends. When a company sends us a dividend payment that just turns up in your bank account, it's tempting to see that as free money, and we all have a mental list of things we'd buy if we happened to stumble upon a little lotto win or small inheritance.

If you give in to that temptation, you'll be seriously wounding your compounding journey.

The answer is boring, but effective: Take steps now to help 'future you' avoid that temptation. We'll go into it later (yes, this is becoming a theme, but this chapter is the set-up for almost everything that follows!), but a little automation or what psychologists call 'pre-commitment' is your friend here.

The short version: Open a completely separate bank account for your investing. Put your regular savings in that account. Get your dividends put in that account. Don't touch it... ever!

'Yeah, but ...'

Can I ask you to indulge me for a minute?

See, when I have this conversation with people, the doubting Thomas' sometimes raise a couple of objections.

And, on the basis that there might be one or two reading this book, I want to address them.

The first objection they have is that I'm not using inflation-adjusted data. They're spot on. But who of us lives an inflation-adjusted life?

Yes, the purchasing power of $889 000 or $75 000 will be much less in 50 years. I could give you the inflation-adjusted numbers, but the thing is, the dollar values don't change.

And—and here's the kicker—would it change *anything* about the plan or what you should do? Not. One. Iota. It's an academic question, and worth discussing on those grounds... but totally pointless when it comes down to the question of how we should invest.

(Indeed, inflation is one of the best reasons *to* invest... otherwise your cash is being eaten away every year by that silent thief!)

Second, the one that *really* gets up my nose: Those people who say 'You can't use those examples... *who would invest for 30 or 40 or 50 years*?!'

Insert scream of frustration here.

Who would?

Me. Warren Buffett. Everyone with superannuation. And, I hope, everyone who reads this book, and is motivated by the potential that long-term investing offers.

Who would do it? Hopefully people who like money.

People who want to retire in some comfort.

People who want to invest for their kids or grandkids.

People who understand that a little sacrifice, now, will add up to a lot of life choices later.

I've been investing now for over 30 years (please, don't do the maths). I hope to be investing well into my 90s, the good Lord willing and the creeks don't rise.

Who would invest for 30 years? Everyone who understands the huge opportunity that compounding offers.

And now, after reading this chapter, that includes you.

Compounding is the engine.

Now, we need to decide whether you're building a machine designed to go the distance... or one that falls apart when the road gets rough.

What really matters

- Compounding turns small, consistent investments into extraordinary sums over time.
- Time is far more powerful than brilliance when it comes to building wealth.
- The biggest advantage an investor can have is simply starting early and staying invested.

5

WHY 'INVESTING' EATS 'TRADING' FOR BREAKFAST

> *In investing, patience* beats *activity—and culture beats strategy.*

There's a wonderful quote that I suspect will ring true for almost anyone who's worked... well, anywhere really.

It's usually attributed to management guru Peter Drucker, though others have cited Apple founder Steve Jobs or long-time General Electric CEO, Jack Welch. Regardless of the source, the line is:

'Culture eats strategy for breakfast.'[15]

And it's a killer line because it's dead right.

Imagine you have the wrong people who have the wrong values trying to implement the right strategy. How far do you reckon you're going to get?

On the other hand, if you have the right people with the right values, they're probably going to do the right thing anyway—and the result is likely to be a good one.

So what's that got to do with investing?

Everything.

Because investing is a culture.

Trading and speculation are strategies.

And culture eats strategy for breakfast.

Investing isn't just shares

Before we go any further, I want to widen the lens a little. Yes, I'm a shares guy. We'll get to that. But when I talk about investing, I'm not just talking about shares. Shares are one way — and a very accessible and flexible way — to invest, but they're not the only way.

Investing is allocating capital to productive assets. That might mean shares in listed companies. It might mean a rental property that produces income. It might mean bonds or a term deposit that pay interest. It might mean owning or part-owning a private business. It might even mean infrastructure assets or farmland. The label is less important than the underlying characteristic.

The common thread across all of these is *production*.

A productive asset does something. It generates cash flow, produces goods or services, earns profits or rent or interest. It creates value in the economy. And because it produces, it has the capacity to grow. Profits can be reinvested. Rents can rise. Interest can be rolled over. The asset can compound.

Shares, for example, are simply partial ownership of businesses — you're literally getting a 'share' of the business, just as you have a 'share' of a pizza when you grab a slice. When you buy shares in a company, you are buying a small slice of an enterprise that employs people, sells products, solves problems and — hopefully — earns profits. When you buy a rental property, you are buying an asset that produces rent. When you buy a bond, you are lending money in exchange for interest.

Investing, at its core, is ownership of productivity.

And that's a very different proposition from ownership of a price.

What investing really means

When you invest, you are saying something quite specific, even if you don't articulate it out loud. You are saying: 'I want to own this'. Not 'I want to flip this next week', or 'I hope someone else pays more tomorrow', but 'I want to own this asset because I believe it will produce value over time — and that growth in value will make the asset more valuable (worth more!)'.

That distinction sounds almost trivial, but it's a vital difference.

When you invest in a business — whether via the share market or by owning the whole thing yourself — you are backing something that sells goods or services, employs staff, allocates capital, takes risks and attempts to earn a return. If it does those things well, it generates profits. If those profits are reinvested intelligently, the business can grow. And, as the business grows, the value of your ownership stake can grow alongside it.

Imagine you owned the local cafe. Or earthmoving business. Or burrito joint.

Your return does not come from finding someone more enthusiastic than you tomorrow. It comes from the business itself becoming more valuable over time because it produces more. It provides more goods or services to more customers more often.

That is why investing works. Not because markets are magical. Not because charts line up. But because human beings continue to innovate, work, consume and improve their lives. Productive enterprises capture that activity. As owners of those enterprises, investors participate in that growth.

Of course, that doesn't mean every business succeeds. Many fail. Some disappear entirely. Entire industries can decline. But, as a group, productive assets have tended to expand alongside economic progress. Investing is, in a sense, a bet on that progress continuing.

A long-term mindset

Here's another thing: Investing assumes *time*.

It assumes that there will be good years and bad years. That recessions will happen. That markets will fall sometimes. That newspapers will declare crises and commentators will predict doom. It assumes volatility. It assumes uncertainty.

But it also assumes that, over long periods, productivity tends to win.

(Volatility? It's just a fancy word meaning that prices go up and down. The more 'volatile' a company's shares are, the more they tend to wiggle around.)

The thing is, that doesn't require blind optimism. It simply requires an understanding of history. For centuries, despite wars, depressions, pandemics and political upheaval, people have continued to build businesses, develop technologies and create wealth. That process has not been smooth, but it has been persistent.

When you invest, you align yourself with that persistence.

You don't need to predict what happens in the next six or 12 months. You don't need to know what interest rates will be next month, or this time next year. You don't need to guess how markets will react to the next headline.

You simply need to believe that over the next decade or two, productive enterprises will continue to produce, to find new solutions to new and old wants and needs.

That belief, combined with patience, is culture.

Trading: A different game entirely

Trading operates on a very different premise. Trading is about buying and selling assets to profit from short-term price movements. It focuses on what the *market* will do next, not on what the underlying asset will produce over the next five, ten or 20 years.

A trader might try to analyse charts, look for patterns, track momentum or react to news. The goal is to identify potential movements and capture a gain before the opportunity disappears.

Professional traders exist. They compete in a different arena.

Most individuals are not playing the same game. And they have a far lower chance of winning.

It's also hard to replicate and usually requires time, money or both.

For every winning trade, there is a losing trade. Before costs, trading is roughly a zero-sum game. After costs (like brokerage and the gap between the price you want and the price that's paid) and taxes, the pursuit likely becomes a negative-sum game for all participants, collectively. Someone makes money, yes, but on average, participants lose once those costs and taxes are paid.

And who's on the 'other side' of the trade?

Often, it's professional traders. Hedge funds. Big investment companies. Algorithms operating at extraordinary speeds. You are competing in an arena populated by participants with more information, more resources and more time.

I mean, play that game if you want, but remember Warren Buffett's warning: 'If you've been playing poker for half an hour and you still don't know who the patsy is, you're the patsy.'[16]

Australians might replace 'patsy' with 'mug' or 'sucker'. And the meaning is, I hope, clear. If you're playing someone else's game, or a game someone else is better at, you might just be the mug.

Meanwhile, the long-term investor is not competing at all. They are simply participating in productivity. Productivity that has, historically, created extraordinary compound wealth.

That's an entirely different position to occupy.

The dangerous seduction of speculation

Speculation kinda sits alongside trading, but it deserves its own category.

Speculation is buying something primarily because you believe someone else will pay more for it later. Not because it produces income. Not because it generates cash flow. But because *sentiment* might improve.

Speculation relies heavily on narrative. On excitement. On the promise of rapid gains. It thrives on scarcity stories and the fear of missing out. You see it in meme stocks, in early-stage companies with no earnings but compelling 'stories', and in certain corners of the cryptocurrency market.

Like trading, speculation is not immoral, and there'll be some people who manage to do it well. There are times when speculative bets pay off handsomely. But speculation depends on timing and psychology in a way that investing does not.

Investing asks: 'Will this asset produce more over time?'

Speculation asks: 'Will someone else pay more?'

That difference matters. Because if sentiment shifts, speculation can unravel quickly. If productivity continues, investing can endure.

A simple test is useful here. If no-one wanted to buy your asset for five years, would you still be comfortable owning it? If the answer is yes, you're probably investing. If the answer is no, you're likely speculating.

There is nothing inherently shameful about either. But honesty about which game you are playing is essential.

And, I'd submit, of those three games you could play, investing probably offers the best odds of long-term success.

So why don't more people do it? And why do so many get sucked into trading and speculation instead?

The seductive pull of action

Here is where psychology comes to the fore.

Humans are wired for action. We all know that deep down. How many times have you heard 'Don't just sit there, do something'? How often have you felt the urge to 'keep busy' when you feel fearful, stressed or anxious?

The reason that's a good thing to do is because, evolutionarily, that's who we are. In our earliest days as a species, the person who ran at the first hint of danger might have overreacted nine times out of ten. The person who didn't was right those nine times out of ten... and a lion's dinner the tenth time!

We jump at the sound of a car horn that gets honked in close proximity. We shrink from activities that could harm or kill us.

Why? Because that trait, which existed in our forebears, resulted in a long, long line of our ancestors that ended with us. If just one of our predecessors had waited to see if it really *was* a lion, we wouldn't be here today.

The drive for action—and the avoidance of risk—has literally been bred into us. It's our default state.

Now, the alternative isn't recklessness, by the way. Despite that evolutionary selection, we—particularly us blokes—still have plenty of testosterone coursing through our veins (predominantly arteries, actually, but give this medical non-expert a little poetic licence!).

It's also an evolutionary hangover, and can be equally bad. The common link? The tendency for action over inaction.

Yes, we're talking fight or flight.

When something moves, we feel compelled to respond. When markets fall sharply, the urge to sell can be overwhelming, just to stop the pain.

When prices surge, the temptation to jump in can feel irresistible, because, well, FOMO. We just hate to miss out.

Doing nothing feels negligent. It feels passive. It feels like ignoring danger. Or opportunity.

Sitting still just feels... unnatural.

But in investing, activity often reduces returns.

The market does not reward effort. It rewards patience.

Read that again.

Activity feels productive. But in investing, it often isn't.

The investors who build substantial wealth over decades are often those who resist that urge to act unnecessarily. Not because they are disengaged, but because they understand what matters.

Compounding requires time and continuity. Every unnecessary trade interrupts that continuity.

The illusion of control

Trading and speculation offer something intoxicating: the illusion of control. You are clicking buttons, making decisions, reacting to news. It feels dynamic. You feel involved. You feel clever.

You feel like you're taking control. And, deep down, we're all control freaks.

But markets are forward-looking. Information is absorbed rapidly. By the time something feels obvious, it is usually reflected in the price.

The idea that you can consistently outmanoeuvre millions of other participants — many with more money, experience and computing power at their disposal — is appealing. It flatters the ego. And, man, do we like our egos flattered.

But it is also statistically unlikely.

And every attempt to 'time the market' (to pick times to buy, sell, and then buy and sell again) introduces friction. Brokerage costs and taxes, mostly. Tax, in particular, is a quiet drain. Long-term investors defer tax, allowing gains to compound before the taxman takes his share. Frequent traders tend to accelerate tax, shrinking their capital base.

Compounding works best when left alone.

Every unnecessary sale resets the clock.

Being right thrice

Here's the thing about both trading and speculating: To do it successfully, you need to be right three times: once when you buy, then when you sell, again when you buy the next thing. Getting one right is not enough.

Meanwhile, the long-term investor stays seated.

Markets have a habit of rebounding before the news improves. The strongest days often occur close to the weakest ones. Missing just a handful of strong days can significantly reduce long-term returns.

Timing is difficult. Remaining invested is conceptually simple, though emotionally challenging.

But simple beats clever more often than we like to admit.

Here's a simple example: I know of quite a few investors who, in the middle of the COVID pandemic of 2020, decided they'd sell and buy back in 'when the pandemic was over'.

And what happened? We had the fastest bear market (a fall in share prices of more than 20 per cent from a recent high) in history. It was brutal. But then we had the fastest *recovery* in history. COVID was declared 'over' as a global health emergency in May 2023. The ASX, as measured by the All Ordinaries, was already above its pre-COVID *highs*. That is, for everything that happened over those 28 months, you made money—and even more we add in dividends. If you'd bought shares during the crisis, you made even more—the All Ordinaries rise 51 per cent, plus dividends, from its COVID lows by the time the pandemic was done.

To be sure, holding through that period of fear and uncertainty wasn't easy. But the investor who did was handsomely rewarded!

Boredom as a virtue

If your investing feels exciting most days, it may be a sign that you are not truly investing.

Investing is often uneventful. Occasionally uncomfortable. Rarely thrilling. That's not a complaint, by the way. That's how it's *supposed* to be.

Speculation and trading are thrilling. They are fast, social and stimulating. They generate stories. They create drama.

The market will happily provide that drama. It is generous in that regard.

Humans *love* drama. But drama does not build wealth. Compounded productivity does.

Boredom in investing is not a flaw. It is a feature. It is the quiet space in which compounding does its work.

Don't get me wrong, investing is fascinating, if you're wired to enjoy looking at businesses and understanding what makes them tick and what separates the good and the bad.

But 'fascinating' and 'exciting' are different things.

The portfolios that change lives are rarely the busiest. They are rarely the most talked about. They are rarely the most exciting.

They tend to be the most patient.

Culture over strategy

Let's return to culture.

The culture of investing is ownership, patience, discipline, emotional control and humility. It is a long-term mindset that values productivity over price and progress over popularity.

The culture of trading is speed, reaction, short-term focus and competition. It values agility and timing.

Neither is immoral. But one compounds and the other competes.

Over short periods, trading and speculation can look brilliant. They're the stories you'll hear from friends or read in the paper.

But over long periods, productivity tends to win.

Investing harnesses productivity. Trading harnesses price movement. Speculation harnesses emotion.

Productivity compounds. Emotion fluctuates.

Investing is ownership. Trading is guessing. Ownership wins.

That is why investing eats trading for breakfast.

Not because it is flashy or exciting, but because it uses an unstoppable natural force: time.

And in investing, time is undefeated.

Here's why.

'You can't go broke taking a profit': One of the most harmful beliefs when it comes to shares

You might have heard the line, 'You can't go broke taking a profit.'

That's true.

But you also can't make meaningful compound gains by taking a profit, either.

Here are two examples.

Let's start with Amazon. (Full disclosure: I owned shares in Amazon at the time of writing.)

Amazon listed on the US stock market in 1997 at a 'stock split adjusted' price of US$0.075 each.

(A stock split is just taking one share and splitting it into smaller pieces; for example, a company whose shares are selling for $5 each might do a 'five for one' split. You used to own one $5 share, but now you own five $1 shares. It makes no difference to the value of the business, or your shareholding, and is largely just window dressing. In Amazon's case, the actual price was US$18, but each share has subsequently been 'split' into 240 pieces over the last 29 years! Now, back to the story.)

At the end of 2025, those shares traded for US$226 each.

Even if we ignore the dramatic ups and downs along the way (for now—we'll get back to them), that's well over a 3000-fold(!) increase in price. Over roughly 29 years, that translates to a compound annual growth rate (CAGR) of around 31 per cent per annum.

Now, pause for a moment and think about what that means.

A 31 per cent annual return sustained for nearly three decades doesn't just double your money. It multiplies it many, many times over. A $340 investment at the initial public offering (IPO), left untouched, would be worth well over $1 million today.

But that return did not arrive in a straight line. Let's go back to that volatility we 'ignored' earlier.

Amazon fell roughly 90 per cent during the dot.com crash. It also had multiple 30 to 50 per cent falls along the way. At various points it looked 'too expensive', 'too risky', or its market was 'too competitive' or 'too mature'.

Imagine buying Amazon in the early 2000s and watching it double. Sensible investors would have been tempted to take the gain. 'You can't go broke taking a profit', they might have said.

True.

Indeed, Amazon shares went up tenfold from around $0.34 in November 2001 to over $3.40 in May 2009.

An astonishing gain. But if you'd sold then, you would have missed out on another 60-fold(!) increase—on top of that tenfold one—over the following 17 years as Amazon built Amazon Web Services (AWS), expanded globally, and layered new business lines on top of its retail base.

Many people didn't miss Amazon because they failed to buy it.

They missed it because they sold it.

Now let's bring it home. And make it a little more sedate... but still very impressive.

Woolworths doesn't have the drama of Amazon. It sells groceries. Laundry detergent. Pet food. It is not, on the surface (or underneath, sorry Woolies), the stuff of Silicon Valley legend.

And yet, since the mid-1990s, Woolworths has been one of Australia's quiet compounders.

Woolworths listed on the ASX in 1993 at $2.45 per share. At the end of 2025, the shares traded at $29.40. That's a very neat (though unintended) 12 times the 1993 price. Add in dividends — which total more than $24(!) over that time — and the total return has been meaningfully higher.

On a total return basis (price growth plus dividends reinvested), Woolworths has delivered around 11 per cent per annum (plus the tax benefits of franking credits — more on that later!) since 1993. That may not sound spectacular next to Amazon's numbers, but over 32 years, an 11 per cent average CAGR turns $10 000 into roughly $282 000.

(The company also spun off a property business and the liquor division over that time, too!)

And, just like Amazon, that journey wasn't smooth.

There were profit scares. There was the Masters hardware debacle (remember that?). There was the arrival of Amazon in Australia. There were regulatory investigations and media criticism. At multiple points, the stock looked 'too expensive'. At other times, it looked like growth had stalled.

Each of those moments would have felt like a reasonable time to 'take profits'.

And each time, long-term holders who simply stayed in their seats were rewarded.

Woolworths didn't explode upward in spectacular fashion. It compounded. Quietly. Persistently. Boringly.

That's the lesson.

'You can't go broke taking a profit' is technically correct, but meaningful wealth is rarely built by repeatedly locking in tidy gains.

It's built by owning productive assets — exceptional ones like Amazon, or durable ones like Woolworths — for far longer than feels comfortable.

That isn't trading.

That's investing.

And investing, over time, eats trading for breakfast.

But hang on ... that all sounds good, but isn't investing, well, *risky*?

Good question ... let's answer it next.

What really matters

- Investing means owning productive assets that generate value over time; trading focuses on guessing short-term price movements.
- Trading and speculation often become negative-sum games once costs and taxes are included.
- Long-term investors aren't competing with everyone else—they're simply participating in, and benefiting from, growth.

6

RISK (THE SCARY CHAPTER)

> *Volatility doesn't destroy wealth; fear, and what it causes, does.*

Let's be honest: this is the chapter most people secretly want to skip. Either because they don't want to face risk and want to pretend the world is wonderful, or because facing it is demotivating and, well, scary.

I hear you, on both counts. But an investor *must* reckon with risk: what it is, what it isn't and how to deal with it.

Gains are fun. Income is wonderful. Compounding is amazing. Stories about buying great assets and watching them grow into giants are the investing equivalent of campfire stories.

But risk?

Risk is the monster under the bed.

It's the late-night thought that whispers:

- What if I lose it?
- What if I'm wrong?
- What if the market crashes the day after I invest?

If you're feeling that, good. It means you're human.

It also means we need to talk properly about risk — not the way the textbooks do, not the way the newspapers do, and not the way the so-called experts define it.

Because most of them are wrong. And if they can't define it properly, how can they discuss it appropriately?

Because misunderstanding risk leads to poor decisions. And poor decisions — not volatility — are where the real danger lies.

In March 2020, I watched the ASX fall faster than at any other time in my investing career. I had lived and invested through the GFC. I had watched the dot.com bubble burst. I had seen panic before. This decline was different in speed, if not in substance.

Every day the headlines escalated. Borders were closing. Lockdowns were spreading. Airlines grounded fleets. Retailers shut stores. Economists used the word 'depression' without irony. Treasury was worried unemployment would hit 15 per cent. The ASX fell 38 per cent in a little over a month.

I remember sitting at my desk one afternoon, staring at the numbers and doing the maths. Not percentages. Dollars. Real amounts tied to years of effort and disciplined saving. Even after decades of investing, I felt it. There was a tightening in my chest and a subtle but persistent urge to act.

That urge is powerful. As we've already discussed on page 65, when something feels dangerous, doing nothing feels irresponsible. The instinct to respond quickly to a perceived threat is ancient and deeply wired into us. Long before markets existed, reacting decisively to danger improved survival odds. Standing still in the presence of threat was rarely rewarded.

But, in investing, inaction is often the disciplined choice. And that is profoundly counterintuitive.

If the COVID crash felt fast and chaotic, the GFC felt heavier and more systemic. Back then, the fear wasn't about temporary shutdowns; it was about whether the financial system itself might fracture—for years to come.

Banks were failing. Governments were intervening. Words like 'collapse' and 'meltdown' dominated headlines. Investors weren't just worried about earnings. They were worried about bankruptcy.

At its worst, the Australian market fell by more than 50 per cent from peak to trough. And that was a grinding fall that went on for month after month after month.

For investors who were fully invested, portfolios were effectively halved.

The losses did not feel like temporary fluctuations. They felt permanent. It felt as though something fundamental had broken.

And yet, markets recovered. Not immediately. Not smoothly. But steadily enough over time that investors who stayed invested eventually saw their portfolios return to previous highs and move well beyond them.

Those who panicked and sold near the bottom locked in a permanent loss. The difference between those two outcomes was not the severity of volatility.

It was behaviour.

The storm was the same. The response was not.

What risk really isn't

Finance textbooks define risk as volatility — statistical deviation from average returns. It's a neat definition, mathematically elegant and easy to measure. But human beings do not experience statistical deviation. We experience fear, regret, doubt and urgency. And loss.

Volatility is simply price movement. It is the visible expression of uncertainty about the future. It reflects changing expectations, shifting sentiment and evolving information. It is not, in and of itself, permanent damage.

If a profitable business continues to generate cash, adapt to competition and serve customers effectively, a falling share price does not make the underlying enterprise weaker. It makes it cheaper.

Volatility is uncomfortable. But discomfort is not destruction.

As Morgan Housel writes, 'Volatility is the price of admission. The prize inside is superior long-term returns.'[3]

If you want the prize, you must tolerate the price.

The tragedy is not that volatility exists. The tragedy is that investors interpret volatility as catastrophe.

And so do the boffins. A company whose shares fall ever so steadily is considered less 'risky', using the academic definition, than a company whose shares rise strongly over the long-term, but has lots of big rises and falls along the way.

The latter is uncomfortable along the way, but the destination is worth it. And far less 'risky' than actually losing money!

During the COVID crash, markets fell rapidly and dramatically. Entire industries appeared uninvestable. Commentators debated worst-case scenarios daily. If volatility were the same as risk, that period would have represented extreme danger.

And it felt like it... at the time.

But by the end of 2020, markets had recovered most of their losses. By April 2021, the ASX had surpassed its pre-COVID highs. When dividends were included, long-term investors were well ahead.

The quality businesses that survived (and the vast majority did) continued to generate earnings and adapt to new realities. Prices moved violently, but productive assets continued producing.

Imagine two investors during that period.

Investor A sold after a 30 per cent fall, intending to re-enter once things 'settled down'. Markets rebounded quickly, often before headlines improved. By the time Investor A felt comfortable buying again, prices were significantly higher.

Investor B stayed invested and continued contributing regularly, purchasing more shares at lower prices during the downturn.

Five years later, their outcomes were dramatically different.

The market environment was identical for both.

The difference was behaviour.

As Warren Buffett observed, 'The best chance to deploy capital is when things are going down.'[17]

That sounds courageous in theory. In practice, it feels deeply uncomfortable. Which is precisely why preparation matters more than bravery.

I'll tell you a personal story. During that COVID crash, I was worried.

Investing wasn't fun. I was losing money, and I didn't want to keep buying.

But you know what I did? I invested anyway. Not because it felt good, or even *right*, but because I knew I should. That wasn't my first rodeo. I'd been there before and I knew what I had to do.

That doesn't make me a genius or better than anybody else. It just meant that I followed the plan, no matter how bad it felt at the time.

(By the way, some of the companies I bought were bad decisions. I didn't make money on all of them. That's also why diversification and dollar-cost averaging is important. We'll discuss dollar-cost averaging in Chapter 9!)

But the key point here is that it felt terrible and scary, but I was able to separate the emotional part of my brain from the rational part that knew to just keep investing.

I did it because I expected those companies' profits to be higher in five years time. And, if that was right, the share prices should be, too. And the greater the market panic, the bigger the discount I was getting.

The fear is real. But so are the outsized returns, if we're able to keep our heads.

And the difference is not just temporary. It compounds over time. Missing even the early stages of a recovery can materially reduce long-term returns.

Volatility does not destroy wealth. Fear does.

The three real risks

If volatility is not the true enemy, what is?

The first form of real risk is *permanent loss of capital*. This occurs when investors buy poor businesses that never recover, wildly overpay for hype, concentrate excessively in a single industry or theme, or use excessive leverage that forces liquidation at the worst possible time. In these cases, volatility may be present, but it is not the cause of destruction.

Structural weakness is.

The chance of permanent loss is reduced by choosing quality businesses, diversifying sensibly, avoiding excessive debt and maintaining a long-term horizon. These principles are not glamorous, but they are powerful.

The second form of real risk is *behavioural mistakes*. Markets fall, fear rises and investors act. People sell to relieve anxiety, wait for clarity and re-enter only after prices have risen. The damage compounds quietly. Intelligence does not inoculate against this risk. In fact, smart investors often rationalise panic more convincingly.

The third form of real risk is *inaction*. Perhaps counterintuitively, this might just be the greatest risk of all over a lifetime. Cash feels safe because it does not fluctuate visibly and is backed by the government. All true. Yet, as we've learned only too well in recent years, inflation steadily erodes purchasing power. At 3 per cent inflation, money halves in real value roughly every 24 years. Over a 40-year working life — and perhaps another 40 years in retirement — that erosion is substantial, and risks a (perhaps far) lower quality of life in retirement (see figure 6.1, overleaf).

Waiting for certainty feels prudent, but certainty never arrives. The opportunity cost of waiting compounds silently.

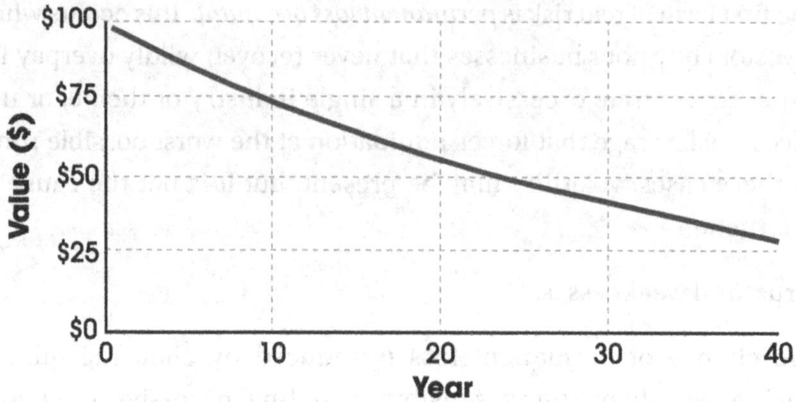

Figure 6.1 Erosion of $100 over 40 years at 3 per cent per annum

Buckle up: The destination is wonderful, but the journey will be bumpy

If you invest for 30, 45 or 60 years, you will likely experience multiple significant market declines.

(Sixty years? Yep. Probably more for most people reading this book. We'll get into why in Chapter 16. For now, just know that your retirement date isn't the end of the investing journey. It's a significant milestone, and might bring changes, but it's nowhere near the end.)

History suggests that markets experience meaningful drawdowns roughly once a decade, sometimes more frequently.

That is not pessimism, it is pattern recognition.

The future will not mirror the past perfectly, but it would be historically unusual for markets to avoid substantial volatility over long periods.

For that reason, you need to make your peace with the inevitability of downturns before they occur. During a crash, emotion will be louder than logic.

If volatility surprises you, it will feel like failure. If it is expected, it will feel like turbulence.

There is a profound difference between being shocked by waves and expecting them. That won't make it fun, necessarily (unless you can really get into a 'buying things on special' mindset), but you'll recognise it for what it is... and respond accordingly.

Prepare, don't predict

Many investors attempt to reduce risk by predicting downturns. They look for signals, headlines and indicators that might provide advance warning. Prediction feels like control.

Preparation is control.

You cannot reliably forecast recessions, pandemics or geopolitical shocks. Just look at the abominable record of economic forecasts and stock market predictions.

Hint: You might know one or two people who correctly guessed the last downturn, but don't forget the many, many hundreds of people who didn't—or those who forecast crashes that never happened!

But you can structure your portfolio to survive those shocks. Preparation includes diversification, sensible position sizing, avoiding excessive leverage, maintaining an emergency fund and investing small amounts regularly.

Preparation does not eliminate volatility. It ensures that volatility does not become catastrophic.

Prediction fails precisely when you need it most. And in two ways. Getting out early costs you the money you would have made if you'd remained invested. And staying in too long means you cop the fall you were trying to avoid.

Frankly, predictions are a mug's game. They make crystal ball gazers and tarot readers look good.

Back to psychology for a moment: Why do these three predictors exist? Because humans hate uncertainty and will turn to self-professed seers and suspend disbelief for the comfort it provides.

Now, it's easy to say, 'You need to make your peace with volatility'. It's harder to explain what that actually means and how to do it.

'Making peace' does not mean indifference. It does not mean enjoying downturns or pretending they do not hurt. It means acknowledging, in advance, that sharp declines are a normal and recurring feature of long-term investing. They are the ticket to the dance.

Most investors intellectually understand that markets fluctuate. Far fewer internalise what that means emotionally. They accept the idea of volatility but still carry a quiet assumption that it will not be severe, or that it will not happen to them, or that they will somehow see it coming in time.

That assumption is fragile. And wrong.

When markets fall sharply, the surprise amplifies the fear. If you believed—even subconsciously—that markets *shouldn't* fall 30 per cent in a month, then a 30 per cent fall feels like a breach of contract. It feels like something has gone wrong.

But if you accept that meaningful declines are part of the mechanism through which long-term returns are delivered, then downturns, while painful, are not shocking. They are unpleasant, but expected.

That shift from surprise to expectation is powerful. It changes how you interpret headlines. It changes how you respond to volatility. It changes whether you view a falling market as a signal to flee or a reminder that this is the price of admission.

Achieving peace is not about removing emotion. It is about reducing the power of that emotion.

Risk tolerance versus risk capacity

There is another subtle dimension to risk that often goes unexamined: the difference between risk tolerance and risk capacity.

Risk tolerance is emotional. It is how much volatility you believe you can handle without panicking.

Risk capacity is structural. It is how much volatility you can afford to endure without jeopardising your goals.

The two are not the same.

A young investor with stable income and decades ahead may have high risk capacity. They can afford significant volatility because time is on their side. But if that investor loses sleep over a 15 per cent decline, their risk tolerance may be lower than their capacity.

Conversely, someone in retirement may have high emotional tolerance — they may feel calm during downturns — but low capacity, because a severe decline combined with withdrawals could materially affect their long-term sustainability. (That doesn't mean you shouldn't invest in retirement, by the way. It means you should *prepare* your financial life accordingly.)

Understanding this distinction matters. It helps you design a portfolio that is both financially appropriate *and* emotionally sustainable.

The goal is not to maximise volatility exposure. The goal is to maximise the probability that you will stay invested long enough for compounding to work. It is to maximise your long-term returns without the risk of being sent back to square one along the way.

For long-term accumulators (hopefully, all of us!), volatility early in life can be annoying and emotionally challenging, but not catastrophic. In fact, lower prices during accumulation years are beneficial, as regular contributions purchase more shares at discounted prices.

But volatility interacts differently with retirement.

'Sequence risk' refers to *when* the downturn happens. Put simply, a 30 per cent fall in the value of your portfolio is less impactful (emotionally and financially) when you're 19 than when you're 69. The retiree has a larger portfolio, isn't adding to it and might have needed that money.

This does not mean retirees should avoid shares entirely. In fact, given the average length of retirement, I think that would be a significant mistake. It means your portfolio should be structured appropriately. Holding adequate cash buffers, diversifying income sources and, at worst, temporarily reducing withdrawal rates are all ways of preparing for or dealing with sequence risk.

Notice the theme again?

Not prediction. Preparation.

No-one knows when the next downturn will occur. But you can build flexibility and cushioning into your plan.

The slow cost of inaction

Earlier, we touched on the risk of not investing. It deserves deeper reflection.

Consider two individuals, both aged 30.

The first begins investing $500 per month immediately, earning an average long-term return of 9 per cent. The second waits ten years, then invests the same $500 per month from age 40 to 65.

The early starter invests for 35 years; the late starter invests for 25.

Despite contributing only $60 000 more over their lifetime, the early starter's portfolio at retirement is *dramatically* larger. The extra decade of compounding creates an advantage that cannot be caught up later.

How much larger?

The early starter ends up with more than $1.5 million (excluding taxes and fees). The late starter would have a little over $600 000 — well less than half.

The difference is not intelligence. It is not superior stock picking. It is simply time.

Time amplifies discipline.

Time punishes delay.

(And if you're looking at that and thinking 'I'm already 35 or 40 or 45', let me remind you of the old proverb from Chapter 4: 'The best time to plant a tree was 20 years ago. The second best time is now.')

The risk of not investing is subtle because it does not produce visible pain in the short term. There are no red numbers on a screen. There are no alarming headlines. There is only the quiet erosion of opportunity.

But decades later, the consequences are tangible. Fewer choices. Delayed retirement. Greater dependence on external factors. Reduced flexibility.

That is real risk, even if it doesn't feel like it at the time.

Literal (and metaphorical) insurance

So we've covered 'not taking enough risk' as one of the biggest risks of all. But if you are taking risk, you should be thinking about insurance.

We insure our homes not because we *expect* them to burn down, but because the consequences would be catastrophic if they did. We insure our income not because we assume disability, but because we acknowledge uncertainty.

Insurance is not a prediction of disaster. It is an admission that uncertainty exists.

Literal insurance is vital.

If your car is worth more than a few grand, it probably should be insured, because the cost of replacing it is meaningfully more than the premium.

If you're renting, and your possessions would be expensive to replace, insure them.

If you own your own home, for God's sake, make sure you have insurance that covers the cost of repairs and — most importantly — replacement. It's bad enough if you lose your home, but if the insurance doesn't cover replacement, you could be stuck paying back a mortgage for a home you can't afford to rebuild.

If you have dependents, consider what would happen to them if you suddenly weren't around. Yes, a cheery thought, I know. But *really* think about it. Would your partner and kids be able to stay in their home? Would they be able to cover the bills on a single income? If the answer is 'no', please consider life insurance. Not for your sake: for theirs.

And what if you were still around, but couldn't work? No life insurance payout there, but the implications will be similar (maybe worse, because you might need to be looked after, too). If your income is important to your family, then income-protection insurance is something you really should seriously look into.

By the way, a word on insurance premiums: They are the worst, most expensive and useless thing in the world. Until you need them, then they're the cheapest and best thing you ever did.

Investing has its own forms of insurance.

- Diversification reduces the damage if you are wrong about a single company or sector.
- Dollar-cost averaging reduces the regret of poor timing.
- Holding quality businesses reduces the probability of permanent failure.
- Maintaining cash reserves reduces the likelihood of forced selling.

None of these eliminate volatility. They do not guarantee smooth returns. What they do is reduce the probability that volatility becomes permanent destruction.

The most resilient investors are not those who avoid storms entirely. They are those who build structures that withstand them.

It is tempting to chase maximum theoretical return. And, in the moment, strategies to get a higher return — leverage, speculation, concentration — can feel justified.

But investing is not an academic exercise. And some risks do become eventualities.

So, as much as I want you to maximise your returns so you can live the life you want, you need to make sure the strategy you choose is one you can sleep soundly with, and one that isn't walking the proverbial tightrope without a net.

If your portfolio causes ongoing stress, or if every downturn makes you feel sick to your stomach, then your portfolio might not be right for you.

Not only is the emotional toll not worth it, but it might also create a worse financial outcome, too: A portfolio you can't live with is a portfolio you will eventually abandon ... and maybe at the worst possible time.

Accepting slightly lower expected returns in exchange for greater emotional durability is rational. It increases the probability that you will remain invested through inevitable turbulence.

You do not build a bridge that functions only in perfect weather. You build one that withstands storms.

Similarly, you design a portfolio that you can stick with when markets are uncomfortable. Because sticking with it is what unlocks compounding.

Over time, you begin to realise that risk is never about the market. It is about how you respond to it.

Stick to the plan

You've already seen the One-Page Investing Plan (page xviii). When it comes to risk, the plan can be distilled to:

- Work hard.
- Save diligently.
- Invest regularly.
- Choose wisely.
- Diversify sensibly.
- Ride the waves dispassionately.

That is not merely motivational language. Or even a wealth maximisation strategy. It is also a risk-management system.

Each of those things, individually, is risk management and risk mitigation. Together, they give you a plan.

Working and saving create resilience. Investing reduces the risk of playing it too safe. Doing it regularly reduces timing risk. Choosing wisely reduces the risk of permanent capital loss. Diversifying sensibly reduces concentration risk. Riding waves dispassionately reduces behavioural risk.

When viewed through this lens, the plan is about delivering impressive compound returns but also about (maybe even 'by') managing threats.

Let's get ready

The next time markets fall sharply — and they will at some point — it will not feel theoretical. It will feel painful and very personal. Headlines will sound convincing. Doubt will creep in quietly. The urge to act will feel rational.

In that moment, the distinction between volatility and risk will matter enormously.

If you remember that volatility is movement, not destruction, you will think about falls differently.

If you remember that preparation matters more than prediction, you will feel less compelled to chase certainty.

Risk is not the presence of waves.

Risk is a boat that can withstand them.

Build well. Expect storms. Stay aboard.

The greatest risk of all is never starting — or starting and abandoning the journey at the first sign of turbulence.

Remember, investing is not about eliminating fear.

It is about designing a system in which fear does not dictate your future by driving your decisions.

Long-term stock market returns have come not in the *absence* of recessions, crashes, wars and uncertainty, but *despite* those things.

Because the very thing that scares most people away (volatility) is the mechanism through which long-term returns are delivered. If markets were smooth, predictable and certain, they would not offer excess returns. The reward exists because uncertainty exists.

That means discomfort is not a flaw in the system.

It *is* the system.

Over time, you begin to see this differently. You stop viewing downturns as verdicts on your intelligence or your plan. You begin to see them as part of the contract you signed when you chose to invest.

The contract reads something like this:

'You will endure periods of doubt. You will experience temporary losses. You will question yourself. In exchange, you will participate in the long-term growth of productive enterprise.'

No-one reads that contract carefully at the beginning.

But every investor lives it eventually.

Those who accept it early suffer less when volatility arrives. Those who resist it experience every downturn as a betrayal.

Now, if I have brought you this far, I'm going to take a risk and push a little further.

We've talked about not giving in, or giving up, when volatility strikes.

But it can also be an opportunity, if and when you're mentally and emotionally prepared to confront it.

And, in time, it can be an opportunity to be harvested. Something perhaps not to look forward to, but a cloud whose lining is shining silver: *I hate that my portfolio is down, but at least I get the chance to go shopping for bargains.*

Risk is not share price movement.

Risk is misunderstanding the nature of the journey.

And once you understand the journey, volatility stops feeling like an ambush.

It starts feeling like weather. And as avid campers like to say, there's no such thing as bad weather ... just bad preparation.

Congratulations! You just made it through the 'scary chapter'. Now we're going to start putting the plan into action.

And to do that, we need to know what we're working with — the building blocks of wealth.

Diversification

Diversification has been called 'the only free lunch in investing'.

It's a nice line. It's also true. If you build your portfolio carefully, diversification costs nothing: no insurance premiums, no trading costs ... just resilience.

So how should you think about it?

The idea is that a properly diversified portfolio will have a range of different risk factors, but without an uncomfortably large exposure to any single one of them.

As I've written elsewhere, you can't diversify by owning all of the Big Four banks, rather than just one. True, you are *slightly* diversified against single company risk (fraud, mismanagement, brand damage etc.), but you remain *very* exposed to funding risks, housing market risks and Australian economic risks.

The same if you own a few miners or a handful of retailers.

That said, if you're going to go full 'Noah' and buy two of everything, you might be well diversified, but perhaps at the cost of your returns. There are some ordinary companies on the ASX, and to own them just because they are different to the ones you already have in your portfolio would be an own goal.

Even if you're investing only in ETFs, have a think about which ETFs you own and what risks are present—and whether adding other ETFs might be useful.

Diversification can be a proactive way to grow your portfolio, too, not just a defensive mechanism. Think about the different types of companies that dominate the different indices. The ASX is full of banks and miners. The US market is dominated by software and consumer companies.

Owning both, together, gives you not only defensive diversification, but access to companies and sectors you can't get, at scale, in just one.

What really matters

- Volatility isn't the real risk in investing—permanent loss of capital and poor behaviour are.
- Market crashes are inevitable and uncomfortable, but historically temporary.
- Investors who prepare for downturns tend to survive them; those who try to predict them usually fail.

7

THE BUILDING BLOCKS OF WEALTH

> *Investing is about probabilities — putting the odds in your* favour *is a good start.*

We've done the set-up. You know what we're out to achieve (long-term wealth creation), and you know the power of compounding. You also know some of the things that can get in the way.

Now we're getting into the construction phase. So, to torture a different metaphor, let's assess the various building materials available to us to understand their inherent characteristics, strengths and weaknesses.

Let's work out what we're going to build with.

And at this point, a not-so-unexpected spoiler alert: I'm a shares guy. Now, I'm not a shares guy because of my day job or because of some sort of ideological or philosophical preference.

I'm a shares guy because I think that's the best way for me to build my wealth (I'll explain why later in this chapter). But, also, let me be clear: If I found a property, or bond, or cryptocurrency that I thought would do a better job, I'd buy it tomorrow.

Because, while I like shares, I like money even more. To ignore a greater opportunity because it didn't fit my preconceptions would be a special form of self-inflicted injury!

Investing is not an abstract philosophical exercise. It is not a Twitter debate. It's not an academic or theoretical argument. It is not a prediction contest. It is a process of assembling assets in a way that serves your goals, matches your temperament and compounds over time.

You don't build wealth with opinions. You build it with ownership.

So what can you own?

At the broadest level, there are a handful of 'asset classes' available to investors: property, shares, bonds and cash, crypto and collectables. (We'll leave things like options and other esoteric 'financial instruments' alone because, well, I think you *should* absolutely leave them alone!)

Each behaves differently. Each has strengths and weaknesses. Each attracts passionate advocates. And each, used appropriately, can play a role in a sensible financial life.

But none are magical. And none are without risk. Most importantly, let's do it dispassionately. God knows there's enough partisan bickering in the rest of our lives. Money doesn't care how it's made, and we shouldn't either. Being on an asset 'team', irrespective of the returns, is ... not smart.

So let's examine them carefully — not through the lens of hype or habit, but through the lens of long-term wealth building.

Property

For Australians maybe more than any other people, property looms large in the national imagination. It is tangible. It is visible. It feels real. You can walk through it, renovate it, improve it. You can point to it and say, 'That's mine'. You just know you can talk about it at your next BBQ, and people will nod along.

That psychological comfort matters more than most people realise.

At its core, when you buy property, you are buying land and a structure. The land may appreciate over time because of scarcity, population growth, infrastructure improvements and economic development. The structure may provide rental income if leased. In many cases, you are also buying leverage, because banks are willing to lend substantial amounts against residential property.

Property has built enormous wealth in Australia over the past several decades. Falling interest rates, expanding credit availability, strong population growth, urban concentration in a handful of cities and tax benefits have combined to create powerful tailwinds. Many households have experienced extraordinary gains in paper wealth simply by owning their home and holding it over long periods.

But it is important to distinguish between what has happened and what must happen in future to deliver the returns we seek.

The returns on property are often significantly influenced by credit conditions. When borrowing becomes easier and cheaper, buyers can pay more. When lending tightens or rates rise sharply, affordability contracts. That dynamic makes property partly a play on the credit cycle, not just on land scarcity.

Property also tends to be highly concentrated. A typical investor might own one or two properties, often in the same city or even the same suburb. That concentration increases risk. If local economic conditions deteriorate, if zoning changes, if oversupply emerges, the impact is not diversified away.

Transaction costs are high. Stamp duty, legal fees, agent commissions and renovation expenses can meaningfully reduce net returns. Liquidity is low. You cannot sell a bathroom to raise capital. Selling the whole asset is often slow and expensive.

Property is also rarely passive in practice. Tenants vacate. Hot water systems fail. Roofs leak. Regulatory rules shift. Insurance premiums rise. There is time and effort involved, even if a property manager handles day-to-day operations.

Perhaps most importantly, property investing in Australia often involves significant leverage. Leverage magnifies returns when prices rise. It also magnifies losses when prices fall. A modest percentage decline in any asset value can translate into a dramatic decline in equity for a highly leveraged investor. But a modest increase in the home price can offer strong returns on the money invested.

None of this makes property inherently good or bad. It simply makes it a specific kind of asset with particular characteristics. It can be a powerful component of wealth. It can also be a source of stress and risk if misunderstood.

Understanding those characteristics is more important than repeating the national mantra that 'you can't lose on property'. And working out whether the future will look like the past is important, too.

Shares

Shares, as we've discussed, represent partial ownership of businesses. That is the simplest and most important definition.

When you buy shares in a listed company, you are buying a claim on its future earnings. You are participating in its growth, its risks, its innovations and its failures. You are aligning yourself with the productive capacity of the economy.

Unlike property, which is largely a play on land and credit, businesses create value by solving problems, producing goods, delivering services, increasing efficiency and innovating. Over long periods, the aggregate earnings of businesses tend to grow alongside — and often ahead of — economic growth.

This is the core reason shares have historically been powerful wealth builders.

It's also worth pointing out that shares are unlike the other asset classes in one important way: They are only a *subset* of the overall asset class of 'businesses' (in this case, Australian businesses).

'Property' is every property in the country. 'Cash', which we'll get to, is all of the Australian dollars. But the ~2000 companies on the ASX are only a tiny fraction of the 2.8 million-odd businesses in Australia. Not necessarily the best — there are some wonderful private companies and some terrible ASX-listed ones — but a specific subset.

And that's an important point to understand, because we're not comparing 'all property' against 'all business', but rather against 'the businesses that, on average, are good enough, big enough and successful enough to be listed'. It is a(n imperfectly) curated set, with above-average returns and potential — something we'll come back to. In short, the average ASX company is better than the average Australian business, and that's an 'unfair' advantage that we can take advantage of.

When companies earn profits, they can use the money to expand operations, develop new products, enter new markets, improve efficiency or acquire competitors. If they generate high returns on capital (basically the ratio of profit to the value of all of the assets and debt of the business) and reinvest that money intelligently, earnings can compound *internally* for decades.

Shareholders benefit from that compounding even if they never add additional capital. Dividends can be reinvested, too. The business itself becomes more valuable over time.

Shares are highly liquid. You can buy and sell them easily. Transaction costs are generally low. Diversification is accessible; with modest sums, you can own dozens or hundreds of businesses across industries and geographies.

But shares come with volatility. Prices are quoted every second, six hours a day, five days a week. They move on sentiment, news, macroeconomic shifts and speculation. They can fall sharply in short periods, even when underlying businesses remain sound.

This always-on pricing is emotionally taxing. It invites reaction. It tempts shareholders to trade, to predict, to respond to headlines. But volatility is not the same as risk, as you've read. Remember, true risk is the permanent impairment of capital. Volatility is often the temporary fluctuation *around* long-term value.

Shares reward patience and discipline. They penalise impatience and overconfidence. They do not require leverage to produce meaningful long-term returns. But they do require the ability to endure uncomfortable periods without abandoning the plan.

Bonds and cash

Bonds and cash are often described as defensive assets. They are typically lower-returning than shares over long periods, but they are also generally less volatile.

Cash is the most stable asset. It provides liquidity and certainty. It does not fluctuate meaningfully in 'nominal' (before inflation) terms. However, it is vulnerable to inflation, which erodes purchasing power over time. Cash is not a growth engine. It is a buffer.

The primary role of cash in a portfolio is not to generate wealth, but to provide stability and optionality. It allows you to meet expenses without selling growth assets in a downturn. It reduces stress. It buys time.

Bonds represent loans to governments or corporations. In exchange for lending capital, the investor receives periodic interest payments and the return of principal at maturity. They're kinda like term deposits but the money is 'deposited' with companies or governments, rather than banks. They're generally less secure than bank deposits, too.

Bonds typically offer lower expected returns than shares, but they can provide income stability and diversification benefits. In many environments, high-quality bonds behave differently from equities during market stress. That divergence can smooth overall portfolio volatility. Lower volatility, in turn, can reduce the likelihood of behavioural mistakes.

Bonds and cash are unlikely to make you wealthy on their own. But they can play an important supporting role in preserving capital and managing risk, particularly if you want or need less volatility, and when you want to have a cash buffer to avoid selling shares or other assets at inopportune times.

The problem? The cost of lower volatility (by holding cash and bonds) tends to be that they lower your overall long-term return. If you need that benefit, and you're happy to pay the price, then they can be useful. But if you don't need volatility protection (or access to a cash 'buffer' for other reasons), that protection can be expensive.

Cryptocurrencies

Cryptocurrency is a relatively new asset class and one that inspires strong opinions (to say the least).

At their core, most cryptocurrencies do not represent ownership of productive enterprises. They do not generate cash flow. Their value is driven primarily by supply constraints, network effects, adoption rates and collective belief.

That does not make them irrelevant or illegitimate. Technological innovation can create enormous value. Digital scarcity and decentralised systems may play meaningful roles in the future financial system.

But, from an investment perspective, crypto will likely behave differently from shares or property in the short and medium term. Without underlying earnings or rental income, valuation is more sentiment-driven. Price movements can be extreme. Gains can be rapid and spectacular. Losses can be equally dramatic.

For investors considering crypto, clarity is essential. Is this a speculative allocation, or is it a foundational wealth-building strategy? The answer should determine the size of the allocation and the expectations attached to it.

And cryptocurrencies, in particular Bitcoin, are likely to have two phases: the adoption phase and the maturity phase. During adoption, the question is how many people will want how much and at what price. At maturity, once adoption has reached its endpoint, it should be expected to largely just hold its purchasing power (and appreciate slowly, but steadily against currencies that suffer from inflation).

At what level will maturity happen? No-one knows. The true believers have their views. The never-crypto lot have their views. The rest of us can only watch in fascination.

But because of that uncertainty, caution is warranted.

Collectables

Collectables include art, classic cars, rare watches, fine wine, trading cards and other items valued for rarity or desirability.

Like crypto, collectables do not generally produce income (the exception tends to be art, which can be leased out for display). Their returns depend on being able to sell them to someone else at a higher price. Demand can fluctuate with fashion, economic conditions and generational tastes.

Collectables can appreciate significantly. They can also stagnate or decline. Valuations are often opaque. Markets are less liquid than public markets. Transaction costs can be high.

There is nothing wrong with owning collectables, particularly if they provide enjoyment independent of financial return. But they are typically better viewed as passion assets rather than core portfolio components.

It would be a brave person who tried to set themselves up for retirement with collectables. That doesn't mean some people won't be able to do it, but it's risky, and generally not advisable. For every person who does it, how many miss out on a comfortable retirement but have a room full of 1970s yo-yos?

Build wealth with productive assets first. Collect what you love once financial foundations are secure.

A quick summary of the pros and cons

Each asset class offers advantages and disadvantages.

- *Property* offers tangibility, income potential and access to leverage, but it is concentrated, illiquid and often heavily dependent on credit conditions.
- *Shares* offer ownership of productive businesses, scalability, diversification and internal compounding, but they are volatile

and psychologically demanding. The best share investments will do much better than property; the worst will do much worse.

- *Bonds and cash* provide stability and liquidity, but lower long-term growth potential. And if the company or government goes broke, the bondholder might be left with nothing to show for their investment.
- *Crypto* offers a potential high upside and exposure to innovation, but extreme volatility and uncertain valuation frameworks. History suggests many (but not all) 'coins' are somewhere between flights of fancy and outright fraud.
- *Collectables* offer enjoyment and potential appreciation, but are illiquid and dependent on fashion and demand cycles.

No asset is universally superior. The question is not which asset is 'best', but which asset (or combination) best serves your goals and temperament.

Why I chose (and choose) shares

This section is really important.

Because I'm going to suggest that a key driver of the One-Page Investment Plan is a slow and steady accumulation of a diversified portfolio of shares.

Not as a rejection of the other asset classes, per se. And not because the others are bad. But rather because I think shares offer benefits that are worth taking advantage of. If you want to substitute your own investment choices into the plan, go for it. It's a little harder to implement dollar-cost averaging or achieve meaningful diversification, but the choice is, ultimately, yours.

With that set-up, here's why I invest in shares, and why I reckon they're an excellent choice for the One-Page Investment Plan.

For clarity—and to avoid just a little hate mail—let's say again and be crystal clear at the outset: Choosing shares was not an outright rejection of property. Don't 'at' me, as the cool kids say.

Property has built enormous wealth in Australia. Sensible buyers in good locations who held for long periods—particularly with disciplined use of leverage—have done very well. A skilled property investor who understands local supply dynamics, zoning changes, infrastructure spending and demographic shifts can absolutely outperform the average. Just as a thoughtful company analyst can outperform the share market. Skill exists in both arenas.

My choice of shares wasn't based on the belief that property cannot or does not work. It was based on the belief that, over the very long-term, shares have structural advantages that make them more likely—not guaranteed, but more likely, in my view—to deliver superior compounding.

First, economic opportunities and constraints

Residential property values, over long periods, are, ultimately, tethered to household incomes. People purchase homes primarily using wages. Even investors rely on tenants whose rent is paid by wages. Banks assess serviceability based on income. Governments set policy around affordability. The entire residential property ecosystem revolves around what households earn.

Credit conditions can stretch and even structurally alter this relationship. Falling interest rates increase borrowing capacity. Looser lending standards expand access. Speculative momentum can push prices beyond fundamental affordability for a time. But over multi-decade periods, house prices cannot sustainably compound far beyond income growth without creating systemic strain.

If property prices consistently grow much faster than wages, several things must happen: households devote a rising share of income to housing, debt levels increase relative to income and affordability deteriorates. There are limits to all three. Eventually, either wages must accelerate meaningfully—which history suggests is difficult and slow—or price growth must moderate.

This does not mean property prices cannot rise strongly for extended periods. They can. They have. Structural undersupply, demographic shifts, urban concentration and infrastructure development can all support multi-year booms. But when we zoom out over future decades, wage growth acts as a gravitational force.

Wages tend to grow steadily, influenced by productivity gains, inflation and labour market dynamics. But they rarely grow explosively over long periods in developed economies. That places a natural ceiling on how quickly housing values can compound across an entire country.

Is that a prediction? No. Investors (should) deal in probabilities, not certainties. Those structural challenges aren't impossible to overcome. It's *possible* that property outperforms shares over the long-term. I just don't think the conditions I've listed make it *likely*.

A business, however, is not constrained by wages in the same way.

When you buy shares, you are buying ownership in an enterprise that can improve margins, increase efficiency, automate labour, expand internationally, launch new products, acquire competitors and capture market share. A company's revenue is not limited to the wages of Australian households. It can sell to global customers.

It can operate in higher-growth markets. It can benefit from technological shifts that increase output without proportionate increases in labour costs.

In fact, many businesses grow precisely by reducing their reliance on wage growth. Automation, digitisation, software scalability and network effects allow companies to increase output while keeping labour growth relatively modest. That dynamic enables earnings growth that can exceed aggregate wage growth.

As I wrote on page 102, listed companies are often (on average) a high-quality subset of the broader business ecosystem. Many of the country's most scalable, profitable and capital-efficient firms are publicly traded. Public markets give them access to capital for expansion and acquisition. Over time, these businesses can consolidate fragmented industries, professionalise operations and take share from smaller private operators.

That structural capacity — to expand beyond domestic wage growth, to improve productivity, to scale across borders, and to capture market share — provides room for earnings growth that outpaces the constraints faced by residential housing as a whole.

Again, this does not mean property cannot outperform in specific locations or periods. A talented property investor can identify suburbs poised for gentrification or infrastructure upgrades. Just as a skilled stock picker can identify undervalued companies.

In sum: As a broad asset class, residential property is more tightly linked to the growth of household incomes. Shares represent ownership in entities that can grow through productivity gains, globalisation, consolidation and innovation — forces that can exceed wage growth over long periods.

That structural distinction is one of the key reasons I expect shares, on average and over decades, to deliver stronger returns.

Second, diversification

With shares, diversification is straightforward. You can own dozens or hundreds of companies across industries — banks, healthcare providers, technology firms, consumer businesses, infrastructure operators. You can spread risk across sectors that respond differently to economic conditions. You can invest internationally and gain exposure to economies far larger and more dynamic than Australia's.

And you can do it easily, by buying a small share in many different companies... or easier again by simply buying a low-cost, diversified, index-based exchange traded fund (ETF).

Property, by its nature, is concentrated. Most investors own one or two properties in one country, often in one city. Even if those assets perform well, they are tied to a narrow set of economic drivers. Shares allow far broader participation in local, national and global growth.

International exposure, in particular, is powerful. Australian residential property is (obviously) tied to the domestic economy. Shares allow you to own parts of businesses in the United States, Europe, Asia and emerging markets, as well as local businesses that serve those markets. You can participate in global innovation, global consumption trends and global demographic shifts.

Third, scalability and consistency

Shares allow gradual accumulation. You can invest smaller amounts regularly. You can dollar-cost average — investing regularly and consistently, regardless of short-term price movements. When markets fall, your regular contributions buy more shares. When markets rise, your earlier investments benefit.

That discipline removes the need to 'time' markets — to try to guess the right times to buy and sell and buy again. It turns volatility into an ally rather than an enemy.

Property investing is typically lumpy. It requires large capital commitments. It is difficult to add incrementally. Shares allow you to build exposure steadily over decades.

Fourth, tax efficiency

Australia's dividend imputation system means that many local companies pay franked dividends — dividends that come with credits for tax already paid at the corporate level. For most Australian investors, those tax credits can materially reduce the tax they have to pay, compared to similar income from other investments — enhancing after-tax returns.

Property has its own tax advantages, including deductibility of certain expenses, of course. But franked dividends provide a structural benefit unique to Australian shares that strengthens the case for owning shares in listed companies.

Finally, not requiring debt

Property investing in Australia often relies on debt to amplify returns. There is nothing inherently wrong with prudent borrowing. But leverage magnifies risk as well as reward. Shares, historically, have delivered strong long-term returns without the need to introduce a bank into the equation.

For me, that matters. It preserves flexibility. It reduces the risk of forced selling. It allows patience.

All of this leads me to a measured conclusion: Property can absolutely play a role in wealth creation, and skill can outperform in any asset class. But structurally, shares have broader growth drivers. They are less tightly constrained by domestic wage growth. They benefit from productivity improvements, international expansion and industry consolidation. They allow diversification, incremental investing and favourable tax treatment.

Of course, they are also volatile. They require discipline. They are not guaranteed. And the range of outcomes for individual companies is much larger than individual properties (though leveraged losses can get big, fast, in property if you're unlucky or make a bad decision).

But for a patient investor thinking in decades, I believe shares are likely to offer a stronger foundation for compounding—precisely because businesses have room to grow in ways that wages, and, therefore, broad residential property values, ultimately, do not.

And that is why I chose them, and think they are an important and useful part of an investing plan.

Mr. Market

Warren Buffett shared a tale told by his mentor, Ben Graham, about a bloke called Mr Market.[20]

Mr Market, in this story, is your partner in a private business. It's an important message, which casts Mr. Market as someone who represents the rest of the people buying and selling shares on a given day.

They're there, every day, offering to buy your shares, or to sell you theirs, if you want. And they—or 'he' in the story—offers you a price.

Most of us are conditioned to think 'well, if BHP shares are trading at a given price, that's what they must be worth'. But Buffett's Mr Market story tells it differently. Mr. Market, you see, isn't a rational person, only focused on the businesses themselves.

He's often erratic and emotional, responding to how he feels on any given day... and focused on the short-term, rather than the long-term. As Buffett says, when he is in a good mood...

> ... he names a very high ... price because he fears that you will snap up his interest and rob him of imminent gains. At other times he is depressed and can see nothing but trouble ahead for both the business and the world. On these occasions he will name a very low price, since he is terrified that you will unload your (share) on him.

But the other thing about Mr. Market is that he doesn't care whether or not you buy or sell. He'll just offer you another price tomorrow. And the day after that. He's always there to buy or sell, if you want. The decision is yours.

But as Buffett also tells us—and this really is the key—Mr. Market is there to trade with only if we want to, but we shouldn't fall under his spell... and we shouldn't assume he's right.

The key line:

> Mr Market is there to serve you, not to guide you... you are free to either ignore him or to take advantage of him, but it will be disastrous if you fall under his influence.

That's what investors need to keep in mind.

What really matters

- Investors can choose from several asset classes: shares, property, bonds, cash, crypto and collectables.
- Each asset has strengths and weaknesses, and none are perfect or risk-free.
- Shares represent ownership in productive businesses and, historically, have been powerful long-term wealth creators.

8

GETTING STARTED, WHERE YOU ARE, WITH WHAT YOU HAVE

> *Investing success doesn't start with stock picking — it starts with behaviour.*

There is a dangerous time that can derail every investing journey. But it's not what you think.

It's the phase where you understand enough to have a handle on things — but haven't yet acted.

Like, well, now.

At this point in the book, you know compounding works. You agree that time matters more than brilliance. You accept that volatility isn't the same as risk. You've thought about asset classes. You've considered shares versus property. You've probably even looked at stockbrokers' websites.

But you haven't quite ... started.

And the longer you wait, the easier it becomes to justify waiting a little longer.

- You'll start when you get the pay rise.
- You'll start when markets settle down.
- You'll start when you feel more confident.
- You'll start when the news improves.

There will always be a reason not to start.

The uncomfortable truth is that investing doesn't begin with picking shares. It doesn't begin with asset allocation spreadsheets or economic forecasts (actually, please don't do those things!).

It begins with behaviour.

(If you've got to this point in the book, you're not surprised to hear that, are you? And yet, it's true.)

Before you buy *anything*, you need to create the conditions that allow investing to work. You need structure. You need resilience. You need cash flow that supports ownership instead of constantly undermining it.

This chapter is not about which ETF or shares to choose. It is about building the engine — the system — that allows you to invest consistently for decades.

Because investing success is not a single decision. It is a system and a process.

And that begins at home.

Beat the budget: Pay yourself first

Many people treat investing as what happens with the leftovers.

They earn income. They pay rent or the mortgage. They cover electricity, gas, groceries, subscriptions, insurance and the discretionary stuff that makes life enjoyable. At the end of the month — if anything remains — they consider saving or investing it.

The problem with this approach is not that it is irrational. It is that it is unreliable.

Human beings adapt quickly. Our lifestyles grow to match our incomes. If more money appears in a bank account, we tend to find a use for it. A dinner out. A subscription upgrade. A small indulgence. None of these feel significant in isolation. But over time, they become permanent.

If investing depends on leftovers, investing will rarely be consistent.

The single most powerful shift you can make is this: *Pay yourself first.*

Treat investing as a non-negotiable expense. When income arrives, a predetermined portion is transferred immediately to savings or investments. Not after spending.

Before.

This is not about extreme frugality. It is about priority. It is about aligning your actions with your long-term goals.

If you say financial independence matters, your decisions — and your cash flow — should reflect that belief.

Harsh? Maybe. But fair.

Now look... there are some people who just can't possibly find an extra cent to invest with. They're flat out just covering the essentials. If that's you, this chapter isn't directed at you (and our society should be structured so that fewer people are in that position — but that's a whole other shooting match).

If you're on the proverbial breadline, you don't need to be told about managing a budget — and there's no point telling you to save and invest. That said, when the extra money does come, and I hope it does, you'll be best placed to have the discipline to start that investing journey.

For the rest of us, here's the tough love bit: You can save and invest — whether you do or not depends on whether you want to confront your spending.

If you *need* the expensive house, the car lease (or two), the private school fees, the twice-weekly UberEats, the expensive wine or whisky, the new clothes, the overseas holidays ... then you're confusing 'needs' with 'wants'.

Now, I'm not sitting in judgement on any of that, by the way. It's a free world. You worked hard for your income, and you're entitled to spend it however you want.

But just remember that choices have consequences. It's what economists call 'opportunity cost'. A dollar spent on one thing then can't be spent on something else. We all know that, deep down, of course. Once the money is gone, it's gone.

So is the opportunity to turn that money into more — much more — in future.

And you're welcome to determine that priority for yourself. But let me be clear, here: You also have to own the consequences.

If the new car is worth more to you than earlier retirement, that's cool — but that's the choice.

If the yearly European holiday now is worth more than a more comfortable retirement, that's your call ... but that's the trade-off.

You get the idea.

And here's where you really need to decide to live, both physically and financially, 'consciously' and (sorry) maturely.

You need to own your financial decisions and their consequences.

It's perfectly fine to choose 'now' over 'later'.

But two things:

1. That means less in retirement and/or retiring later than you otherwise might
2. Don't kid yourself that you're a victim of circumstances and you don't have a choice.

Okay, that last one does kinda sound like fighting words. But I need to be straight with you.

You need to own your financial choices, not fall into the trap of believing you're a victim of circumstances.

Yes, I know inflation has been through the roof. And, yes, I know there are other things in life besides investing. If you're feeling defensive right now, maybe put the book down for a bit. Doubly so if you're feeling angry right now.

But do me a favour. Go for a walk. A long one. While you're walking, think about 'future you'. Imagine looking back on your life, in 20, 35 or 50 years from now.

My favourite framing for life decisions is Amazon founder Jeff Bezos' idea of the 'regret minimisation framework'.[19]

What will you regret more? Not buying (or leasing) that new car? Or not being able to retire earlier or with more?

Would you really miss an UberEats dinner (which probably arrived lukewarm anyway) if the price of that was a more comfortable retirement?

Do you really need that new television, or would you feel less stressed knowing you had money in the bank and you were on the way to financial freedom?

Yes, I'm phrasing those as rhetorical questions, but you might have different answers.

All good — just own those decisions and the outcomes.

Before you do answer them, though, I want to remind you again of the shortcomings of our evolutionary biology. We have evolved to prefer 'now' over 'later'. And that makes sense.

Given the choice of $1 today or $1 next year, I'd take the money today. Why wait?

Given the choice of a hot meal now or a hot meal in three days, I'd take 'today'.

Totally logical.

But compounding is an evolutionary infant, at least in financial terms. We have no inbuilt mechanism to automatically process it. Indeed, on a dietary basis, our desire for sugar and predisposition to (modern) obesity came from the need to gorge when food was plentiful, because that condition may not last.

Just as our impulses haven't adjusted for a state of plentiful food (and ultra-processed food, more worryingly), our reptilian brains haven't yet realised the awesome power of compounding. There was zero benefit in leaving fruit on the tree — either it would fall off and rot, or someone else would take it — but there is incredible potential benefit in leaving money to compound, rather than spending it.

Why am I telling you all this? Because when you do go for that walk, I need you to think really deeply, rather than impulsively.

That's the 'future you' lens I mentioned earlier. And when you do think about future you, make sure you think in compound terms.

Given the choice of a new car now or a new car later, I'd take a new car now.

But compounding isn't a 1-for-1 question. You'll remember in Chapter 4 we discussed the Rule of 72 — an easy way to work out how long it takes for your money to double.

My $2 million mistake

And it's here I want to make a financial confession: I bought a new car in my 20s. Want to know how much that cost?

Would it surprise you to know it cost me more than two million dollars? No, not at the time, but in opportunity cost (there's that phrase again). Stick with me as I wallow in my own misery.

See, in my 20s, I got a promotion at work. And the new position came with a 'car allowance'. You don't see 'car allowances' often these days, but back then, the new position came with a choice: a company car to drive or a yearly 'car allowance' that I could use to put towards my own car.

Now, to be clear, there was no *requirement* for me to buy a car. No minimum price or age. I could have just taken the money and kept driving the car I already had.

But I was—what's that word again? Ah, yes—an idiot.

Full of some combination of ego, testosterone, pride and whatever else, I figured: 'Well, I didn't have the money yesterday, so it's not like I'll have less if I buy the new car!'

Which was true ... and stupid.

Don't get me wrong, I loved driving that car. But it was a dumb decision. Really dumb.

The car cost $65 000. (I used a car lease with a 'balloon' payment at the end, so it actually cost even more, considering the interest, but let's not rub my face in it.)

I can't actually remember the year (a self-defence mechanism?), but let's assume I was around 25 at the time. And let's invoke the Rule of 72, and assume the stock market's long-term average return of about 9 per cent per annum.

Had I invested that $65 000 instead, by age 33 (72 divided by 9 means I'd double my money roughly every eight years), I'd have had $130 000.

By 41? $260 000.

You're already ahead of me, aren't you? But just to really, *really* rub my nose in it, let's finish the series.

49: $520 000

57: $1 040 000

65: $2 080 000

Bloody hell.

Was the car fun to drive? You bet. Did I feel good driving it? Absolutely.

Will I look back at 65 and want to wring 25-year-old Scott's neck? I already do, and that pain is only going to get worse!

The cost of that new car, combined with hubris? A cool $2 million.

(And, by the way, if I invested that $2 million at 9 per cent in retirement, I could buy a new car every six months, and still have money left to pay exorbitant car wash prices every week!)

Again, I'm not going to tell you what you should do (but you really, really shouldn't get on the car lease treadmill). I'm just going to remind you that the impact of your decisions now will be far, far greater over time — for good and for ill.

Choose wisely.

Speaking of choices, what's the right choice to make, in terms of how much money you should invest?

If you're an Australian reading this, the great news is that thing called superannuation. If you work for a wage or salary, 12 per cent of your pay is being put aside for 'future you'.

And here's the thing: plenty of working people complain that 'the money is mine' and 'I should be allowed to choose what to do with it'. But do you know how many retirees complain about super? None.

My memory might be failing me, but I can't recall a single retiree ever telling me they were unhappy that they were forced to save for retirement! Funny that.

So, you're already off to an excellent start, thanks to some prescient and future-looking government policies.

(A word here for the self-employed. I know your business is important. And, like the worker who has to choose between spending and investing, you're thinking, 'I could use this money to grow my business, instead'.

Don't. Please, don't.

Maybe the business will boom and you'll be raking in the cash, and sell the business for a motza. Or maybe it'll just putter along. Worse, perhaps it fails and you lose everything. Please don't take that gamble. Like the wage-earner, please pay yourself first. Pay yourself super. (You'll thank me later.)

Okay, so that's 12 per cent of your salary. Isn't that enough? It might be, actually. And some of the investing education that follows in later chapters — the how — applies to both your super as well as money you invest yourself, so if you decide not to add more, please keep reading anyway.

Me? I invest outside super as well. Why? Two (related) reasons:

1. I want to have a more comfortable retirement than super alone might bring (including the opportunity to help family and give to charity, among other things).
2. I want to choose the timing of that retirement and/or have flexibility if retirement is thrust upon me (if I lose my job and can't get another one).

Now, it's true that I'm getting older, and slowly closer to being able to access my super. If my health remains good (touch wood), I continue to enjoy my work and my boss continues to think that my work is worth paying for, I won't need to use that flexibility.

But I might.

And flexibility is one part of the financial freedom I discussed at the beginning of this book.

And, as I've mentioned, I'd simply also like to have the choice, and the portfolio, to give me options before and during my retirement.

So, I reckon saving 10 per cent of your take-home pay is probably the right number. Especially — and the car numbers I talked about bear this out — earlier in your career, if you can manage it.

(I know housing affordability is a stupidly big issue. That'd be the topic of *yet another* book! And I know that makes it hard to save. Again, if you absolutely, objectively can't save, then that's where super comes to the fore. But if you can, please do, as early as possible.)

And, if by some strange quirk of fate, this book lands in the hands of someone who doesn't have super — either because they're working outside Australia or they're self-employed or have spent long periods outside the workforce, 10 per cent is the *absolute* minimum you should be aiming for ... and probably more.

That's why it's important to pay yourself first. And make those conscious decisions to free up the money required to achieve your goal.

But what decisions?

Ways to find money to invest (#getabetterrate!)

I've lost count of the people who've told me they'd invest 'if only they had more money'.

But, as I mentioned above, lifestyle inflation is real. Here's another example:

When I got my first full-time job, I earned $24 500 per year. And I couldn't spend it all!

I mean, I could have, if I tried, but I was living at home, driving a car I'd paid my parents a small amount of money for, and other than weekly board, that was it. I paid rego, car insurance and petrol.

I didn't wear fancy clothes. My desires were limited (not having social media surely helped!), and without trying, I had money left every fortnight.

When I got a pay rise, to $27 800, I was *rich*.

Fast-forward a few years, and I… had found ways to spend money. My income increased significantly as I got a new job, and then a promotion. At first, there was lots of money left.

But then… almost nothing.

Now, I'm not saying you should move back home (but I'm not saying you shouldn't, if that's a viable option that you can live with while you save!).

I'm just saying that lifestyle inflation is real.

And, as I mentioned earlier, that's probably the greatest potential source of savings to free up money to invest.

The next is discretionary spending. Using the 'regret minimisation' framework, ask yourself if in ten years' time, you'll still be glad you spent that money.

On the fancy dinner. The new TV. The new phone, when the old one is only 18 months old. On the dress, pair of jeans or new jacket. Sofa. Holiday. You get the drill.

Sometimes you need to replace stuff that's worn out. Other times… you're just spending because it feels good.

(It's okay if the answer is 'yes', too. Sometimes, a fancy dinner is just what the doctor ordered. Just... don't get carried away.)

The third category, though, is money for jam. Not only does it rarely hurt, but the savings can be meaningful. And, because they weren't really 'choices' in the first place, money saved here can and should be put straight to investing, because it doesn't hurt your lifestyle at all.

And what's this category? It's what I call #getabetterrate

Let's start with the largest expense for those in their own homes: the mortgage. There are literally hundreds of mortgages out there.

So, statistically, what's the chance you have the best one for your circumstances? It's not zero — you likely shopped around for the right combination of fees, conditions, features and interest rates when you took the loan out.

At the time, it was probably one of the best 10 or 20 options you could have chosen.

But now? After rate changes, new loan products? After you paid down some of the principal and maybe got a pay rise?

Maybe it's still the best loan for you. *Maybe.*

But I reckon if I got just 1 per cent of the savings that every Australian made by shopping around and moving to a better loan, I could retire tomorrow!

The benefit? You don't have to sacrifice your lifestyle one bit. The lower repayments are literally free money. The cost? Some googling. A phone call. You spend more time scrolling Instagram and talking to telemarketers!

Instead? Find out what your bank is charging you. Google or use a comparison website to find similar loans (loan length, amount, fees) and call your bank. Tell them you want a better rate or you'll leave.

Much of the time, they'll either meet that other loan, or give you a lower rate than you're currently on. That is literally free money you've 'earned' by picking up the blower.

And if they don't? Okay, changing banks will take a little additional effort. You might have to fill out a few forms and get some payslips. That's annoying.

But the payoff could be in the hundreds or thousands of dollars a year. Done over the lifetime of a mortgage, it'll be many, many times that.

Think of how far you'll go out of your way to save a few cents a litre on petrol, or how you'll justify buying something that's on special to save a few bucks.

If the 'cost' of maybe saving thousands of dollars is a few forms and a couple of emails? Time to harden up and just do it, I reckon.

Now, that's mortgages, but the savings don't stop there. Think about all of the areas in which a little effort to #getabetterrate can save you a small fortune:

- Car insurance
- Home and contents insurance
- Life and income-protection insurance
- Health insurance
- Electricity
- Gas
- Mobile phone
- Internet
- Home loans (as discussed)

- Personal loans
- Credit cards
- Cash in the bank (not a case of 'saving' but rather 'earning' more by making sure you're getting a good interest rate).

Imagine saving $10 a month here and $20 a month there. Pretty soon, you're getting to some serious savings. And remember, it's *free money*. You're not getting lower levels of service or satisfaction — you've just been able to #getabetterrate, and the savings are yours!

There's one other way to save a few bucks, and we're skipping forward a little here. We'll cover the proverbial rainy day fund in a bit, but when you have enough in that fund (and make sure it's earning the best possible interest!), you can afford to increase your insurance excess. You probably know all about that, but essentially insurance companies require you to pay the first chunk of any claim (the 'excess'), and they pay the rest. Now, the higher the excess, the lower the monthly or annual insurance premium. Yes, to some degree you're betting against luck, but if you kick the excess up from a couple of hundred dollars to double that, or even more for home insurance, your premium can drop considerably. That'll save you a lot of dough.

Now, here's the deal: Promise me (and yourself) that every dollar you save from that exercise will be earmarked for investing, not just allowed to be soaked up by other spending! (We'll talk about how to best do that in a minute.)

One last point: I was raised to believe that loyalty is important. My parents were dead right: It's a very important personal value ... with the exception of your finances. If you don't know the name of the person on the other side of the transaction, assume you're just a number to the company you're dealing with.

There was a time when you and the bank manager knowing each other was important. And loyalty that went both ways was appropriate and valuable.

These days? What do you get from being loyal to your bank? Your insurer? Your electricity company?

Nothing.

In fact, new customers usually #getabetterrate than existing ones!

The 'loyalty tax' has been estimated at potentially well over six figures over the life of a $1 million mortgage. It would be less for smaller bills, of course, but it's still very real.

And, one last time: As long as you move to a product with the same benefits, the savings are completely free, other than a few minutes of your time.

Shop around. #getabetterrate. And compound those savings.

Build your 'oh, shit' fund

With apologies for the language, shit happens. We all know that. And there are two versions.

The first is the best/worst-case scenario, where we curse our luck or circumstances. We curse the fact we've had to spend money on something that broke, stopped, got stuck when it should move or moved when it shouldn't. We fix the problem and move on.

The second is the same, up to the point of spending the money. In the second version, maybe we simply can't fix the problem because we don't have the money. Or we have to use a credit card, borrow the money from the bank or risk our kneecaps with the bloke in the corner of the pub.

I don't need to tell you which version is better.

What I do need to tell you is that based on surveys, an extraordinary number of people don't have the cash set aside to meet these unexpected, unwelcome yet unavoidable periodic obstacles. The data varies, but it's usually somewhere between a large minority and a small majority of people who couldn't find the money to solve those problems.

Call it a rainy day fund (as in 'saving for a rainy day'), if you prefer. Me? It might be uncouth, but it's the 'Oh, shit' fund. Money put aside for when the proverbial hits the fan.

As I wrote on page 119, some people just don't have the financial ability to save. After housing, food and bills, there's just nothing left. That's awfully precarious — and just plain awful. But then there's the group that, consciously or otherwise, have the ability to prepare for those outcomes but just… don't.

Whether they don't think about it, or don't think it'll happen to them, or just can't bring themselves to save money that they could otherwise spend, they're taking some big risks.

Risks that just aren't worth taking.

Think about it. For those people, in a 'best/worst-case' scenario, they save money they'll never need, *and* earn interest on it in the meantime.

In the 'worst/best case', when disaster strikes, they still curse whatever gods may be, but pay the bill and move on.

The worst/worst case is debt, interest and moving further away from the eventual goal.

Next time you have an unexpected expense that makes you think 'oh, shit', hopefully you'll have the money ready to go.

Which begs the question: 'How much?'

There is obviously no single answer that's right for everyone. It depends on the circumstances and the size of the unexpected disaster.

It also depends on your circumstances: whether you have kids, whether you have a partner who is working (or could work, if needed), and more.

But back to our motto of 'prepare, don't predict', here's how I think about it.

The worst-case scenario is usually losing your job. The fridge might blow up, but that's a fixed replacement or repair cost. Ditto a car that breaks down. But if you lose your job, it could take months to find another one. Meanwhile, the bills keep coming in.

My *minimum* 'Oh, shit' fund would be three months' worth of *unavoidable* expenses. That is, you can cancel the gym membership and a streaming service or three. You'll be okay eating baked beans rather than takeaway burritos for a while. But you'll still need to pay the rent/mortgage, electricity bill, school fees, car repayments and the rest.

So, add up the monthly cost of all of the things you can't avoid, multiply it by three, and make that your target.

And as I said, that's a minimum. Ideally? Ideally, I'd aim for six months, particularly if you're the sole breadwinner, you're renting and/or you aren't ahead on your mortgage repayments.

Oh, and make sure the money is in a high-interest online savings account, rather than one of those no-interest accounts the banks will offer you.

You may never need it — in which case it'll give you some nice regular interest payments and a lot of peace of mind. But better to have it and not need it than need it and not have it, I reckon.

Get rid of bad debt (and bye-bye Afterpay!)

You might have heard a quote attributed to Einstein, about compounding? He probably didn't actually say it ... but it's a good one. Most people have heard the first sentence:

> 'Compound interest is the eighth wonder of the world.'[13]

They imply, in their heads, the second sentence of the 'quote':

> 'He who understands it, earns it.'

But few remember — or internalise — the third:

> 'He who doesn't, pays it.'

Compounding is wonderful when your money makes money.

The problem is that your debt makes debt ... or at least makes interest that makes your debt harder to get out from under.

You know that tough love thing from earlier? It's back.

This time in the form of your grandparents.

They used to have a saying: 'if you can't afford something, don't buy it'.

You didn't use Afterpay. You didn't use credit cards. At most, you put it on lay-by, which was kinda like buy-now-pay-later, but it was pay-over-time-and-get-it-when-you-finish-paying.

No, not as catchy, but it kept them out of debt.

Let me be really clear here: *consumer debt is financial poison.*

What's consumer debt? Debt you take on to buy an asset that falls in value, or a product that is consumed and used up.

Mortgage debt? Perfectly good (as long as the house is reasonable value and you can make the repayments).

University debt (HECS/HELP in Australia)? Excellent, as long as it helps you get the career you want.

Debt to buy that new stereo, pair of jeans, television or holiday? Hell. No.

Oh sure, you can justify it at the time, but what was it again that your grandparents would have said? If you can't afford it, don't buy it.

Boring? Yep. Old fashioned? Yep. Annoying? Sure.

But just common sense financial management. Your grandmother didn't say it because it was fashionable ... she said it because it was — and is — right.

Are you ready to hear something that seems almost sacrilegious these days? Good.

Delete your Afterpay account. Get rid of Zip. Don't buy-now-pay-later — save-now-buy-later instead.

These aren't 'budget management tools' as the providers call them — that's complete and utter BS.

They are tools that prey on our desire to have something now, turbocharged by social media. And they are terrible for your financial health — not so much because of the size of the debts, but because of the habits they help you form.

That goes doubly for younger people who are just learning to manage their money.

Speaking of financial poison, next cab off the rank is credit cards, some of which charge up to 25 per cent interest. Literally one-quarter of your debt in interest every year.

You have two choices here: either pay your entire balance, in full, every month ... or cut the bloody things up. No, you don't need a credit card to buy stuff online — use a card company's 'debit' card option instead. Or link your savings account to PayPal (Disclosure, here: At the time of writing, I owned shares in PayPal, but I'm pretty sure this mention won't move the share price!).

Carrying a credit card balance is the financial equivalent of leaving the tap running. It just leeches away your income even before you get it.

By the way, if you're thinking, 'well, they're bad for other people, but I'll be responsible', just remember that 90 per cent of us think we're above-average drivers! We all think it'll be the other guy, but so do they! Some of us will end up being the other guy ... don't take the risk.

Oh, and one last thing: Telling me you're using the credit card 'for the frequent flyer points' is like reading *Playboy* for the articles. It might even be true, but by the time you've paid the annual fee and any other interest on the way through, you'd likely be better off just putting the annual fee directly towards your next flight!

Your financial fitness 'to-do' list

Okay, that's some Frankenstein's monster combination of encouragement and tough love, right?

I hope I got the balance right.

Either way, it's time to put this stuff into action so you can get ready to invest.

Here is a list of the actions you need to take, to get yourself on the right track. Some people will find it easy — others will find it hard. This stuff falls into the 'simple, but not necessarily' easy bucket. But you can do it.

Here's what you need to do in order. And it's dead simple:

1. Delete the buy-now-pay-later apps. No ifs, no buts. This is the first step on your journey.
2. Have a look at your credit card statements. Hand on heart… Did you pay the balance, in full, every month over the last year? Frankly, I'd rather you cut them up either way, but if you have a track record of doing so, and you really can't wean yourself off the habit, then keep going, but keep it conservative! Actually, bugger it. If you are paying the bill in full every month, just use your savings account for those expenses in the first place! And if you didn't, pay in full every month, cut up the cards now! You'll still have to pay the debt, but at least you're not adding to it! (Can't imagine life without buy-now-pay-later or credit cards? Feel like you'd be 'missing out' or somehow 'not normal'? That's precisely *why* you should get rid of them. The finance industry has got its claws into your psyche. Time to cut it loose!)
3. No need to do a full budget, but roughly estimate what you can afford to save and invest every month. How much would be left after the unavoidable bills? If the answer is 'at least 5 per cent of my income', you're on the way. If it's 10 per cent, even better!
4. #getabetterrate. Spend 10 minutes each lunch break this week calling your providers, and demand a better rate (leave if they won't give you one). Keep track of how much you'll save each month as a result.
5. Add the savings from your personal #getabetterrate campaign to the 5 to 10 per cent you can reasonably save by cutting back a bit on the discretionary spending. Consider it a donation from 'present you' to 'future you'. A donation that will multiply many times over before 'future you' gets it.

For some people, that's more painful than for others. Some will feel the loss of that discretionary spending as something that almost physically hurts because it crimps their lifestyle. Others will really get into the 'game' of trying to save more.

Either way, if you really do want financial freedom and choice — whatever that means for you — this is how you start the process.

Like a snowball rolling down a hill, even the smallest start can turn into something massive as it goes. And that's what I want you to cling to for now. Because when you start to see your money making money — share prices rise, dividends coming in, your portfolio growing — you'll start to see that snowball getting bigger.

And that's when the payoff starts, and the motivation gets easier.

Now, it's time to pucker up and give that money a job to do ...

What really matters

- The most dangerous phase of investing is the moment when you understand enough but still haven't begun.
- Paying yourself first—investing before spending—creates a system that allows compounding to work.
- Small lifestyle decisions today can have enormous long-term benefits... or costs.

9

KEEP INVESTING SIMPLE, STUPID

> *The simpler your investing plan, the easier it is to follow when it matters most.*

What? Am I calling you stupid?

No. Not even a little bit. But I reckon you've heard of the KISS acronym. And its point is to remind you to keep your investing simple.

There is no shortage of people and organisations who will try to make investing sound complex. Maybe they believe it. Maybe they hope you'll become so bamboozled that you'll engage them to 'help' you — for a fee, of course!

And if you *want* to find complexity in investing, there is no shortage of rabbit holes you can go down. But do you need to? No. Is it advantageous? Often, also no.

Can it be sometimes? Probably, but which times? Which strategies? Which advisers? At what cost?

Or, you can keep it simple, and just harness the immense force of compounding.

Soon, we'll get into what to invest in. But for now, let's get the structure working for you.

In the last chapter, we talked about organising your financial life to get ready to invest — finding and setting aside the money that is going to be the kindling for the fire that provides financial freedom.

But, to torture yet another metaphor, let's talk about how to get that fire lit, and how to keep it burning.

So ... what makes a difference?

The maths of investing is pretty straightforward, with three broad inputs:

1. How much you invest
2. How long you invest for
3. Your return rate

That's probably in rough order, too.

You can double your monthly investment (to a point!) more easily than you can double your holding period. And you can double your holding period more easily than you can double your rate of return (your annual gain).

There are, of course, exceptions to each — if you're 98, none of the above will have a huge impact (sorry!). And you can't go back in time and start investing any earlier.

But if you're asking me how someone could improve their long-term returns, I'd say 'invest more, start earlier and improve your annual rate of return, in that order'.

This chapter is all about helping you think through the framework of how to start, and keep, investing — for the long-term.

Work, save, invest

'Earn more over time' is the second part of the One-Page Investing Plan. And for some, it might fall somewhere between obvious and condescending.

Fair enough.

The point, though, is that you can only invest what you save. And you can only save what you earn.

In the last chapter, we talked about ways to save.

And I'm not going to spend too long here preaching about hard work. Frankly, other than those who attach a religious fervour to it, I'd take easy over hard, all things considered!

But I don't mean 'work hard' in that context. I mean it in the sense of maximising your income, so you have more to invest.

That actually might not be about work at all. It might be about getting another qualification — letting you get a job that you might enjoy more, be better at and stick with longer.

It might be thinking about ways to work better or smarter. To deliver more value to your boss and workplace. Because, outside award-wage changes or general company-wide pay rises, demonstrating your value to your boss is one of the best ways to get a pay rise or a promotion.

But it might also actually be working harder, too. Overtime. A second job. A side hustle. No, I'm not saying you have to — or even should — do these things. And I'm not passing any moral judgement. I'm just suggesting that there are two ways to increase the amount you save: earn more or spend less. Or some combination of both.

If you're a young person reading this, can I encourage you to really work hard on understanding the business or organisation you're in, and working out how to demonstrate value?

I have no stats on this, but my best guess is that it's those people who tend to come to the notice of their boss (and their boss) when it comes to opportunities for more responsibility and promotion. The person who shows an eagerness to work hard (and well) will put themselves at the top of those lists pretty quickly — and will likely learn more in the process.

As both an employee and as a manager, I've seen firsthand the success had by others who've really dug in and have committed themselves to being valuable.

And if you think that's just some corporate version of 'sucking up', you're welcome to that view — but I kinda reckon an employee should be earning, not just receiving their wage. But even if you're just entirely self-interested, the opportunity for more responsibility tends to be more satisfying and, importantly for this context, tends to come with a higher income, all else being equal.

I'm not asking you to sell your soul. Don't become a corporate drone. Just treat it as an opportunity to learn, to show your skills and experience and to be rewarded for them (or, to be more employable by another company if you do leave). That probably leads to a more satisfying work life, and it probably means a higher income, too — which, if you save a decent portion of it, takes you ever closer to financial freedom.

Then what? I mean, we've talked about earning an income, spending a little less and saving the difference.

We've talked about 'paying yourself first'. But how?

I'm glad you asked.

This is one of the most fundamentally important parts of the whole process. The road to hell is, as they say, paved with good intentions.

Intending to save is important. Actually doing it is vital.

And this is where the rubber hits the road. The good news is that just a little organisation, using some incredibly simple ideas, can turn your intention into action — and your action into some, hopefully, very impressive compound returns.

Your 'get started' plan (and checklist!)

One of the more annoying things about being human is the difference between good and bad habits. Annoying, because bad habits are easy to form, while good habits tend to be far harder!

So what are we to do? The field of behavioural finance has some answers, but they largely come down to one (wonkish) word: pre-commitment.

That is, deciding a course of action in advance so that we're not waylaid by temptation and circumstance at the time of action itself.

For our purposes, here's how it works:

First, set up two online, high-interest accounts: one for your 'Oh, shit' fund and one for your investment cash. If they send you an EFTPOS card to go with them, cut it up. These accounts have one simple rule, with one slight variation.

The 'Oh, shit' account can only be touched for *two* reasons:

1. In the event of an 'Oh, shit' moment
2. To transfer the interest payments to your investment account.

The investment account can only be touched for *one* reason:

1. Retirement.

Before that, money goes in, but never, ever comes out. Ever. No, not even for that reason, or that reason. Only when you retire.

And the investment account has two functions:

1. To receive the regular savings (more on that in a bit); and
2. To receive dividends from your investments.

How are we going so far? (There's a checklist at the end, so no need to take notes).

All you need to remember at this point is that these accounts never, ever get touched for anything else, no matter how badly you want that phone/jacket/trip/couch!

Now you have the accounts set up, you're going to fill them in order: The 'Oh, shit' fund needs to be fully funded with whatever amount you decided in Chapter 8.

Then when it's full, you're going to direct your regular savings to the investment account. The only reason you'll stop putting that regular amount in the investment account is if/when you need to refill your 'Oh, shit' account if you need to use it to deal with some unexpected drama.

Now, here's one of those 'pre-commitment' things: If your pay office allows it, get your pay split between your current bank account and this new one. Grab the form, and nominate a dollar amount each payday to go into your investing account, with the rest to go into your regular account. That way, the money will never touch your bank account, and you won't be tempted to spend it!

If your pay office won't allow split payments, don't fret. Work out what day payday is, and set up a regular direct deposit the day after to transfer your investing money to your new investing account. So, if you get paid every Thursday, or every second Wednesday or on the 15th of the month, the money will come out the next day (don't do it the same day, in case the transfer goes out before the money arrives!), and while you'll see it in there, you won't have a chance to spend it before it's whisked away to continue building your financial future.

Next, you're going to open a brokerage account. Frankly, if doesn't much matter which one you choose, as long as you keep the costs relatively low, and resist their marketing entreaties to trade more often (remember, most brokers make money, not if you are successful, but if you trade a lot... so you know what they're going to get you to do!).

At the time of writing, I have brokerage accounts with CommSec, Pearler and Sharesies (for different reasons). All three are perfectly good options. When you're comparing, by all means look for the lowest fees — the money is better in your pocket than theirs! — but also make sure you get a feel for which seems easiest to use, and which has the best information to help you make it as easy as possible to set up.

Then ... pick one. You can always change later. Don't let yourself get caught up in trying to decide, and end up inadvertently doing nothing because you can't choose. When you open your brokerage account, the broker will either have a cash account to transfer money to, to buy and sell, or will ask you to nominate your own bank account.

Here's the thing: You can't *ever* nominate your normal bank account! One of the most important contributors to your long-term compounding will be dividends. It's important that your dividends (and the proceeds of any shares you sell) go into your investment account, and you then buy more shares with that money. If you have them paid into your regular bank account, you know it'll be tempting to just spend them.

Then, when there's enough money in your investment account, buy some more shares (if you can, try to keep the brokerage fee to under 1 per cent of your investment each time. But if it's a little more, no drama—investing, and staying invested, is better than trying to get cute on brokerage fees.)

And now you have a lovely little virtuous circle going. Here's the plan: Money goes into your investment account, you use it to buy shares, those shares go up over time *and* pay you dividends, and you use those dividends to buy more shares.

(No, they won't always go up. No, you won't always receive dividends. But if you've chosen your shares well, and history is any guide, both will happen over time, and your portfolio will compound away nicely!)

One list, no excuses

Okay, so here's all of that in a single list:

- Open a high-interest, online 'Oh, shit' savings account. Shred the EFTPOS card that comes with it.
- Open a high-interest, online investment savings account. Shred that card, too.
- Ask your pay office to send a regular dollar amount into those accounts, one at a time, every payday.
- If they won't or can't, set up an automatic direct debit from your regular bank account the day after payday.

- Open a brokerage account. One of the bigger ones. Doesn't matter which.
- If your brokerage account doesn't have its own 'cash account', get the dividends and share sales paid into your investment account.
- When there's money in your investment account, invest it!

Got it? Good.

That's not *entirely* all there is to it, but that's all the framework you need!

But before we get to what's available to buy (and worth buying!) on the ASX, this is a great place to introduce you to one age-old idea and another boring but very powerful investing concept.

Aesop was right

Turns out that the older we get, the more we realise our parents really are right about most things. Painful, but true. My younger self has a lot to apologise for.

Also turns out that ancient wisdom is ancient wisdom for a reason: It persists because it's right.

And so it is with investing and Aesop. No, not the skincare brand, the Greek storyteller of Aesop's fables fame. Among them was the one we were taught as kids: 'The tortoise and the hare'.

The hare mocked the tortoise for his lack of speed. Sick of the carry on, the tortoise challenged the hare to a race. You'll remember that the hare sprinted the course then, full of action and ego, decided to take a nap, given how far the tortoise was behind. And when he awoke, the tortoise had won the race.

There are many lessons to take from this fable, but the one I want to draw out is the one we know: Slow and steady wins the race.

It is tempting to want to be the hare. And, in this sense, we can deviate a little from the original fable to expand the idea. The hare is the patron saint (patron bunny?) of the 'get-rich-quick' scheme. He is the spirit animal of the speculator. He is the pin-up rabbit of the day trader. The hare is the idea that we can somehow prevail through short cuts and easy options.

Now, if I thought hare-ness would work, you bet I'd do it. If I thought I could get rich quick, why wouldn't I?

The answer, of course, is because it's rarely possible, and the number who try, but fail, are legion compared to the few who manage it. In this sense, the hare really is the exception that proves the rule.

Aesop's tortoise, on the other hand, did a simple thing repeatedly. He put his head down, and plodded along faithfully. No excitement, no haste. No short cuts, no silly risks. He was slow and steady ... and he won the race.

'Aha!' you might exclaim, 'but what if the hare hadn't slept, and just ran the whole way to the finish?' Then the hare would have won, handsomely. But that would have gone against the hare's very nature. The hare lived and (metaphorically) died by the sword. The hare could no more have shelved his ego than he could have won the race.

The day trader, the get-rich-quickster and the short-cutter are the hares. The things that lure them into those pursuits are the very things that stop them being able to avoid the hare's metaphorical nap, mid-race.

I know of no way to help you get to financial freedom if you insist on being the hare, however sleek his form and enticing his speed and energy. Because those things go from asset to liability very quickly.

I do know that, for the last 125-odd years, the tortoise has kept just doing his thing, and the gains have been extraordinary.

Now, lest we get permanently lost in metaphor, the tortoise isn't one particular investor. Or even a particular subset. The tortoise is long-term investing — and the market as a whole.

The worst label for one of the best ideas in investing

Here's a phrase only a boffin could make up: 'dollar-cost averaging'.

It kinda feels like some sort of tax calculation or a phrase accountants would use, right?

I should make it my aim to come up with a better term, but, well, I'm a finance nerd, not a creative genius, so instead, I'll give a Freddo Frog to anyone who can come up with a better one.

Especially because it's a really important idea that will not only help you build long-term wealth, but also ride the waves of volatility.

Here's the idea.

Previously, I talked about saving money every pay day, and investing that money as regularly as you can (keeping costs low as you go).

Let's use a hypothetical example. You decide to invest every month. In the first month, the shares are $9 each. Next month, $10. The month after, $9.50. Then $11, $10 and $10.50.

At the end of six months, that $10.50 price is higher than some of the prices you paid, but lower than others.

But what if you'd bought only once? Maybe you'd have paid $9. At the end of that six-month period, you'd have made a nice gain and probably feel pretty good.

And if you'd only bought once, say, in month four? You'd have paid $11, and be nursing a small but disappointing loss.

Now, in an investing lifetime, one company, bought once isn't going to make or break you. Even buying a few companies a few times won't.

But if you're making only very occasional, large purchases, you're putting a lot of store in your ability—or luck—to buy for the right price at the right time.

Dollar-cost averaging, by comparison, suggests that buying small amounts regularly smoothes—or 'averages'—your cost. Hence the (clunky) name. It removes the need to try to 'time' the market, by giving you an average(-ish) price.

Let's say you invest $200 per month for a year. Sometimes the price is up. Sometimes it's down. It'd be nice for the share price to just go up after you bought, of course, but there's something else at play here. Just look at how your purchasing power expands when the price falls (see table 9.1).

Table 9.1 Dollar-cost averaging in practice

Price per share	Number of shares purchased
$9.00	22
$10.00	20
$9.50	21
$11.00	18
$10.00	20
$10.50	19

No-one likes a smaller portfolio. But because you keep buying, in the 'down' months you get more shares for your money! You own more of the company now than if the share price had simply only gone up.

Here's the other way to look at it through a behavioural psychology lens: If you buy today at $10, and the share price drops to $9, you get to buy the next lot at a cheaper price. And if you buy today at $10 and the share price rises to $11, you've made money.

Now, that's selective use of data and arguments of course, but the point is that it helps keep us on the investing straight and narrow, and keeps us buying.

See, I've heard plenty of people take one of two opposing views based on how they feel about share price movements:

When a share price falls, some people will say 'Great, it's cheap. I should buy more', while others will say 'Nah, it's falling... I'm not buying'.

On the other hand, when prices rise, some worry that 'I've missed it', while others say 'It's going up... I'll buy'.

I'll level with you: None of those approaches is right, based only on share price movements.

Maybe the stock that's gone up is now too expensive. Maybe the one that fell is down because the business is tanking. Or maybe the shares are up because the business is growing strongly, or down because of sentiment, not business reality. In other words, there is nothing to learn from past share price movements!

But dollar-cost averaging, when committed to as a strategy, allows you to put those psychological demons to rest. It allows you to make your investing more mechanical — adding regularly as long as the company is worth investing in at the current price.

It won't give you the lowest price ever — but then nothing other than luck will ever do that. And you could be more involved if you wanted, picking which company's shares you buy when, if that's your preference.

But for many, perhaps most, people, dollar-cost averaging is a form of the 'pre-commitment' we discussed on page 151. And it can be a serious help when it comes to getting invested, remaining invested and adding to your investment snowball as it rolls steadily downhill, picking up more snow as it goes.

Now, let's unpack one of the most powerful acronyms in investing.

The Pareto Principle

You might have heard of a bloke called Pareto, after whom the Pareto Principle is named.

You've almost certainly heard his idea expressed more simply as the 80/20 Rule.

The idea is that 80 per cent of a result comes from 20 per cent of the effort.

Maybe 20 per cent of a company's customers deliver 80 per cent of the revenue.

Maybe 20 per cent of a company's customers are responsible for 80 per cent of complaints, too!

(Apparently — or apocryphally — Pareto discovered 80 per cent of the peas he got from his garden came from 20 per cent of the plants!)

You get the drift. It's common sense, and a concept that you probably have personal experience with, even if you didn't consciously think about it as the 80/20 rule.

It won't surprise you to learn that the same thing applies—directionally, at least, Pareto is essentially a rule of thumb—in investing.

Except it might be closer to 90/10 or 95/5.

The vast bulk of your return will be driven by your savings rate and investing horizon. A little extra (the 5, 10 or 20 per cent) might come from the time, effort and energy you put into trying to outsmart the market.

Maybe.

The Pareto Principle isn't an iron law—but it is an observation that getting a few big things right is generally the key to success in most endeavours.

In investing, that's probably your savings rate, your investment horizon, diversification, dollar-cost averaging and patience.

By all means, chase the extra return if you have the opportunity... just make sure it doesn't backfire on you, instead.

What really matters

- Complex strategies rarely outperform simple, disciplined approaches.
- Diversification and consistency matter far more than cleverness.
- Simplicity makes investing easier to stick with when markets become volatile.

10

THE WTF OF ETFs

> ***ETFs make it possible to invest broadly, cheaply and sensibly without needing to pick individual winners.***

Stockbroker CommSec put out some data in late 2024 that laid bare one of the biggest seismic shifts in modern investing: the move from individual stock picking to the widespread adoption of ETFs.

The report showed that the top-five investments traded by over 40s were all individual shares, while the top-five investments traded by under 40s were all ETFs.

That is, to put it plainly, huge. There is something between an evolution and a revolution underway on the ASX.

And if you're reading this, you probably already know that. But not all ETFs are equal. Some are wonderful. Others, in all likelihood, might just be bad for your wealth. So it's worth spending a little time on the topic here.

And we'll start with a definition and a little potted history, because it shows the distinction between the good and the not-so-good quite nicely.

An ETF is — somewhat unusually for the finance industry — exactly what it says on the tin. Let's break it down.

A 'fund' for our purposes is simply a name for money from different sources pooled together and invested as a group. Traditionally, someone would set up a 'managed fund' (often called a 'mutual fund' in the USA) and invite investors to join the fund by sending in money.

Thereafter, all investors shared in the gains, in proportion to their investment. If the fund gained 10 per cent, every investor — whether they invested $1000, $10 000 or $100 000 — would gain 10 per cent of their investment. The fund manager would often charge a set per cent of the fund value to manage the fund, and another per cent if they managed to beat a preset return rate.

Essentially, the idea was to hand over your money to the experts, who would invest it for you, in theory, better than you could invest it yourself.

Spoiler alert, here: Most research suggests that well over half of all managed funds actually fail to beat the market benchmark. The thing was, back in the day there was no easy way to access the return of 'the market'. You'd have to buy shares in all of the big companies, in proportion to their size, to get a return that approximates the return of, say, the ASX 200 or the US S&P 500.

Jack of one particular trade

That was, until a bloke named Jack Bogle came along. He wondered if the managed fund model could be used, not to actively pick stocks, but to help investors simply and easily get the market's average return.

Instead of each of us having to buy shares in the top 200 Australian companies or the top 500 US companies, his idea was to have a managed fund that would track a stock market index. He created a fund manager called Vanguard, and the 'index fund' was born.

Later, Jack would say, 'Don't look for the needle in the haystack. Just buy the haystack.'[20]

Bogle was also incredibly investor-focused. Rather than starting the fund and making a motza by collecting fees for his own benefit, he created a structure where the fund investors owned the fund — and that meant fees started out small and have only become smaller as a percentage as the funds have grown. Warren Buffett said that Bogle: 'has probably done more for the American investor than any man in the country'.

Buffett wrote:

> If a statue is ever erected to honor the person who has done the most for American investors, the handsdown choice should be Jack Bogle. For decades, Jack has urged investors to invest in ultra-low-cost index funds. In his crusade, he amassed only a tiny percentage of the wealth that has typically flowed to managers who have promised their investors large rewards while delivering them nothing... of added value.
>
> In his early years, Jack was frequently mocked by the investment-management industry. Today, however, he has the satisfaction of knowing that he helped millions of investors realize far better returns on their savings than they otherwise would have earned. He is a hero to them and to me.[21]

I agree.

Fast-forward a little more, and Vanguard decided that they could make it even easier for the average investor. Instead of having to transfer money to the fund manager, and then request that money back when it was desired, Vanguard decided to list its index funds on the stock market itself.

And (brace for the huge reveal) when you have a *fund* that's *traded* on a stock *exchange*, it gets called an exchange traded fund, or ETF.

Compare the pair

And Vanguard's index-based ETFs were and are wonderful. At the time of writing, the average management fee for the Vanguard Australian Shares ETF is 0.07 per cent per year. Other than being James Bond cool, that 0.07 per cent means that you'd pay only $7 per year to have Vanguard manage $10 000 in that Australian shares ETF.

Management fees for active funds can often be somewhere in the range of 0.5 per cent to 1.5 per cent (some are lower and some higher), but just taking a midpoint of 1 per cent means you'd be paying $100 per year — some 14 times higher!

Now, if your fund beats the market, that fee might absolutely be worth paying (though the fund probably also charges a performance fee for that outcome, so check carefully!), but it's a pretty high starting point, I reckon.

Their Vanguard U.S. Total Market Shares Index ETF charges even less: just 0.03 per cent, or $3 for every $10 000 they manage. Even if you had $1 million in that ETF, your fee would be $300 per year!

Now, in my day job, I pick stocks for a living. I love analysing businesses and trying to work out whether the prices are attractive enough to offer what I hope will be market-beating returns. So you might suspect I see index ETFs as the enemy.

I mean, they kinda *are* the enemy, when it comes to whether or not people join the investment services we offer, but I love index ETFs, and own some myself! For many people, who don't have the time, interest or temperament to own individual shares, index ETFs are brilliant. And, frankly, for people who try, unsuccessfully, to beat the market by picking stocks, pivoting to investing in ETFs instead is a great idea, too.

Index ETFs are also great for things like diversification in a portfolio (whether or not you directly own individual companies' shares as well) and access to other markets — for example, the ability to buy an S&P 500 ETF here on the Australian Stock Exchange, rather than needing a US brokerage account.

They're also great because they keep the other fund managers focused by providing an alternative benchmark on both performance and fees.

Index-based ETFs are the best example of what we know as *passive investing*. Passive, in the sense that you're not picking stocks or sectors or anything else. You're just (hopefully regularly) adding money to the fund and getting the market average return, less some tiny fees.

(The stock-picking investors — whether individual investors or fund managers — are known, in contrast, as *active* investors.)

Now, every now and then someone writes an article or gives an interview about how passive investing is somehow going to kill the market. That is, well, garbage.

They say it'll reduce activity and so-called 'price discovery' — the idea that when there are lots of buyers and lots of sellers, the 'wisdom of the crowd' will get the price roughly right. Except the market functioned perfectly well for long-term investors 40 and 50 years ago, when trading volumes were a tiny fraction of what they are today.

I mean, *maybe* if passive ETFs controlled 95 per cent of the market, we *might* start to worry. Until then, feel free to assume those people are just looking after their own interests rather than providing unbiased commentary.

Speaking of active versus passive investing, you need to be aware of (and perhaps a little sceptical of) those ETFs that have arrived more recently, riding on the coattails of Bogle's invention.

See, the term ETF was originally applied to the only ETFs that existed at the time: low-cost, passive, index-based ETFs, like Vanguard's funds (and some others). And because they were — and are — so good, the phrase 'ETFs are great' was willingly applied by anyone with half a clue.

And then ... it changed when those coattailers arrived.

Why ETFs can't have nice things

Perhaps, these people surmised, ETFs don't need to be only low-cost, passive and based on a market index like the ASX 300 or the S&P 500.

Perhaps they could also be applied to high(er) fee, active ETFs that they could create for the purposes of 'clipping the ticket' (claiming a fee as a percentage of the invested cash) ... you know, funds that were created to offer investors the opportunity to have a punt on lithium or AI or crypto, or ...

Yes, I'm being cynical. But also, in yet another rare case of the finance industry dispensing with the jargon, funds are known in the industry as 'product manufacturers', and that's just what they do — work out if they can make money flogging a trend, fad or speculation. And, even better if you can put the new creations under the 'ETF' umbrella and bask in the reflected glow of Bogle's creation!

Now, let me be clear for a second. Not all 'active' ETFs are bad. And investors are grown-ups who can make their own decision whether or not they want to buy a double-leveraged 'bear' ETF that makes money if the market falls, but loses heaps if it doesn't. It's even possible that some of the product manufacturers believe in what they're offering.

I suspect, if you asked them, they'd give you an answer somewhere between 'hey, we don't make people buy them' and 'well, if we didn't, someone else would'. They might even be right.

My (main) issue isn't really with them. Well, not much. It's just to make sure you know that when people like me (and plenty of others) say 'low-cost, passive, index-based ETFs are great', you need to pay attention to the words that come before 'ETFs', because the label now applies far more broadly than it used to, and it's important to know which one is which, when it comes time to add ETFs to your portfolio.

What are you really buying?

While I'm here, though, one additional comment on the investment merits of those active ETFs. Most investors who consider them think, 'Trend A is strong and growing, and I think I could make money investing in that trend'. That's a perfectly reasonable starting point, too — something that's growing and might be more popular in future is an indication that there might be something there.

But because you're buying a whole basket of these things, here are some questions you probably should be able to provide a considered and grounded answer of 'yes' to:

- Is the trend real?
- Will the trend continue?
- Who will the trend make money for?
- Are those companies in this ETF?
- Is the ETF selling at an attractive valuation?

I want to give you an example: the airline industry.

If you'd have told me in 1975 that the number of airline passengers might climb from around 600 million to almost 10 billion 50 years later — a gain of 13 times — you would have conclusively — and accurately — answered the first two questions.

And I might have mortgaged the house, sold the kids and put all of the money into airline stocks.

The problem is that while air travel boomed, airlines did terribly. Woefully. Some went broke two or three times over that time. The trend was real, but the benefit went to consumers as competition drove the cost of air travel lower.

Airports did okay, but airlines lost a fortune. As Warren Buffett (yes, him again) said:

> … if a farsighted capitalist had been present at Kitty Hawk, he would have done his successors a huge favor by shooting Orville [of Wright Brothers fame] down'.[22]

Now let's turn to, say, lithium.

Is the trend real? Yes, so far. Absolutely.

Will the trend continue? Probably, but that assumes battery chemistry doesn't evolve away from lithium.

Who will the trend make money for? It's hard-to-impossible to know. If more lithium is discovered and mined, that could keep a lid on prices, which would mean miners will be okay, but consumers will win. Or maybe supply struggles to keep up with demand, and prices rise. Who knows?

Even if you think it'll be the latter, are those companies in a given lithium ETF? Maybe. But you'd have to check each one to make sure, rather than assuming (Visa and Mastercard, for example, are in some 'crypto' ETFs!).

Is the ETF selling at an attractive valuation? How could you know, unless you work out which companies are in the ETF, and what their profitability and prospects were, and compare that to their prices, before adding it all up to see whether the ETF itself was attractive?

In other words? In other words 'Lithium demand is growing, so I should buy a lithium ETF' might be just a *little* too simplistic, however exciting the ETF marketing material makes it sound.

For that and other reasons, you might reasonably assume I'm pretty cool on these non-index-based ETFs. And you'd be right. I'm not saying they could never have a place in a portfolio under certain circumstances, if and when an investor had done all of the above work. But I am saying I reckon too many investors buy them without doing that work... and that makes them potentially dangerous for your wealth.

Bogle is still right

But the low-cost, passive, index-based ones are still an absolutely great tool for investors, if they're looking for the sort of hands-off diversification they can deliver.

I want to finish with a word of caution, though: Just because they're diversified, doesn't mean you can't lose money from time to time when the whole market drops. An ASX ETF didn't prevent you from losing 38 per cent during the COVID crash. In fact, it was the opposite — because it followed the index precisely, it *guaranteed* you'd lose that much! But it also guaranteed you'd benefit from the subsequent recovery.

Just don't use index ETFs to save you from volatility—they won't, because they're not designed to. And that's a feature, not a bug, because if the market continues to create value and rise over time, those ETFs will grow in value, too. And that's what I fully expect them to do.

But well-chosen ETFs will provide you with low-cost simplicity and diversification—and that's well worth taking advantage of, I reckon.

(For the record, at the time of writing, I own various Vanguard and Betashares ETFs.)

What really matters

- ETFs allow investors to own many companies at once with minimal cost and effort.
- ETFs dramatically lower the barriers to diversification for everyday investors.
- They can form the backbone of a simple, low-cost long-term portfolio.

11

YOU'RE BUYING A BUSINESS, NOT A STOCK

> *If you wouldn't buy the whole business, think carefully before buying the shares.*

I mentioned in the introduction that my old man considered the stock market akin to a casino. Frankly, his concerns then are even more valid now.

The vast, *vast* bulk of trading these days is done by computers. Short-term trading predominates daily market activity. So-called 'derivative instruments' like options and contracts-for-difference offer more opportunity to take a punt, and leveraged ETFs (that is, ETFs that use borrowings to magnify share price movements) continue to grow.

And, look, if you want to try to make money that way, be my guest. I don't think the odds will be in your favour, given the effort you need to put in and the people (and computers) you're selling to or buying from, but that's your call.

Contrast that with much of what I've been telling you so far in this book. About how humans seem pre-wired to want to find new and better solutions to new and old problems. About the ability for business to harness that human ingenuity. About the astonishing compound gains that have been made not only by one or two businesses, but by the stock market as a whole.

About the multi-decade returns that turned a hypothetical $10 000 into more than $130 000 by being invested across the market, then simply left alone.

If you've decided to take the trading route, you don't care about any of that. And you *shouldn't* care about it either. You're playing the 'guess the short-term movements' and the 'beat the other guy' games.

But if you chose the other path? The path that has, for more than 125 years, created incredible wealth? Then you're hitching your wagon to business. Not 'a' business, but business in general. To the clever allocation of scarce financial and human capital to the task of coming up with something that people will want, now and in future.

No, capitalism isn't perfect. And businesses usually do the right thing, but sometimes... they don't. There has always been, and will always be, fraud, mismanagement, collusion and more.

And yet... to steal (and embellish) a line from Winston Churchill, democratic capitalism is the worst system except for all the others that have been tried.

In other words, despite its imperfections, we're yet to come up with a working version of anything that's better.

And I use 'democratic capitalism' rather than just 'capitalism' because I don't believe in a completely free market. That'll get me branded as a communist by those who think anything less than absolute freedom is evil, but I've got broad enough shoulders to carry their disdain.

No, I use 'democratic capitalism' because governments — and duly elected governments at that — should, I reckon, have an important role in making sure the economic system gels with, and fits into, our larger society, and to make sure that capitalism is working properly — that competition rules are followed, that polluters pay and that kids aren't sent down the salt mines!

It's that system of democratic capitalism — for all of its faults — that we live in today, and that has provided the backdrop and the framework for that century-and-a-quarter of incredible progress and prosperity.

But government hasn't been *responsible* for delivering it. That's been the net result of people and businesses working together to meet the wants and needs of our society.

The *good* type of capitalism

It is the people who figured that a department store under Town Hall in Sydney should probably be called Woolworths, and should move from a full-service store to a self-selection supermarket. Those who figured a newly discovered silver deposit in Broken Hill might be mined profitably. That banking services might be needed, and whose provision might be profitable. That telling people the news — and giving them somewhere to advertise — might make for a successful enterprise.

These days we can add software makers, insurers, medical device companies and more to the list of some of the biggest and best businesses on the planet.

We didn't (and don't) make progress because the per-share price of some three-letter ASX code wiggles up and down on any given day.

We make progress because people combined together as shareholders and as managers and employees to create and deliver value, and to be appropriately compensated for doing it. (The shortcomings of, and remedies for, our system of democratic capitalism would be the subject of yet another book! It's just important to recognise that there are issues to address, but also that the benefits hugely outweigh those problems.)

Now, my readers are smart people. You know there are businesses behind those codes. And yet… how easy it is to fall into the trap of thinking not about the company, but the share price.

Be careful of your thoughts… they become habits

And for the professionals, too! My colleagues will tell you, with something between a wry smile and slight annoyance, that I have a funny-not-funny requirement at work. Taking the lead from a US colleague, Bill Mann, I have forbidden my team from using stock codes at work or in our communications with our readers and members.

'WOW has an announcement out', one will say.

'Oh, I've never heard of WOW, what do they do?' I'll respond with a physical or an emoji smile.

Is it necessary? No. Silly? Maybe. But back to our behavioural finance understanding, it's my way of making sure we don't slip into bad habits.

It's a not-so-subtle reminder that we're (in this case) talking about Woolworths the business, not WOW the share code. And when you do that, you remind yourself to think not about a chart of where the company's price has been over the last month or year, but instead about its pricing strategy, its store rollout, its margin management and its debt levels.

And doing that takes you out of the casino. Oh, sure, some will still play it as a casino because, well, that's the game they want to play. That's up to them. But when you think not about 'stocks' but about 'companies', you're deciding to play a different game.

You're choosing to be a part owner in a productive enterprise. You're choosing to (hopefully) benefit, not because someone else pays 1c more for your shares, but because the business manages to delight its customers a little better, to expand or open another office or store, to invest in automation or marketing, and everything else that goes into running a successful business.

What would Jake do?

It's why I love trying to put myself in the shoes of Jake, the bloke who owns my local cafe. He does a sensational job, and I couldn't do what he does. But he's not a 'cafe trader', he's a business owner. He doesn't get a quote on the value of his business dozens of times every trading day. There is no All Cafe Index quoted on the news each night. His cafe doesn't have a three-letter code and a price chart that he obsessively updates on his phone.

He just runs his business. The shop is clean and tidy. His staff are capable and friendly. The coffee beans are fresh and the machine is spotless. The food is delicious and the prices are competitive. His focus is on providing the best experience for his customers, knowing that when he does that, they'll enjoy themselves and come back. And when they do, the cafe will make more sales, covering his costs and delivering a profit. I have no idea if he'd sell the business, but I'm pretty sure he knows that the best chance of getting the highest price is to run a really good business, rather than setting up price alerts on his brokerage app.

And that's how Australian businesses have progressed and flourished for more than a century, too.

Right now, you might be thinking, 'cool story, bro' (that's what the kids say, right?), and I get that. But there is an important implication for investors. And assuming you're not trying to play the trading game, it's vital that you understand it.

And that's the case whether you're buying shares in individual companies or buying ETFs. Because, once you understand the game you're playing, it helps you think about volatility more clearly.

Let's go back to Jake on a bad day. Let's say the economy isn't growing and interest rates are up. I'm going to take a stab in the dark and say that Jake probably isn't happy about that. It's even possible that, if he bothered to ask a business broker, he'd probably be told that there aren't many people looking to buy cafes, and that the price would be lower if he wanted to sell today.

But here's the thing: I suspect Jake wouldn't even bother asking. Why would he? He's running a business, not 'trading cafes'. Sure, he might feel better if he knew cafes were selling for a fortune, and a little worse if someone told him that cafe prices have fallen, but he's a business owner and manager, so he'd probably just shake it off and get back to work.

He might change his menu or his prices. He might work harder to get people in the door or review his staffing levels. But a good business manager does that as a matter of course anyway.

But my bet is that Jake would take the economic circumstances in his stride. He wouldn't sell at a depressed price just because that's what cafes were selling for. He wouldn't give up on running a cafe because prices were lower. And he wouldn't let the market for cafes impact his mood. Why would he? He's not selling.

I suspect if I asked him about all of that, he might just tell me that he's going to keep doing what he does best and focus on running the best cafe he can, setting the place up for long-term success. That whatever the ups and downs of the economy or inflation, or the time they did roadworks out the front and customer numbers were down for a few weeks, it's execution that matters. And the future.

That approach is *precisely* the one investors should take, too. It's natural and normal to look at a rising share price and feel good, and to see a falling share price and feel unhappy. It makes perfect sense. Richer is good. Poorer is bad. Obviously.

I'm sure Jake would be happier if someone wandered past his open door and yelled, 'Your cafe is worth more today!' and less happy if the same bloke walked past the next day and shouted, 'You're poorer today!'

Be like Jake

Remember I said on page 102 that, as a shareholder, you're a part owner in a productive enterprise? You are. Sure, you don't have your name on the door, and you don't sign the cheques — but you're a part owner, regardless. Your shares are literally you sharing in ownership of the company.

And owners — proper, long-term owners — make money when their companies are more successful. When they are more relevant to more people, more often. When they turn that into more sales, and then, combined with prudent cost management, turn those higher sales into higher profits.

As a shareholder, wouldn't it make sense, then, to think like Jake, rather than thinking like a day trader?

I think so.

And that's the case whether you invest in individual businesses, like Woolies, BHP or ANZ, or you invest in an ETF — which is just a ready-made combination of those companies anyway.

And if you're doing that, you need to separate the two parts of your brain: the part that (justifiably) feels the joy and the pain, and the part of your brain that controls your actions.

Don't get me wrong — that's not easy. When shares are up, the sky is a little bluer, the birds are a little louder and, well, I feel a little smarter (the ego wants to take credit for me being a wonderful investor!). And when they're down, it feels like all of the doom-and-gloomers are right, and this whole investing thing is for the birds!

But we'll get to all of that.

For now, the point is that investing — proper, long-term investing — is owning pieces of businesses that measure their success in years, not minutes, days, weeks or months. And whose *value* is a function of those years of effort, even if the *price* is just a popularity contest from day to day.

But let's say you are buying shares in individual companies. There are books and books written on valuation and financial statement analysis. A few of you will be unhappy that I don't intend to delve into that, here, but I suspect many of you will breathe a sigh of relief!

I will, though, stick with the theme of this chapter and talk a little about what makes a good business. And I'll give you some indicative thoughts on how to think about price. But no maths and especially no algebra — I promise!

What makes a good business?

Everyone will have their own take on the answer to the question of what makes a good business, and general 'rules' won't fit every single circumstance, but I reckon it usually comes down to the three Ms: *moats, margins* and *management*.

1. Moats

Even if your awareness of medieval castles only extends as far as *Shrek*, you'll be familiar with the use of moats as defensive emplacements. Full of water (or crocodiles or lava or sharks-with-lasers, depending on your choice of comedic device), once the drawbridge was up, they stopped the baddies getting into the castle... or at least slowed them down.

In investment terms, they're usually used as metaphors for those things that can separate a business from its competition. And, extending the metaphor, a good business will maintain and even widen that moat as much as possible.

Warren Buffett has long used that metaphor when talking about investing, and even wrote about it to his managers in the wake of the September 11 terrorist attacks in the US:

> What should you be doing in running your business? Just what you always do: Widen the moat, build enduring competitive advantage, delight your customers, and relentlessly fight costs... [A]lmost all operating decisions that made sense a month ago make sense today.[23]

And it's that three-word phrase—'enduring competitive advantage'—that matters here.

Think about Coke. How hard would it be for a competitor to build a better cola brand?

Think about Microsoft. How hard would it be for companies using its software to suddenly switch?

What about Amazon? Who could match that company's scale and breadth?

Or Carsales.com.au? Many, many have tried to muscle in on its turf, but its network effect (buyers attract sellers who attract buyers who attract sellers ...) has been unbreakable.

Now, not every company has a moat. And growing companies arguably may not be able to have one, at least at first ... but you bet they're trying to create one!

Think about Woolies and Coles. How hard would it be to replicate their store network?

On the flip side, Aldi can happily coexist because their moat is 'small stores, cheap products, limited range'.

Or consider Apple's enormous margins, compared to almost all of its competitors combined. Its profit margin is the result of having a wide moat—the incredible brand loyalty of its customers.

There are heaps of examples.

And that Apple story also illustrates the problems with *not* having a moat: It's really hard to compete successfully.

Now to margins.

2. Margins

See, the other thing about moats is that they don't just provide longevity (though they usually do), they also allow for higher profits than competitors.

Consider Woolies and IGA. Who do you reckon makes more money?

Apple trounces its competitors on that front, too. The costs aren't that different, but the brand allows it to charge a much higher price ... and that means far higher profits.

Moats can and do erode over time, so their maintenance and 'widening' should be the first job. If that's done well, profits usually follow.

And, frankly, it's hard for any business to maintain a significant level of profitability for any length of time without one.

They'll be okay. They might limp along. They might even have some periods of higher-than-usual profitability.

But higher profits, over the long-term, rarely come without a wide and defensible moat. And if you're going to be a long-term investor, the best companies to own are those that continue to grow and become more prosperous over years and years — and they tend to be the ones with those deep, wide and scary moats.

3. Management

This takes us neatly to management. Because, as we just said, there aren't many moats that are self-sustaining without that care and maintenance. And that's the job of management.

A bad or self-interested manager might try to make hay while the sun shines. They might cut back (actual) maintenance to lower costs and make profits look better. They might pull back on marketing or product development or investments in technology. They might put prices up to a level that the market can tolerate for a while, but that eventually prove too high.

And, even if the CEO doesn't consciously think that way, the big bonuses and shareholder pressure can weigh on the decisions that they make.

On the other hand, a *good* manager will accept that sometimes forgoing short-term profit is a good thing if it means you can deliver over the long-term. A great example is during recessions: A quality manager of a quality company won't cut costs just because sales are flagging. They'll keep the staff, continue to run ads and keep delivering great service. Why? Two reasons: It maximises the chance that the company survives, maybe at the expense of weaker competitors, and it means that when the worm turns, as it always does, the business has momentum and comes out fighting. Short-term pain, long-term gain.

A good manager will also be straight with investors. No spin, no nonsense — 'just the facts, ma'am'. In short, they'll act in the interest of shareholders, and treat them as they would want to be treated if they were in their shoes.

Now, none of those things — moats, margins or management — either separately or together, guarantee business success. But, if you were going to identify three things that made success more likely — and that success could potentially compound for years — I reckon these are the things you'd choose.

And speaking of the future...

Growth and value

Now, if there are three (other) things that I'd want to triangulate when buying shares, they would be quality (covered above by the three Ms), growth and price.

In that order.

And for the reasons you'd probably think.

First, if you have a low-quality business, growth is harder to get, and it's hard to pay a low-enough price! If I gave you camera-maker Kodak or video-rental company Blockbuster three years out from each company's eventual bankruptcy, trying to find a way for them to grow, or a price that was low enough to pay, would have been incredibly hard.

On the flip side, if you start with a quality business with those attributes, it'll probably withstand a lot. And if it's a business that can likely grow for a long time, that compounding will probably work in your favour.

Then we get to price. Way too many pages have been written on how to work out the right price for a company's shares. And fair enough too — even the best business in the world will be a disappointment if you pay a ridiculous price.

Still, the average investor can afford not to obsess over price. Not only will you never pick the bottom of the market, but the future is inherently unknowable. And this is where the stuff we've just talked about comes into play.

Let me quote Warren Buffett yet again:

> *It's far better to buy a wonderful company at a fair price than a fair company at a wonderful price.*[24]

Now, he doesn't say 'high price' or 'silly price', so neither Buffett nor I am suggesting you should write a blank cheque. But a company that can grow profits for years to come will make any valuation mistakes far less important than a company that can't.

So how much should you pay? 'It depends' is the uncomfortable answer. And it mostly depends on the future.

If you had two companies, each making $1 million in profit this year, it can be tempting to think you'd pay the same price for both. But I suspect you're already ahead of me here... it depends what happens next.

Let's go back to our Blockbuster example. At different times in their corporate lives, Netflix and Blockbuster would have made similar levels of profit: Netflix on the way up and Blockbuster on the way down. So, even though the profits were the same, the future was very different — as was the price you should have been prepared to pay.

Now, I'm going to make a *lot* of assumptions with what I say next. Please don't take this as gospel or use it to make investment decisions without doing your own research!

But, *if* you wanted the long-run return of the market at around 9 per cent, and if you thought the average company could sustainably grow profit at about 3 per cent per year, you'd probably pay around 16 times that company's earnings (what the finance types would say was a price/earnings (P/E) ratio of 16).

Why 16, by the way? Well, I promised to keep the maths out of this book as much as possible. I'll save you the calculations, but you might have heard — or not — about something called a 'discounted cash flow' or DCF analysis. It's basically just working out how much you'd pay for a given company, based on your assumptions of the desired return and the company's growth prospects. The faster it grows, the more you'd pay. If it was earning $1 a year in profits, and you thought those profits would grow at 3 per cent per year, how much would you pay?

Plugging a 9 per cent desired annual investment return into the equation would tell you to pay $16 for a company currently earning $1 in profits, growing at 3 per cent per year. If a company can grow faster than that for a long period of time, you should be prepared to consider paying more.

If it can't grow that fast (think: old, slow, mature companies in flat or declining parts of the economy), you'd want to pay less—perhaps much less—or avoid the company altogether.

And if it's going to be an average company (which isn't a bad thing at all!), then around that number might be a useful starting point.

Now, a huge point: That's just a rough rule of thumb to start your own research. And, yes, if you're a finance nerd you might say 'yeah, but...' And you might even be right! This is not a treatise on valuation. It's to give investors or would-be investors a bit of a yardstick—a centre of gravity, if you like—to build their own understanding.

Now you have some of the tools to start thinking about the sorts of businesses you might want to put in your portfolio—or that make up the ETFs you might buy instead or as well.

But, then what? It's time to think about when to buy, hold and sell...

What really matters

- Shares represent ownership of real businesses, not just numbers on a screen.
- Thinking like a business owner encourages patience and long-term thinking.
- Market prices fluctuate constantly, but the underlying business value changes far more slowly.

12

BUYING, HOLDING AND ... SELLING?

> *The hardest part of investing is often simply holding on.*

By now you know the principles.

You know that compounding works. You know that volatility isn't risk. You know that owning shares means owning businesses. You know that behaviour beats brilliance. You know that trying to outguess the market is usually a losing game.

Which means that what comes next isn't about knowledge.

It's about what you do.

This chapter is where investing stops being theoretical and becomes deeply personal. Because the biggest damage to long-term returns is almost never caused by recessions or rate hikes or geopolitics.

It's caused by us.

It's caused by what we do — or fail to do — when prices move.

Buying, holding and selling sound like simple verbs. They aren't. They are emotional decisions dressed up as financial ones.

(Not just investing, by the way. There's a widely held school of thought that most of our decisions are made emotionally, and then we — subconsciously — rationalise them and tell ourselves we're logical!)

So, unless we're deliberate about how we approach those decisions, the very instincts that kept our ancestors alive will quietly undermine our portfolios.

Let's slow down and take them one at a time.

Buy 'to' hold not buy 'and' hold

That tiny preposition matters more than most investors realise.

'Buy and hold' used to be — mostly still is — the creed of the long-term investor. And totally appropriately... to a point. Or maybe it's just that the naysayers have fun with the wording, which means we need to be more specific.

Here's why.

'Buy and hold' sounds definite. Permanent. Unquestioned. Which can lead some people to make mistakes and can make others feel like they've got a 'gotcha' ready for people like me.

In the first instance, 'buy and hold' can make people feel like they don't have to ever do anything else. Just buy and let the miracle happen, right? I mean, maybe. Or maybe you decided to 'buy and hold' Kodak. Or Blockbuster. That can be a mistake.

The troublemakers use the same idea as a criticism: 'How can you say "buy and hold"? Anything could happen!' (They usually then spruik their new you-beaut trading system. Funny that.)

And there is a kernel of truth that both are pointing to.

I am a big proponent of long-term investing. The data shows that it has worked astoundingly well. And I don't think that's likely to be any different in future.

I also hope to still be holding some of the companies and ETFs that are currently in my portfolio in five, ten, 20 years. In fact, if my kids don't end up inheriting some of my current holdings when I die, I'll be disappointed (also blissfully unaware, but you know what I mean).

But I'm not going to hold them just because I already own them. I'm only going to keep holding if it makes sense. So whether you're someone trying to live the 'buy and hold' mantra, or you're someone who is muckraking about it, I'm going to switch things up just a little bit.

And that's where 'buy *to* hold' comes in.

It disabuses both the unaware and the unkind of the idea that 'buying' is the end of the process. That ownership must only ever be 'until death do us part'.

It talks, instead, to an intent. To a plan. To an idea. And to a strategy.

It says that, all being well, the aim is to obtain a part share in a business, with a preference for not selling. It says, 'I'm a long-term investor, and I believe that my gains will compound over the long-term by staying invested, not by chopping and changing'.

That's where the real power of both long-term investing and 'buy to hold' comes from.

'Buy and hold' tells us to stay in the game. To stay the course. To let time, and quality businesses, do the heavy lifting. It's exactly the right idea.

And 'buy to hold' takes that and just reminds us not to be ideological or stubborn about our portfolios (and to remind us not to fall for the 'buy and hold means you'd never, ever sell, no matter what, and that's crazy!' sales trick of the trading software salesperson).

It means that holding — not selling when the shares are volatile, or there's some scary headline, or your mate tells you you own a 'dud stock' — is our default setting.

It turns the old saying on its head: It's not 'don't just sit there, do something', but 'don't just do something, sit there', instead.

Remember in Chapter 4, when I talked about the people who snidely say 'Yeah, but who'd just invest and not touch the money for 30 years?'

I hope by now — or at the very least by the time you've finished reading this, you can answer that answer very clearly with one word: 'Me!'

But here's the key: You don't have to hold the same thing — necessarily — for 30 years. I mean, it'd be an ideal outcome if you could find an ETF, or a group of companies, that you *could* hold for that long. But if you're one, five, 15 or 29 years into that journey and you realise that you no longer have confidence in one of your holdings, you should be prepared to make a change.

The catch is that you have to buy something better, rather than leaving the money in cash or, worse, taking it out of the market and spending it.

Yeah, I know. I'm being *that* guy... taking all of your fun away. But 'future you' will thank 'present you' (and me, I hope!) when you resist the temptation.

Now, here's where I want to really stress-test your new confidence.

Remember: According to Vanguard's 30-year index chart, a hypothetical $10 000 would have compounded at 9.3 per cent per annum, on average, between 1995 and 2005, turning your ten grand into $143 000.

Amazing, right? And easy! You didn't have to do anything. More precisely, you had to do *exactly nothing*. You had to leave it alone.

Now, if I'd made you that offer in 1995, I hope you would have taken me up on it!

But let me share a short potted history of some big (approximate) falls over that period, and their causes:

- 1998: –22 per cent (Asian currency crisis and the failure of hedge fund LTCM)
- 2000–3: –50 per cent (dot.com crash)
- 2007–9: –54 per cent (GFC)
- 2010: –16 per cent (Euro debt scare)
- 2011: –21 per cent (Euro crisis and US debt rating downgrade)
- 2015–16: –22 per cent (China slowdown and the related commodity slump)
- 2018: –15 per cent (US Federal Reserve increased interest rates)
- 2020: –37 per cent (COVID crash; this took only a month and four days to happen!)
- 2021–22: –18 per cent (high inflation and higher interest rates)
- 2023: –12 per cent (fears of sustained inflation and ongoing higher interest rates)
- 2025: –20 per cent (Trump's tariffs and trade war)

That's some list, huh?

- Eleven times in 30 years, the market fell more than 10 per cent.
- Seven of those times, the fall was more than 20 per cent.
- Three of those were a fall of more than 30 per cent.
- And twice the market lost half of its value.

Now, reread it slowly, and ask yourself how each one of those would have felt?

If your answer isn't 'I'd be stressed and scared', either you're Mr Spock from *Star Trek*, or (how do I say this gently?) you're lying to yourself.

It's okay—healthy, actually—to admit that. I was there. I hated it. I was scared, worried and, during some of those long, slow deep losses, it was hard not to just want to chuck it all in.

What matters—to your financial future, anyway—isn't how you feel, but what you do.

I stuck it out through each fall. Not because it was fun, but because I was convinced that 'buy to hold' works.

Thankfully, that's what the past told me then, and it's what it continues to tell us today. I can make no promises nor give you guarantees about the future, but my money (literally, because I'm fully invested) says the future is likely to look pretty much like the past.

When should I buy?

Speaking of making your peace with things, you'll never succeed as an investor if your goal is to 'buy at the bottom'.

If you've spent any time looking at past price charts, you've likely thought to yourself 'Imagine if I'd have bought *then*' as you look at the points at which share prices hit their lows and started to recover.

And then your thoughts probably turned to 'Well, that's what I'll do next time!'

The bad news? I'm sorry to tell you this, but it ain't going to happen.

Instead, almost every time you buy, you'll be buying after the shares have already gone up or before they fall further.

Actually not 'almost' every time. Unless you're the luckiest investor in the world, it will be *literally* every time. That's just life.

If you can't make your peace with that, you're really going to struggle as an investor.

We've already talked about the beauty of dollar-cost averaging (the idea, not the clunky phrase itself!), and that's part of how we manage our emotions and keep ourselves on track.

The other is to aim to be 'roughly right, not precisely wrong'.

Because you know what's worse than buying after a share price rise or before a fall?

Waiting.

Because, for all of the falls in the list, remember that the market *still* managed to rise more than 14-fold over 30 years!

Here are two truths I want you to internalise:

1. The market's incredible long-term compound return happens despite not in the absence of semi-regular, hair-raising, stomach-churning falls.
2. The ASX (and the US market for that matter) has never yet failed to get back to, then go higher than, a previous high.

Please tattoo those things (I'd suggest metaphorically, but hey, you do you) somewhere. They are the two talismans you can and should cling to before, during and after the next big market falls.

Internalise the idea. Expect those falls. Imagine how you'll feel. Plan how you'll respond. Then, when it happens, the pain might be slightly less, but the real benefit is that you'll be far, far less likely to succumb to it.

(And, if it helps, whack a Post-it note on this page or dog-ear it and read it again next time the headlines are scary or the market falls.)

One more (but not the last) time, too: I can't promise the future will be like the past. But don't you reckon that's the most likely outcome, especially when the same forces are in play? I do.

But I still haven't answered the question, have I?

When should you buy?

Today. Tomorrow. Next week. Next month. Next year.

More directly: Don't try to 'time' your purchases. Don't get me wrong, I'd do *exactly* that… if it were possible. But it's not.

So, the next best thing? Put compounding to work. Remember the three ingredients: the amount you invest, time and your return. *Not* investing is betting against both history and time.

Yes, sometimes you'll buy and markets will fall. They might even fall slowly for months and months, like during the GFC. But you'll be dollar-cost averaging, so you're getting more for your money if that happens and you keep buying anyway.

There's only one caveat: While I don't reckon you should time the market, I also don't think you should pay just any old price.

So… buy regularly, just make sure you're not paying a completely silly price, or buying a bad business, as we talked about in the last chapter.

(This is assuming you have your 'Oh, shit' fund topped up and you've gotten rid of all of your consumer debt. If you haven't done that yet, that's the priority.)

Don't wait until 'the coast is clear'; it never is.

Don't wait for a 'better price' — the market goes up over time, and quality shares and ETFs will likely rise, too.

Don't wait for a fall — many investors have missed a 20 per cent gain while they waited for the shares to fall 10 per cent.

Diversification: The only free lunch in investing

Now, I'm not suggesting you should put on your happy face, assume the best and dollar-cost average all of your money into that tiny loss-making, speculative miner that your brother-in-law's mate's barber's Uber driver likes.

But also, don't do it with *only* Woolies, CBA or Telstra either.

Don't get me wrong, I think those are big, dominant companies are likely to be around for a long, long time to come. But will they perform as well in future as they have in the past? And don't rule out the chance that, in the fullness of time, one of them — or another massive company that *everyone* likes — won't go broke at some point.

I mean, how many of the biggest companies in 1950, 1970 or 1990 are still on the ASX today?

No, that's not designed to scare you. I think it's incredibly likely that those three companies will exist in one form or another in 30 years. But I might be wrong. Or, as I said, the performance of those businesses might be very ordinary between now and then.

So what's an investor to do?

Diversify.

Diversification is not putting all of your eggs in one — or even a few — baskets. Not because you think the baskets are poorly made ... you wouldn't invest in them at all if you thought that.

But because, despite your best efforts, you want to protect against being wrong or unlucky or sideswiped by circumstance.

You might have heard of these well-known ASX-listed companies:

- One.Tel
- HIH Insurance
- ABC Learning
- Dick Smith

Each was delisted and investors got nearly — or exactly — zero.

Could you have avoided them all? Maybe. Probably.

But it's not just about the outright disasters.

I mentioned Telstra earlier. At the time of writing, the shares were still well down from their highs of over $8 in 1999 — some 27 years earlier.

Myer shares were well over $3.50 in late 2010, and had lost almost 90 per cent of that value by early 2026.

AMP was trading for over $14 a share in 2001, and had fallen to less than 90 cents by late 2023. They've since recovered ... a tiny bit.

Now, there are many, many companies that have done incredibly well over that same period — that's how the market managed to grow 14-fold despite the terrible examples listed here.

The point is that if you were to buy just one, or a few, companies, you might have hit on one of the absolute rocket ships, and be reading this book in the Bahamas with a cocktail in one hand. Or you could have completely, or almost completely, done your dough.

Worth the punt? Nah, not with your life savings. Making a motza would be wonderful. Having to go back to square one (or two or three) would be financially devastating. In Chapter 9, I discussed the maths of investing (spoiler: how much you invest for, how long you invest for and your return rate). The key here is *time*. If you cancel out a few years, or a decade or two, and have to go back to the beginning, there's little-to-nothing you can do to get those years back.

So, we're back to Aesop. The hare buys one or two stocks and naps. The tortoise, as you'd expect, diversifies. He's mathematically *guaranteed* to get less than the lucky bastard who buys Fortescue at 30c in 2004 and watches it go to almost $30 in 2024 ... but he's also very, very likely to do better than the person who bought a concentrated portfolio of AMP, HIH and Myer — and won't have to join them back at square one.

Here's the other thing about diversification: it is likely to make your portfolio less volatile. If you own one company and it falls 50 per cent, you'll feel physically sick. If that company is only 5 per cent of your portfolio, your wealth will still take a 2.5 per cent hit ... but that's far more manageable, financially and emotionally.

And how should you diversify?

Let me tell you two things not to do.

First, buying shares in all four big banks or three large retailers or both telcos isn't diversification. Diversification is about having different industries, sectors, geographies, currencies and risk factors. So that if one industry or country or type of customer gets into trouble, your portfolio is not too exposed to that group.

Second (and, on the surface, contradicting the previous point): You're not Noah ... you don't need two of everything. Just because an industry or sector exists, don't feel compelled to invest in it, even for the sake of diversification. You should have variation in your portfolio, but you don't need every suit of cards in your hand to win a trick.

Diversification is about avoiding concentration, not spreading yourself so thin you've stopped focusing on buying quality businesses.

Lastly, while low-cost, broad, index-based ETFs are a wonderful way to get instant diversification across a single index, don't forget to think about geographic and currency diversification, or the opportunity to invest in sectors that aren't particularly large here in Australia. In other words, don't forget to think internationally.

Don't be penny-wise but pound-foolish.

By now, you've probably realised that Warren Buffett is one of my investing heroes. He is, without peer or argument, the GOAT.

But let me tell you how he cost Berkshire Hathaway about $10 billion. Actually, I can go one better. Here's Buffett's retelling:

> I cost us about $10 billion. I set out to buy 100 million shares of Walmart, pre-split, at about $23. And Charlie [Munger] said it didn't sound like the worst idea [I] ever came up with, which is — from him, I mean, it was just ungodly praise. And then, you know, we bought a little and then it moved up a little bit. And I thought, 'Well, you know, maybe it will come back' or what — Who knows what I thought? I mean, you know, only my psychiatrist can tell me. And that thumb sucking, reluctance to pay a little more — the current cost is in the area of $10 billion.[25]

By the way, that's US dollars. I won't make it worse for Uncle Warren by converting it to Aussie dollars!

Now, Buffett isn't suggesting — and I've made the point already — that you should pay any old price. Everything needs a cut-off at some point or you'd always be able to justify 'just a little more'.

But when you're buying — especially a company with a long growth runway ahead — you need to balance the desire for a 'better' price with the risk of missing out altogether.

In fact, Buffett's company Berkshire Hathaway is another wonderful example of something that always looked expensive in dollar terms, but consistently went on to higher heights (see figure 12.1).

Figure 12.1 Progress of Berkshire Hathaway shares[26]
Source: Yahoo Finance

- In 1980, the shares traded for around US$400.
- By 1985, they were over US$2000. That is ... a lot.
- By 1990? More than US$6000.

Feel like you've missed the boat? I would have.

But by 1995, the shares were almost US$30 000!

Waiting for a dip?

You finally got one in 1999, when they fell 20 per cent... to over US$50 000 from over US$60 000 the previous year!

(A reminder not to wait for dips!)

I'll put you out of your misery — by early 2026, the shares changed hands for a whopping US$750 000 each. That's more than a million Aussie dollars apiece!

And if you're saying, 'Well, they're *obviously* too expensive now', you might be right... but that's what some people could have — and did — say at each of the points I mentioned!

(There are two classes of Berkshire shares: the Class A shares mentioned previously and Class B shares — a 'split' version — that trade for 1/1500th of the price. Unfortunately for me, I own some of the latter, but none of the former!)

Yes, the price you pay matters. But, unless that price is way too high, the compounding potential of the business often matters more.

Hold. Just hold.

I have a 13-year-old son. He plays rugby with his school team. As a training aid, and to coordinate themselves on the field, they have a line they repeat together while they're waiting for the ball and the opportunity to tackle their opponents. (If you're not a rugby fan, the defenders can't move past a tackled player until the ball comes out of the mess of bodies known as the ruck after a tackle is made.)

'Hold... hold... hold... up!'

The 'hold' bit is to keep them all disciplined and in a straight line. The 'up' bit is the point when the ball is out and they can move forward.

And lately, it's been something I keep in mind as a little investing mantra, too.

As I've said already, buying can be hard. But I reckon holding is harder. That human instinct for activity — for action — is strong. Very strong.

And another line for you to tattoo, this time an echo from Chapter 2: 'Successful investing might be best defined as the ability to subdue our evolutionary impulses.'

Especially in the face of ongoing, overwhelming stimulus.

Share prices that are updated by the second.

Daily news headlines.

Regular economic data.

Talking heads (yes, including me!) giving their thoughts on the state of the economy and markets.

Our impulse is to add those things to what we already know, and to alter course accordingly.

Except, almost without exception, that stuff is almost entirely useless and irrelevant to any serious long-term investment in a quality business.

Oh, it might impact share prices in the short and medium term — traders and other investors can get skittish, and are prone to bouts of deep pessimism and irrational optimism from time to time.

But does it change your long-term expectations of what the company will do? Only if those events threaten to permanently change the profitability — or in extremes, the existence — of the companies of which you are a part owner.

Sometimes, gains can take a while to appear. Car maker Tesla's shares were around $14 a piece in late 2014. They moved around a little, but were selling at the same price in late 2019. That's a long time to go nowhere... especially if the market is going up and you're missing out. The second half of the story? By late 2024, another five years later, they were selling for more than $430! No, it wasn't guaranteed, but those who believed in the story — but sold because they couldn't wait — have a helluva sob story to tell.

That doesn't mean you'll never have a reason to sell — we'll get to that next. But if share prices of quality companies go up over time — and they tend to — then our job is to make sure we're not scared out of owning them by a combination of fear, exuberance, impatience and a need for action.

And given they do tend to go up over time, then the rugby mantra is a good one.

So, chant it with me: 'hold... hold... hold... up!'

Sometimes you really should sell

Yes, I want you to buy. Regularly.

Yes, I want you to hold. Because the gains are made in the holding.

But sometimes you should sell.

But when?

You can put the answer into three buckets:

1. When you no longer believe in the company's future.
2. When the price is so high, relative to earnings, that you just have to take the money.
3. When you find something you like better.

Befitting our 'buy to hold' approach from page 186, we're not going to spend too much time here, because the long-term investor hopefully spends far, far more time and effort in the buying and the holding and relatively little in the selling.

This is another of those times when you might have people telling you that 'buy to hold' is lazy, and you'll miss opportunities if you're not selling regularly, 'rotating' into better ideas to try to maximise your returns. They're right, in theory. Some might even be able to do it, sometimes. A very few, regularly. But as baseballer Yogi Berra famously said (and it's one of my very favourites): 'In theory there is no difference between theory and practice. In practice there is.'

So, in the real world, for those of us who are determined to be Aesop's tortoise, let's break those three areas down just a little.

1. You no longer believe in the company's future

I hope this first one is pretty straightforward. At some point in Blockbuster's descent into oblivion, I hope most of us would have said, 'You know what? I bought a company that was a leader in video rental, and I thought the future was bright. But now I realise that streaming is increasingly a thing.' And at that point, the expectations we had for our investment are dashed. Or, in the jargon you might hear used, 'our investment thesis is broken'.

(By the way, please never, ever sell *just* because a price is up or down. Even Berkshire Hathaway has had big jumps and falls. A falling price doesn't indicate either a huge opportunity or an impending disaster. It *might* be one of those two things, but you can't tell just by looking at the price. The same with a rising price, too.)

2. The price is so high that you just have to take the money

The next is probably the hardest one. As we discussed earlier, it's hard to know a 'reasonable price' for a company, because the future is unknowable.

But if I offered to sell you a genuine diamond ring for $1, you'd know it was a bargain. And if I offered to buy it from you for $1 million, I hope you'd take the money! In the context of selling, we're not trying to work out valuation to three decimal places—that's some 'false specificity' that we can leave for those who don't realise the mistake they're making.

Now, I don't know the prices of diamond rings particularly, but if the price I offered to buy yours was somewhere around the market price, I suspect you'd probably just keep it, because you weren't offered a really good price.

If you get an offer that's too good to refuse, you probably should take it. Otherwise, let your quality company or ETF keep doing its thing and remain a part owner.

3. You find something you like better

This last one is somewhat of a combination of the other two, to be honest, because it includes elements of both quality and price. And we'll switch up the metaphor, too. You might have a perfectly good car. You bought it at a good price, it hasn't lost much of its value, it's cheap to run and reliable. Perfect.

But you're perusing Facebook Marketplace (as we all do) and you notice a car for sale. It's different to the one you're currently driving—maybe it's a different model, different style and is available for a different price. But you look at it and think, 'You know, I really like my car, but if I sold it and bought that instead, I reckon it'd be a very good trade. That one is cheaper than it should be, and that model tends to hold its value, whereas people are paying a lot for the model I currently drive.'

In shares-speak, let's say you own Coles shares, and they look a little expensive because sales and profits aren't growing as fast as they used to. Then you look at Westpac, and figure those shares look pretty attractive, given the price and the bank's growth. It might make sense to sell your Coles shares and buy Westpac instead.

But a warning here, too. Whenever you sell something to buy something else, you need to be right twice: once when you sell Coles and again when you buy Westpac. It's not impossible, but just remember that extra degree of difficulty.

There's also the question of tax, when you sell ... and that's coming up. The short version? Consider tax implications, but don't let it drive your investing.

But first, you now know enough to build wealth.

Now let's talk about what happens when the world tries to stop you.

Let's stop and take a breath

Before we talk about crashes—and yes, they do (and will!) happen—let's come back to the One-Page Investing Plan.

Because we're now about halfway through it.

And because nothing we're about to discuss changes it.

What's important is being able to take what we've already covered and put it into context before we move on.

I hope you can see the plan coming to life. I hope you feel more informed and more confident—about the plan itself and your ability to follow it.

Remember, the plan isn't a 'tactical response' plan.

It's not an 'in case of emergency, break glass' plan.

It *is* a 'slow and steady wins the race' plan.

Supported by more than a century of evidence, decades of experience and the powerful maths of compounding.

I hope this is the plan that anchors your investing.

That gives you solid ground to start from, and return to, as you build your future.

So, have another look, a few minutes of reflection and then let's press on.

THE
ONE-PAGE INVESTING PLAN

INVEST. ADD. WAIT.

Know your why
Be clear about what you're investing for — security, freedom, generosity — and write it down so you have a north star when markets wobble.

Earn more over time
Grow your income through skills, effort and opportunity — you can only invest what you don't spend.

Pay yourself first
Automatically invest around 10 per cent of your take-home pay every single payday, before your lifestyle expands to consume it.

Spend intentionally
Focus on what truly matters, avoid lifestyle creep and protect the surplus that funds your future.

Build your 'oh, shit' fund
Hold three to six months of expenses in cash so emergencies never force you to sell.

Invest regularly
Add money on a schedule — no matter what.

Own diversified, productive assets
Buy diversified, broad, low-cost ETFs and/or quality shares representing real businesses earning real profits.

Reinvest and minimise costs
Reinvest dividends, avoid unnecessary trading, and keep fees and taxes as low as possible.

Stay the course — even in retirement
Expect volatility, shift gradually from growth to income when needed, but let compounding start (and keep) working for decades.

That's it. That's the whole thing. Everything else is details.

What really matters

- Buying well matters, but the biggest investing returns usually come from holding good assets for long periods.
- Investors often sell for the wrong reasons—fear, boredom or impatience.
- Selling should be reserved for genuine changes in the underlying investment case.

13

THE NEXT CRASH IS COMING

| *Prepare for crashes—don't try to predict them.*

The next crash is coming.

I don't know when. I don't know why. I don't know what, or who, the headlines will blame.

But it's coming.

If that sounds dramatic, it's not meant to be. It's just... history. Markets have always risen over time, but they don't rise in straight lines. They lurch. They panic. They overshoot. They fall far further than feels reasonable. Then, eventually, they recover.

And I've been there for a few of them.

I remember the GFC not as a sharp drop, but as a slow, grinding, relentless erosion. It wasn't a single dramatic 'down 30 per cent today' moment. It was months. And months. And months.

You'd check the market at the end of the day. Or the week.

You'd tell yourself it couldn't get worse.

It... got worse.

Banks were on the brink. Financial institutions that had existed for a century simply disappeared. Governments were stepping in. The phrase 'systemic collapse' became commonplace ... and serious risk.

That one felt genuinely scary.

It didn't feel like a buying opportunity. People were saying we were witnessing 'the end of capitalism'.

Then there was COVID.

If the GFC was a slow suffocation. COVID was a punch in the face. From Mike Tyson.

In January 2020, markets were humming along nicely. We'd heard of what felt like 'yet another flu mutation', but it didn't feel any worse than those what had come before.

Then, between late February and late March, the ASX fell more than 35 per cent. The fall took just over a month. Borders essentially closed. Planes grounded. Offices emptied. Entire industries shut overnight.

It wasn't *financial* contagion this time. It was *biological*.

You couldn't go to work. You couldn't go to dinner. You couldn't visit your parents.

It felt like the world had stopped. It kinda had.

And when the market was down 30 to 35 per cent, most people weren't asking whether shares were cheap. They were asking whether they should sell everything 'until this settles down'.

It never feels like a temporary fall at the time. The combination of fear and uncertainty can be toxic. It always feels like maybe 'this time it's different'.

Let's go back a bit further (I'm old!).

The dot.com crash in the early 2000s was a different flavour again. That one began with essentially unchecked euphoria. Companies with no profits — and sometimes not even any revenue — had market valuations of hundreds of millions of dollars. You didn't need earnings; you needed 'eyeballs'. Or 'clicks'. Or something that sounded futuristic.

Then reality arrived.

The NASDAQ halved. Then halved again. Tech darlings disappeared. People who thought they were financial geniuses discovered they weren't.

That one hurt differently. It wasn't systemic collapse. It was a wake-up call. Bewilderment that became regret. Too many people had bought 'stories', not businesses. The boom had been so incredible that it truly warped reality for many investors who were persuaded by the momentum and threw out their proven investment strategies in favour of what seemed like a new world.

Until it wasn't, and they learned that gravity really did still exist. (For the record, I didn't get whacked too badly, but I did own some shares that lost a *lot* of their value!)

And then there's 1987. I was younger then, but I remember the stories on the TV and in the paper. The stories of that 'Black Monday' are seared into market folklore, and it's only in the past few years that investors have stopped marking the anniversary.

Down more than 20 per cent... in a single day. Imagine that. Not over months. Not over weeks. In one day.

The Great Depression? That one sits above them all — the archetype. Down almost 90 per cent from peak to trough in the US. Years of economic hardship. Bank failures. Bread lines. A genuine collapse of confidence.

Different triggers. Different speeds. Different narratives.

Same emotion.

Fear.

Not academic fear. Not 'hmm, that's concerning' fear.

Visceral fear.

The kind that makes you pause to prepare before you open your brokerage app. The kind that makes you wonder if maybe the cautious people — the pessimists — were right all along. The kind that tempts you — just quietly — to do whatever it takes to make it, and the accompanying pain, stop.

Here's the thing, that's easy to say in hindsight and hard to feel in real time. None of those crashes were obvious buying opportunities when they were happening.

Looking back now, the GFC trough in March 2009 looks like a gift. COVID in March 2020 looks like a gift. Even the dot.com wreckage, if you'd focused on the right companies (hello, Amazon), looks like an extraordinary long-term entry point.

But in the moment?

In March 2009, the headlines were not 'Shares look cheap!' They were 'Financial system on the brink'. In March 2020, they weren't 'Once-in-a-decade opportunity'. They were 'Global pandemic shuts down world'.

That's the part people forget.

(By the way, two of the most famous business magazine cover stories come out of the dot.com boom and bust. The first was the 'What's Wrong, Warren?' story about Buffett being too old fashioned and out of touch to join the tech gravy train when stocks were booming (he was right). And then the 'Amazon.bomb' story about the savage fall in the company's share price from over $4 to as little as 50c (adjusted for stock splits). In early 2026, it was over $200 — more than a 400-fold gain. Sometimes, magazine covers — or the modern equivalents — can be a counter-indicator!)

When markets are falling hard, it doesn't feel like volatility. It feels like danger.

And this is where the theory you've read in the earlier chapters collides with reality.

You can understand, intellectually, that volatility isn't risk. You can nod along to the idea that markets recover. You can appreciate that time and compounding are your allies.

But when your portfolio is down 20 per cent, 30 per cent, maybe 40 per cent (more?) … those ideas feel thin.

You don't think about compound annual growth rates. You think about the dollar amount that just vanished from your screen.

You don't think about 30-year charts. You think about whether this is the start of something much worse.

You don't think 'buy to hold'. You think, 'Should I just step aside for a while?'

I've been there. Done that. I know that feeling intimately.

During the GFC, there were moments when I wondered whether this time really was different. During COVID, there were moments when I thought, 'Maybe I'm wrong. We just don't know how bad this will get.'

The difference wasn't that I didn't *feel* fear.

The difference was what I *did*.

I remained invested. And kept adding.

Not because I'm particularly brave. And I'm rarely the smartest guy in any room. And it's not because I enjoy watching red numbers (indicating losses) flash on a screen.

I remained invested because I had already decided what kind of investor I wanted to be.

I had already made my — imperfect, sometimes fragile — peace with the idea that crashes are part of the deal. That if I want the long-term compounding that markets have delivered over more than a century, I have to accept the price of admission.

And the price of admission is temporary, sometimes wrenching, losses.

The next crash will not announce itself politely.

It won't arrive at a convenient time. It won't wait until you feel 'ready'. It won't care whether you just increased your super contributions or finally built up a meaningful portfolio.

It will just arrive.

Sometimes, it'll be for reasons that people have been warning about for years. Other times — most often — it'll be out of the blue.

The question is not whether it will happen.

The question is who you will be when it does.

The emotional timeline of a crash

If you've never lived through a proper crash as an investor, you probably imagine it as a single dramatic moment.

One big red day.

One horrible headline.

One decision.

That's not usually how it works.

Crashes have stages. Not neat, evenly spaced stages. But recognisable ones. And if you know them in advance, you're far less likely to be blindsided by them.

Here's a quick summary.

Stage 1: Shock

It starts quickly.

Markets fall 5 per cent. Then 8 per cent. Then 12 per cent.

'It's just a correction', someone says on the internet or TV. 'It's healthy', says someone else.

You check your portfolio and think, 'Well, that's unpleasant'.

But you're not panicking yet. Your pulse quickens, but you're observing.

There's still confidence. Still optimism. Still the hope that it's a short fall and regular programming is about to resume.

Stage 2: Rationalisation

The fall continues.

You start explaining it to yourself.

'It's just inflation.'

'It's just geopolitics.'

'It's only going to impact one sector.'

'It'll be over soon.'

'It's just overvaluation.'

You instinctively, subconsciously search for narratives that make the fall temporary. Limited. Explainable.

You start to look at charts, even though you know they're not predictive. You read more articles than usual. You listen to more podcasts than usual. You want information. Because information feels like control.

But the market keeps falling.

Stage 3: Fear

Now the drop is serious. 20 per cent. Maybe 30 per cent.

Your portfolio isn't just 'down a bit'. It's meaningfully down.

You stop thinking in percentages. You start thinking in dollars.

'That's a new car.' 'That's a year's salary.' 'That's a house deposit.'

This is when the evolutionary wiring kicks in.

Your brain does not distinguish well—if at all—between financial threat and physical threat. Nor between volatility and permanent loss.

Loss feels like danger. And your instinct when faced with danger is simple:

Make it stop.

Selling feels like action. Selling feels like relief. Selling feels like control. This is the most dangerous stage.

Stage 4: Just make it stop

You start to bargain with yourself. Sometimes rationally, other times trying to rationalise your emotional state.

'I'll just move half to cash.'

'I'll wait until it stabilises.'

'I'll buy back in when it's clearer.'

This is where a lot of long-term wealth quietly dies.

Not because the investor was silly. Or thoughtless.

Because they were human.

They didn't want to be wrong. They didn't want to feel pain. They didn't want to watch it fall further.

So they acted.

And very often, they locked in the loss.

Stage 5: Exhaustion

If the downturn drags on — like the GFC did — something else sets in.

Fatigue.

The headlines are still negative. The portfolio is still down. But the drama dulls.

You stop checking as often. Not because you're calm — because you're tired.

This is dangerous, too.

Because fatigue can morph into disengagement.

You stop contributing.

You stop buying.

You stop believing that investing is worthwhile.

And the market, indifferent as ever, continues doing what markets do.

Stage 6: Disbelief

Then something strange happens. At least, it feels strange, based on recent history.

The market starts to rise.

Not dramatically. Not in a neat upward line. But it lifts.

But, burned by the falls, you're sceptical.

'This won't last.'

'The real crash hasn't happened yet.'

'There'll be a double-dip recession.'

The irony is thick. At the bottom, it felt like permanent decline. On the way up, it feels like a trap.

Opportunity never feels safe. It feels suspicious.

Now, here's what I want you to take note of:

None of these stages are about data or information.

They're about emotion.

The economic cause — rates, inflation, pandemics, debt crises, tariffs — changes every time.

The emotional sequence doesn't.

Shock.

Rationalisation.

Fear.

Make It Stop.

Exhaustion.

Disbelief.

And then … recovery.

But … if you can internalise that process before the next crash arrives, an interesting change starts to happen.

When you feel fear — because you will — you don't think, 'This is wrong'.

You think, 'Ah. Stage three.'

When you feel the urge to sell, you don't think, 'This is rational risk management'.

You think, 'This is Make it stop'.

Naming the stage doesn't remove the discomfort.

But the process gives you a marker. A milestone. And something to grab onto as the waves surge around you.

It lets you put a small gap between 'feelings' and 'actions'.

And in investing, that small gap might just be the difference between compounding and capitulation.

Why opportunity never feels like opportunity

There's a particular cruelty to markets.

Writer Morgan Housel captured it perfectly:

> Every past decline looks like an opportunity; every future decline looks like a risk.[3]

Read that again slowly. What does it tell us about big falls?

Past crashes look like opportunity.

Future crashes look like risk.

A couple of changed words, but a world of difference

Pull up a long-term chart of the ASX or the S&P 500 and find the bottom of the GFC — March 2009.

With the benefit of hindsight, it's a gift. A flashing neon sign. A once-in-a-generation entry point.

The usual refrain? 'I wish I could have bought then. What an opportunity!'

But in March 2009, the headlines weren't celebratory.

Banks were failing. Governments were nationalising institutions. There were serious conversations about whether the global financial system might not survive intact.

That was the story being told. And the risk we all felt, with markets down ... a lot.

It didn't feel clever buying in March 2009.

It felt somewhere between reckless and financial self-harm.

Now fast-forward to March 2020.

Markets fell more than 30 per cent in a matter of weeks. Entire economies were shutting down. Borders closed. Offices empty. Schools shut. Hospitals were preparing for the worst.

It didn't look like an opportunity.

It looked like the end of normal life.

Airlines were grounded. Retailers were shut. Restaurants were empty. People were losing jobs.

If someone had said to you in that moment, 'You know what this is? A huge buying opportunity', you might reasonably have thought they were delusional.

Others went to cash, waiting for it all to be over.

And yet, look at a chart now. March 2020 is a sharp V-shaped dip. A blip. A blindingly obvious opportunity.

But here's the crucial truth:

Opportunity only looks obvious after it has worked.

At the time, it just feels like risk.

It feels like uncertainty.

It feels like stepping towards danger when everyone else is taking cover. And the data — the falling market — tells you that they're right.

Which is precisely why so few people manage to buy at those cheap prices.

It's not because they lack intelligence.

It's not even because they're emotionally lacking.

It's because they lack emotional *insulation*.

When prices are falling sharply, the narrative is always compelling.

'It's different this time.'

'Structural shift.'

'New era.'

'Paradigm change.'

Housel again:

> Pessimism always sounds smarter than optimism because optimism sounds like a sales pitch while pessimism sounds like someone trying to help you.[3]

The story is always persuasive because it explains the fear you're already feeling.

In 2001, it was the bursting of a tech bubble built on fantasy.

In 2009, it was systemic financial collapse.

In 2020, it was a global pandemic.

Each time, the explanation felt definitive.

Each time, the fear felt rational.

And each time, diversified long-term investors who stayed the course were eventually rewarded.

Handsomely.

Now, let me be clear: I'm not saying every individual company survives. Some don't. We've already talked about that.

I'm not saying markets bounce back instantly. Sometimes they grind lower for years and then the recovery takes years more.

I'm giving you the broad explanation: Markets overreact to fear.

When uncertainty spikes, prices often fall further than is justified — just as they overshoot on the upside during euphoric periods.

But when you're inside the fear, it doesn't feel 'unjustified' ... you feel like something is wrong.

In sum? The best long-term buying opportunities are created by maximum discomfort.

The moments when you most want to retreat are often the moments when future returns are most attractive.

But you cannot rely on *feeling* brave in those moments.

You won't. I don't.

If you wait to feel confident, the opportunity will already be behind you.

This is why 'buying at the bottom' is mostly a myth.

You won't know it until it has passed. And even then, you don't know if there's another big fall coming.

As prices recover, you'll hear plenty of people predicting the next one is just around the corner.

And it's emotionally taxing, too. Volatility on the way up, just as there was on the way down. The headlines continue to tell you about the ongoing or future risks.

'They don't ring a bell at the bottom' is a stock market maxim. There's no 'all clear' signal, either.

And with markets being markets, there's only a small pause between the Chicken Littles and the doom-and-gloomers switching from 'the worst may not be over' to 'well, now prices have recovered, there's another fall on the way'.

Another aphorism: 'The market climbs a wall of worry.' By the time it *feels* safe again, prices *are* meaningfully higher.

The market is a cruel master. We're wired to seek safety. But the stock market rewards patience in the presence of discomfort. The solution? Understanding that your emotional state is not a reliable market timing tool.

When you feel safest, markets are often expensive. When you're most fearful, they are usually near their cheapest. If you can internalise that — truly internalise it — the next crash won't feel like a signal to flee.

It will feel like a test. And you'll already know the answer.

Why causes don't matter

Every crash has its cause. That's part of what makes them so convincing.

There's always a story. A rational explanation.

In 1987, it was portfolio insurance and automated selling.

In 2000, it was the bursting of a speculative tech bubble.

In 2008, it was subprime mortgages and excessive leverage.

In 2020, it was a global pandemic.

Different catalysts. Different bad guys.

And yet… strip away the narrative detail, and the pattern looks remarkably similar.

Prices rise.

Optimism builds.

Something shifts.

Uncertainty spikes.

Fear spreads.

Selling accelerates.

Then, eventually, stability returns. Confidence returns. Prices recover. (Sometimes in the reverse order!)

The cause changes, but the human reaction doesn't. Why is that important? Because, if you believe that understanding the cause will allow you to predict the outcome, you'll feel compelled to analyse it deeply.

You'll gather more information, and spend more time trying to find explanations. You'll get deeper into the weeds, which can actually rob you of perspective.

You'll ask:

'Is this worse than 2008?'

'Is this more structural than 2000?'

'Is this truly unprecedented?'

And you'll convince yourself that if you can just get the analysis right, you can position yourself perfectly.

But here's the thing.

Did anyone in 1987 know whether the one-day collapse would spiral into depression?

Did investors in 2008 know, in advance, if, how and when the GFC would resolve?

Did anyone in March 2020 know how long lockdowns would last, how quickly vaccines would be produced or how governments would respond?

Of course not.

And so... doesn't it make the effort to understand and predict what will happen look somewhere between silly and, well, just a little unreasonably arrogant?

See, sensible, diversified, long-term investors who own quality businesses don't need to know those things. Oh, it'd be lovely if we could, but that's the point. We can't—so we set ourselves up accordingly.

We just need a few things: people to continue to seek 'better' answers to questions, solutions to problems, and products and services to meet wants and needs.

And despite wars, pandemics, political upheaval, financial crises, oil shocks, currency collapses and technological upheavals, that ongoing reality has proven to be remarkably resilient and enduring.

The danger of obsessing over 'causes' is twofold: The temptation to believe that understanding leads to the ability to predict, and the folly of 'this time it's different'.

Of course things change.

Process. Mechanisation. Automation. Computerisation.

Governments. Interest rates. Taxes.

And some companies will absolutely fall by the wayside.

The ETF you own today will look very different in 20 and 30 years time.

But in general? The things that change are circumstances, not principles.

And that's the point.

You don't need to know exactly how a particular crisis will resolve. You just need to believe that collectively, humans (including those inside businesses) will adapt and adjust.

We progress *through* problems, not in the absence of them.

We grow *out of* crises, we don't succumb to them.

Innovation creates value, even as it disrupts others — and sometimes itself.

The cause shapes the circumstances. But those circumstances have always led to greater prosperity for our society and our businesses as a whole.

Now, this is not blind optimism. It's not Pollyanna stuff.

It's grounded in both history and sensible investing.

History is the story of humanity struggling, overcoming and prospering.

Sensible investing is buying quality, diversifying and dollar-cost averaging.

In every crash and downturn, if you owned a broad range of productive businesses across sectors and geographies, the cause — though scary at the time — did not mean permanent destruction.

Not even close.

The market falls because uncertainty rises. Uncertainty eventually falls. And when it does, prices rise.

Trying to forecast the precise trajectory of each crisis is intellectually stimulating. It's tempting to want to learn, understand and conquer it. I'm sorry to be the bearer of bad news, if that's your thing, but it's very, very rarely financially useful.

I do TV and radio interviews quite a lot. And relatively often, I'm asked, 'How are you positioning your portfolio in the face of [insert issue of the day here]?'

I'm sure those journos, and many of their viewers and listeners, would love me to tell them how I'm changing this and tweaking that. It makes good TV/radio, and gives people a sense of being able to 'do something'.

Frankly, I don't think I've ever said anything other than 'I'm not'.

The full answer is something along the lines of 'I'm not, because the principles of good investing haven't changed. It might prompt me to make sure I haven't inadvertently strayed from those principles, but that's as far as it goes.'

Because while you can't control pandemics, inflation, central banks or geopolitics — you can control whether you sell.

The three biggest mistakes investors make in crashes

When markets fall hard, most of the damage isn't done by the falls themselves.

It's done by reactions.

The crash itself is temporary but the decisions made during it can be permanent.

Over the years — through the GFC, COVID, the inflation sell-off and everything in between — I've seen the same three mistakes repeated again and again.

Not by bad, silly or thoughtless people. By normal people, feeling normal emotions.

Let's walk through them.

Mistake #1: Selling to 'stop the bleeding'

This is the big one.

The portfolio is down 10 per cent… 25 per cent… more…

Every day seems to bring more falls. More headlines. More talk.

At some point, your initial confidence shifts to concern.

It starts to feel irresponsible to hold. Even more irresponsible to buy more. You want to go into protection mode.

Selling feels prudent. Responsible. Mature. And when you don't sell, and prices fall further, it only convinces you that you should make the move before it gets worse.

In reality, you are probably converting a temporary decline into a permanent loss.

Many investors who sold in early 2009 didn't get back in until years later — if at all.

Many who moved to cash during COVID waited for 'clarity' or for the pandemic to be declared 'over'. The clarity arrived alongside sharply higher prices. The pandemic ended years later.

The worst bit?

Selling is emotionally rewarding, because it provides immediate emotional relief as the numbers stop going down. You feel better when the volatility stops being a constant companion. You can feel the anxiety disappear, and that feels like proof you did the right thing.

And the cost will never appear in black and white on your statement, because we never experience the road not taken.

But that road is real, and the cost is in the returns you missed out on while you were holding cash.

Actually, that might not be the worst bit after all. The worst bit might just be when you do the maths on what might have been, but can never be recovered.

Mistake #2: Stopping contributions

This one is quieter — and just as damaging.

You might not sell — that's a huge win. But you do stop buying.

You stop saving. Or you save, but don't invest. And you tell yourself you'll restart when 'things settle'.

That's only sensible, at least on the surface. Who wants to throw good money after bad?

But think back to our old friend from Chapter 9: dollar-cost averaging.

When markets fall, prices drop. When prices drop, you get more shares for your money. And when prices drop, expected future returns rise. (Why? Think about a company whose shares are selling for $15. Then, during a crash they go to $10. Eventually, they hit $30. At $15, you'd be doubling your money. At $10, it'd triple—hence the higher future returns from a lower price.)

But right when shares are cheaper than they were six months ago is precisely when many investors choose to stop buying.

It's rationally silly, but perfectly understandable, given our human evolution and hardwired instincts.

We're wired to prefer buying when things are rising (because it feels safe) and to avoid buying when things are falling (because it feels dangerous). But long-term wealth is built by consistently investing through both.

During the GFC, the investors who kept contributing bought at depressed prices for *months*. And for much of that time, their purchases lost value in the days, weeks and months afterwards.

Doesn't that feel kinda dumb? It should, at least instinctively. But over the following decade, those purchases paid off in spades.

If you want to do one thing right in the next crash: Keep contributing.

Not because you want to. You won't. Not because it feels good. It'll feel awful. Not because the shares will go up. They mightn't, for a while.

But just grit your teeth. Be like Nike. Just do it.

Mistake #3: Consuming fear

This one doesn't show up in the numbers. But it can cloud everything.

When markets fall, our appetite for news explodes. '$X billion wiped off share market' is the headline, and we all click and read, rubbernecking our own financial car crash.

We're drawn to check prices more often, to read reports and analyses. We're wide-eyed as the losses mount. And we talk about it to each other.

Whether we know it or not, we're looking for certainty. For an explanation. Because humans are deeply uncomfortable with not knowing (just check out the popularity of tarot readers and seances).

But what we usually find is amplification.

Media incentives don't change during crashes — they intensify. 'If it bleeds, it leads' isn't suspended during downturns. It's turbocharged.

And the more fear you consume, the more urgent the need for action feels. Plus, just think of the social media algorithms. How easy it is to fall into an echo chamber that almost imperceptibly changes what we see and hear … and eventually how we feel.

It's that temptation to understand so we can act. But it changes our perspective along the way.

There used to be a rule of thumb that you became more like the five people you spend most time with.

That's turbocharged in our modern media and social media environment where you choose the news, and then the news chooses you.

The thing is, consuming fear doesn't improve your timing. It doesn't improve your investment analysis either.

What it does is weaken our resolve. Distort our perspective. Shorten our time horizon.

It drags us away from our own strategy and towards something else.

Sometimes the most financially productive thing you can do in a crash is turn the volume down.

• • •

So, here's what's interesting about those mistakes. They're not made from ignorance or inability or a lack of intelligence.

They are the product of emotion.

Selling to stop pain.

Not investing to feel safe and sensible.

Overconsuming information — which becomes doomscrolling — to regain control.

All perfectly human. Just also damaging to long-term compounding.

Which is why this chapter isn't about being brave. It's about being prepared.

Because when markets fall sharply, you *will* feel the pull toward these three behaviours. You won't be immune. I'm not, either.

Remember, the goal isn't to eliminate emotion. It's to separate emotion from action.

And, ideally, to know what actions you've already decided to take when the proverbial hits the fan. Which is where the playbook that follows comes in.

The 'market crash' playbook

It's one thing to understand past crashes.

It's another to survive future ones.

When markets are falling hard, theory evaporates quickly. What matters then is not how well you can explain what's happening — it's whether you've already decided how you'll respond.

So let's make this practical.

This is *not* market timing advice.

It's a behavioural framework. It's pre-commitment. It's a script you can follow when your emotions are loud and your clarity is low.

When the market falls 10 per cent

Do nothing.

Not because 10 per cent doesn't matter. It does. But 10 per cent declines are normal. They happen regularly. If every 10 per cent fall demands a response, you will spend your investing life reacting.

So at minus 10 per cent.

No selling.

No changing strategy.

No portfolio tinkering.

No frantic rereading of economic forecasts.

Just breathe.

Continue your regular contributions.

And remind yourself that volatility is the admission price.

When the market falls 20 per cent

Now it feels *serious*.

Talking heads will use the phrase 'bear market'.

Friends start asking questions. The doom and gloom starts to crowd out the optimism. This is where the temptation to 'just move a bit to cash' creeps in.

Resist it.

At minus 20 per cent: Keep contributing.

Remind yourself that you're a long-term investor. Remind yourself why you own what you own.

Reduce price-checking. This is not the moment to try to change horses, midstream. It's the moment to remain consistent.

When the market falls 30 per cent

Now we're in deep discomfort territory.

Your portfolio looks meaningfully smaller. This is when doubt becomes persuasive.

So this is when discipline matters most.

At minus 30 per cent: Remind yourself of why you bought the shares you own, and your long-term expectations for those companies and ETFs.

Are you invested in productive businesses? Has their long-term ability to generate earnings permanently changed?

Check your emergency fund. If your 'Oh, shit' fund is intact, you don't need to touch your investments.

But also, narrow your inputs:

Fewer headlines.

Fewer opinions.

No doomscrolling.

Notice what's *not* on the list?

Selling.

Because unless the long-term earnings power of productive businesses has been permanently impaired, falling prices are a shift in sentiment, not necessarily a shift in value.

That is the creed of the long-term investor.

When the market falls 40 to 50 per cent

This is rare. It's painful. It's memorable.

It's the sort of decline that produces documentaries later.

At this level, your job narrows dramatically.

Don't try to 'optimise'. Don't 'reposition'. Don't try to out-trade the rest of the market.

Instead, your job is to *endure*. To stay the course.

Winston Churchill probably didn't say these words that are ascribed to him, but if he didn't, he should have. And they're words that will matter when your portfolio is looking like the result of a tropical cyclone: 'If you're going through hell, keep going.'

Here's your simplified playbook:

- Keep contributing if you can.
- Do not reduce your time horizon.
- Avoid irreversible decisions.
- Do not 'wait for clarity'.

This is when you'll hear the most confident predictions (and remember, pessimism sounds smart, because it feels like people are trying to help):

'The recession will last years.'

'The recovery will be slow.'

'There's a structural change in the market.'

'We're in a new normal.'

Maybe.

But remember this: The market does not require certainty to rise. It requires improvement at the margin.

The worst headlines are often still being written at, and after, the market has bottomed and has started to rise.

And history suggests that by the time clarity arrives, prices are often higher. Maybe much higher.

The most important rule

Make decisions in calm times.

Execute them in turbulent times.

That's it.

We talked about automating your saving and investing earlier, which is a form of pre-commitment. It removes the need for you to make a decision right at the time when that decision is going to be hardest to make.

The same applies to how you handle downturns and crashes.

Your response should not be improvised.

It should be predetermined.

If you wait until your portfolio is down 35 per cent to decide how you feel about volatility, you'll be too late, and your emotions will be too raw to make a rational decision.

If you wait until headlines are screaming to decide whether you believe in long-term compounding, you'll be too late.

Decide now.

Write it down.

'When markets fall sharply, I will continue investing.'

'When markets fall sharply, I will not sell unless the company's long-term prospects have significantly worsened.'

'When markets fall sharply, I will reduce noise, not increase it.'

This isn't bravado.

It's insulation.

A subtle shift

Here's something interesting.

Once you've lived through one or two proper crashes and stayed the course, something changes.

The next one still hurts. But it doesn't surprise you.

It doesn't feel like an anomaly. It feels like weather. Unpleasant weather. But weather, nonetheless.

You don't sell your house because it rains. You don't abandon investing because of the lightning and thunder.

You stay inside for a bit. And, eventually, the sun comes back out.

Crashes are *violent*, but they are not *verdicts*.

They are *volatility*.

And if you own productive businesses and give them time, volatility is noise — sometimes very loud noise — during a long upward trend.

The only thing that matters

When markets fall hard, everything feels urgent.

Headlines feel like they need a response. Opinions are telling you to act. Decisions feel necessary.

Your portfolio shrinks and your brain screams: 'Don't just sit there. Do something!'

But you'll need to step back. Zoom out. Remember history.

Because what actually determines whether you build long-term wealth?

Not whether you correctly predicted the cause of the crash. Not whether you perfectly timed the bottom. Not whether you felt calm while it was happening.

Only one thing truly matters: Did you remain an owner of productive businesses long enough for time to do its work?

That's it.

Crashes don't destroy long-term wealth. Permanent exits do.

Fear doesn't derail compounding. Behaviour does.

The market *will* fall again.

(I'm not allowed to make promises or give guarantees, but I'll happily walk right up to the threshold of that prohibition here. Recessions happen. Falls happen. Crashes happen — less often, but they *do* happen.)

Is it likely that history will stop repeating just because I've written these words or because you've started investing or for some other reason?

Nope. Not even a little bit.

The market will fall. I don't know when, but it will.

It may fall 20 per cent.

It may fall 40 per cent.

It may fall quickly or the grind might play out over months.

But it'll happen.

And when it does, none of the historical charts will *feel* comforting. None of the statistics will *feel* persuasive. None of the averages will *feel* relevant.

What will matter is whether you trust the process you've already chosen.

Whether you trust that businesses adapt.

Whether you trust that human ingenuity doesn't suddenly disappear as the result of a recession.

Whether you trust that the long arc of democratic capitalism bends — messily, unevenly, sometimes frustratingly slowly — upward.

You don't need certainty.

You need commitment.

Commitment to stay invested.

Commitment to continue to save and invest.

Commitment to not shorten your time horizon just because prices are volatile.

Remember: You are not trying to outwit the market. You are trying to outlast your own impulses.

Every major crash in history has eventually been followed by recovery.

Not instantly.

Not smoothly.

Not without casualties among individual companies.

But the broad market — the collective engine of business, innovation and human effort — has recovered and moved higher.

Every. Single. Time.

Not because someone rang a bell.

Not because the headlines said it would.

Because people kept working.

Kept building.

Kept solving problems.

Kept allocating capital.

And if you remain a part owner in that process, time works for you. Indeed, as Warren Buffett would remind us, we should *'Be fearful when others are greedy, and greedy when others are fearful'.*[8]

The next crash is coming.

It will feel different. It will sound different. It will have a different villain.

It will still test you in exactly the same way.

The only thing that matters is this: When it comes, will you still be in the game?

If the answer is yes—calmly, deliberately, pre-decidedly yes—then the crash is not your enemy.

It's simply the toll booth on the road to compounding.

Pay it.

And keep driving.

Now, to two little words that can make a massive negative impact on your portfolio.

What really matters

- Market crashes are inevitable parts of investing and have occurred throughout history.
- Every crash feels terrifying in real time but obvious in hindsight.
- Investors who stay invested during downturns are usually rewarded when markets recover.

14

UNDERSTANDING FEES AND TAXES (WITHOUT BEING BORED TO DEATH)

> *Tiny percentages can quietly cost you a fortune.*

There are few things in investing more dangerous than a percentage point.

Not market crashes. Not recessions. Not even your own emotions.

A percentage point.

Let me ask you a question.

What's the difference between 1 per cent and 2 per cent?

Most people shrug. One percentage point? Not much. Certainly not enough to lose sleep over.

We instinctively compare it to the 'whole' — 100 per cent. The difference between 1 per cent and 2 per cent? Almost nothing in that context.

But our instincts let us down in lots of ways when it comes to money, as we've already discussed. And here's just one more.

Let's run some numbers.

Imagine you invest $10 000 at a 9 per cent annual return for 30 years.

At 9 per cent with no fees, you end up with just over $133 000.

That's huge. And in keeping with what we've discussed already. Compounding doing its thing, almost unnoticed day by day, but astonishing over long periods.

But now let's assume you're paying a 1 per cent fee to have that money managed, reducing your return to 8 per cent.

You'd have $100 000, instead.

And at a 2 per cent fee? About $76 000 (see figure 14.1).

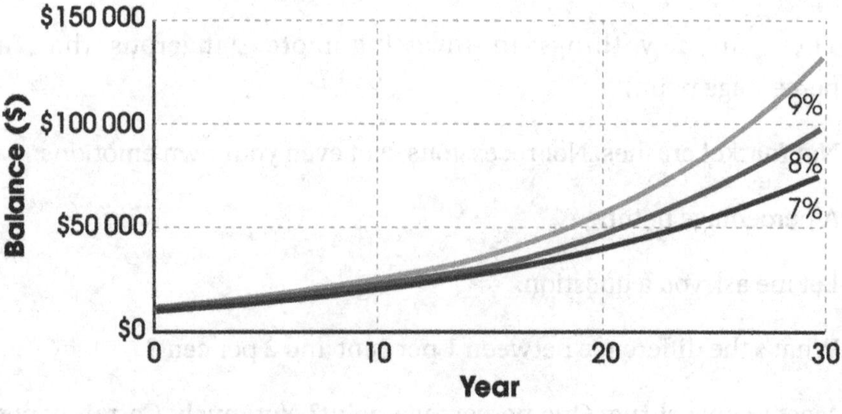

Figure 14.1 Compounding growth of $10 000 over 30 years

That's in the same market. With the same investments. Held by the same investor.

The only difference? A single percentage point, each time.

(Yes, this sounds like the 'compare the pair' superannuation ads. For good reason! It's exactly the same concept.)

That 'tiny' 1 per cent difference didn't cost you 1 per cent. It cost you more than $30 000. A full quarter of your wealth!

Two per cent stole more than 40 per cent of it. Forty per cent!

Now think larger.

Instead of $10 000, imagine it's your superannuation balance.

Instead of 30 years, imagine 40.

Instead of a single lump sum, imagine contributions every year of your working life.

That percentage point doesn't just nibble at your returns.

It gorges on your retirement... not just the numbers, either—your very lifestyle in your golden years.

I hope your eyes are just a little wider at this point.

(Bonus points if you're a little annoyed or angry, and wondering how much it's cost you, thus far, and if you're ready to make a change!)

Here's the uncomfortable truth: A 1 per cent fee doesn't take 1 per cent of your money.

It takes a(n often massive) slice of your future.

And the longer you invest—which, as you now know, is exactly where the power of investing really shines—the bigger that slice becomes.

Compounding is magical when it works *for* you. It's merciless when it works *against* you.

Let's talk about how.

How seemingly small costs can skewer your portfolio

The reason fees are so dangerous isn't that they're large. It's that they compound, just as your wealth does... but in the opposite direction.

When a fund charges you 1 per cent, it doesn't just take 1 per cent this year and call it a day.

It takes:

1 per cent this year...

And the growth that 1 per cent would have earned next year...

And the growth on that growth the year after...

And... for decades.

It's *negative* compounding.

Imagine two investors.

Both earn 9 per cent before fees.

One pays 0.2 per cent in total costs. The other pays 1.2 per cent.

After fees, one earns 8.8 per cent. The other earns 7.8 per cent.

That one percentage point difference doesn't sound dramatic. But over 40 years, it becomes enormous.

Let's imagine a 25-year-old investing $10 000 to start, then adding $10 000 every year for 40 years.

At 8.8 per cent, they'd end up with roughly $3.5 million.

At 7.8 per cent, they'd end up with around $2.7 million.

That's about $800 000.

Gone.

Not because they picked worse companies.

Not because they panicked in a crash.

Not because they tried to time the market.

Because of a single percentage point.

That's the tyranny of compounding costs.

This is why costs matter so much in long-term investing. They don't just reduce your return. They reduce the return on your return.

Now, before we go full anti-fee crusade, let me say something important.

Fees aren't evil.

You should pay for value. If someone genuinely improves your outcomes, helps you avoid behavioural mistakes, builds a proper plan or gives you peace of mind—that can be worth every cent.

We'll get back to maximising returns rather than minimising costs later, but here's some simple (rhetorical) questions:

Would you rather earn 9 per cent and pay a 0.2 per cent fee, or 12 per cent and pay a 2 per cent fee?

Would you rather pay a 1 per cent fee to someone who helps you remain invested during a downturn or pay no fee at all and sell at the bottom?

Fees aren't the problem. The extra return you get for those fees is what you should be focused on.

If the extra return is greater than the extra fee, fill your boots.

If it's not... we're in negative compounding territory and that's stealing your returns.

And it's often really hard to beat the market by the amount required to justify the fees you might pay.

If a fund charges 1.5 per cent per year, it has to outperform an alternative fund charging 0.2 per cent by 1.3 per cent every single year (on average) just to break even.

That's a very high hurdle.

And that's before we even get to performance fees. These are fees managers charge when they beat a specific benchmark... and which can be 15 or even 20 per cent of that 'outperformance'... but which most don't give back if they subsequently underperform.

Again, I'm not anti-manager. I'm pro-maths.

And the maths is relentless, particularly if it's a set percentage.

And here's the thing: The larger your portfolio gets, the more money you pay in fees... for exactly the same service.

So where are these little leaks hiding?

Where are they stinging you and how can you avoid it?

The good news is this: You can't control markets. But you can control costs.

And if you can't control the investment return, but you can control fees, doesn't that make the latter an obvious place to start?

Let's look at the usual suspects.

Superannuation

This is the big one.

Super is, for most Australians, their largest investment outside their homes. It's also the one we tend to pay the least attention to.

On one hand, that's good — if you're not obsessively watching it, you're far less likely to succumb to the temptations of over-trading and reacting to falls.

On the other ... those fees might go unnoticed.

Inside your super you'll typically find:

- an administration fee
- an investment fee
- indirect costs
- possibly insurance premiums.

And some people have multiple super accounts all charging separately.

If you're paying 0.4 per cent in total fees, that's one thing. If you're paying 1.5 per cent, that's another entirely.

(Those aren't made-up numbers either. They were the minimum and maximum, respectively, for a $100 000 super balance in the default investment strategy, found by the regulator APRA, in a 2022 study.)

Over a 40-year career, that difference can easily mean six figures less at retirement.

So here's a simple super health check:

- Do you know your total percentage fee?
- Do you have more than one super account?
- Are you paying insurance premiums you don't need?
- Is your investment option appropriate for your age and risk tolerance?

You don't need to obsess. But you do need to know. Because the system will happily keep charging you whether you're watching or not.

Managed funds and ETFs

Fees here vary wildly. And I mean *wildly.*

Some broad market ETFs charge less than 0.05 per cent per year, and have no performance fee.

Some actively managed funds charge 1.5 per cent or more plus performance fees.

Again, the question isn't 'active or passive?' It's 'is the cost justified?'

Remember, you can get the market's average return — less a very tiny fee — by buying a low-cost, passive, index-tracking ETF. Now, if a fund charges 1.5 per cent and consistently does better than that ETF — after fees — that's wonderful. But 'after fees' is the key phrase.

The hurdle is higher than most people realise.

How high? Study after study finds that the vast majority of funds fail to earn a higher return than the market average after fees. And that's not because these people are (necessarily) bad stock pickers.

Think about it: Investors as a group get the average return (by definition). And because it's an average, (roughly) half of investors will do better and (roughly) half will do worse.

(It's not mathematically *absolutely* true — the amount of money managed by each investor will skew those results a little. But for our purposes, it'll be close enough to true.)

Now, let's say the 50 per cent of actively managed funds that outperform *before fees* charge 1 per cent.

The group who beat the market before fees, but by less than 1 per cent, all of a sudden become *below average* after fees are included, leaving (far) less than 50 per cent still beating the market.

And that means your odds of finding an after-fee outperforming fund manager are ... not good, statistically speaking.

We're going to dip back into some Buffett wisdom, here. In his 2005 letter to shareholders, he wrote about a family called the 'Gotrocks'. They owned all of the shares of all of the companies on the stock market. So, they benefit entirely from the growth in profit, and value, of those companies. That's a pretty good deal—some companies do better, and some worse, but all of the benefit goes to the family.

But then, 'Helpers' come along, offering to help a few family members beat the others. For a fee, obviously. So the family buy and sell among each other, paying the 'Helpers' for their work.

And after all that? Well, the family still owns all of the companies, as a group. But they've paid the 'Helpers' for the privilege of assisting with the game of musical chairs. Meaning that they're actually worse off, overall, because while the total return remains the same, they're now leaking money to those Helpers. The family is poorer than they would have been, had they just held on to what they already owned.

Then more Helpers arrive, in many forms. Fund managers, asset consultants, stock brokers... lots of (to use an unkind metaphor) snouts in the trough, all reducing the returns the family would otherwise have kept for themselves, for no net gain.

Oh sure, each 'Helper' says they'll make money for each family member. Some might actually do it, too. But others won't, and the fees, in total, are a drag on the overall return.

The family is poorer for engaging the services of these Helpers, than if they'd just left well enough alone.

As Buffett says:

> The Gotrocks still own all of corporate America; the trades just rearrange who owns what. So the family's annual gain in wealth diminishes, equaling the earnings of American business minus commissions paid. The more that family members trade, the smaller their share of the pie and the larger the slice received by the Helpers. This fact is not lost upon these broker-Helpers: Activity is their friend and, in a wide variety of ways, they urge it on.

Again, it's possible that some Helpers can truly add value. But as a group, as Buffett's analogy shows, they can only detract from the total value of the market. Read that again: the 'Helpers', who offer to improve your returns, can only, as a group, detract from them.

While Buffett was using an American example (and spelling), the same applies wherever fees are paid.

It's not just the direct fees, though, that threaten your returns.

There's also turnover. Funds that trade frequently can trigger capital gains inside the fund, which may flow through to you. That's another layer of hidden friction.

Doesn't sound much like a recipe to maximise returns, on average at least, does it?

We've already set out our strategy as low turnover, low cost, long holding periods.

Which ... doesn't sound much like many funds, does it?

Brokerage and churn

Every time you trade, you pay.

Brokerage. The bid-ask spread. Possibly tax.

If you buy and sell monthly 'just to be active', you're not just risking poor timing. You're adding friction.

Investor A trades a few times a month, paying $20 each way. That's $1440 a year in brokerage alone. Over 20 years, that's almost $30 000 — before you account for lost compounding.

Investor B buys quality businesses and holds them for decades. Brokerage becomes almost irrelevant.

And again, brokerage fees themselves aren't (necessarily) unreasonable. Brokers are performing a service.

The thing is, they don't make money when you get rich. They make money when you trade. Which ... kinda feels like investors and brokers are at cross-purposes, doesn't it?

If frequent trading is likely bad for your wealth (and it is), and your broker wants you to trade more often ... are they a helper or a pusher?

One more nuance: Not all brokers are built that way. But you should be sceptical and on your guard against suggestions, incentives and inducements to trade more often.

This'll sound completely contradictory, but there's also another wrinkle to consider: While you should keep your overall brokerage costs down, it doesn't mean you should (necessarily) choose the broker with the lowest per-trade fee.

Huh?

We've already talked about the investor (trader, really) who buys and sells every month, and the costs they incur at $20 per trade. It's… a lot. Now, it would absolutely make sense for that investor to find the lowest possible brokerage cost.

But, as in the example of Investor B, previously, if you buy regularly (but not every week) and rarely sell, it might actually make sense to prioritise things like website ease-of-use, customer service and reliability over trying to save $5 in brokerage each time you buy.

But if you're over-trading, the market doesn't need to beat you. Your own activity can do that just fine. Ouch.

Now, fees are at least visible. They appear on statements. You can look them up.

Tax is sneakier.

Tax basics for investors: Capital gains tax and dividend franking

Tax matters.

But like fees, it's best understood calmly rather than emotionally. Put away your thoughts on government waste or your ideology about who should pay what tax.

We're going to look at the world as it is… and the impact of tax, based on what you do and don't do.

(A quick note here. Nothing that follows is tax advice, and the information is correct at the time of writing. But laws change, so make sure you're up to date, and seek advice from a tax professional.)

Capital gains tax (CGT)

In Australia, you pay tax on profits when you sell an asset.

Not when it rises.

Not when it's 'up on paper'.

Only when you realise the gain.

That matters.

Because unrealised gains compound tax-free.

If you buy a great business and hold it for 20 years without selling, the gain grows untouched by tax until the day you sell.

Let's go back to our imaginatively named investors again.

Investor A buys and sells within months, repeatedly locking in gains and paying full tax each time.

Investor B buys, holds for five, ten or 20 years, and then sells. They benefit from years of tax-deferred compounding.

Same businesses. Different behaviour. Different outcomes.

Tax isn't the enemy. But impatience is expensive.

Dividend franking

Australia has something many countries don't: a dividend imputation system. Or what's colloquially known as 'franking'.

When a company earns $100 in Australian profit, it might pay $30 in company tax. If it distributes the remaining $70 as a dividend, it also attaches a $30 'franking credit'.

As a shareholder, you receive:

$70 in cash *and* $30 credit for tax already paid.

If your marginal tax rate is lower than 30 per cent, you may even receive a refund of the difference.

This prevents double taxation and makes after-tax returns more attractive for many Australian investors.

By the way, this is one of the least appreciated benefits of owning dividend-paying shares. If you earn $70 in bank interest, you pay full tax. If you receive $70 in net rent (after expenses), you pay full tax. But if you receive a $70 'fully-franked' dividend, you'll get a $30 tax credit and pay much less tax (the numbers depend on your marginal tax rate) than in the other two cases.

It also means that comparing dividend yields internationally without considering franking can be misleading.

Now, another quick point: Not all dividends have franking credits attached. If the company hasn't got a large 'franking credit balance', it can't distribute those credits to shareholders. A common cause would be for profits earned (and taxes paid) outside Australia. Franking credits only apply to *Australian* taxes paid by a company.

But here's the key point: Franking credits are part of your total return, even if you don't see them quoted in the dividend you see when you search a company's share price online.

Which brings us to the most important idea in this chapter, and one of the most important topics in investing—no matter the asset class you invest in.

Don't minimise your tax (maximise your after-tax return)

Can I make a confession? I hope I pay a stupidly high ... eye-wateringly high ... amount of tax over my lifetime.

As Julia Roberts might say, 'Big. Huge'.

And while I do want to contribute my share of the national bill because I think it's a civic responsibility, there's another altogether more selfish reason. But we'll get to that.

First, let's talk about the problem that can stem from focusing on minimising tax: Investors sometimes become so focused on avoiding tax that they sabotage themselves.

They refuse to sell a deteriorating business 'because of the CGT'.

They make suboptimal investment purchases 'to minimise tax'.

They chase deductions rather than returns.

I'm not going to pick on property investors, but I suspect the number of them who in the past invested not to 'maximise their returns' but to 'pay less tax' is...large.

So hear this: Avoiding tax should not be your goal.

Please read that again. There are some powerful incentives — financial, ideological, greed-induced — that lead people to focus not on making as much money as they can, but on paying as little tax as possible.

So, again, avoiding tax is not the goal.

Building wealth is.

If a business you own is structurally weakening—losing competitive advantage, taking on too much debt, being disrupted—or is priced at a ridiculously high price, making future returns likely small or negative, clinging to it purely to avoid tax can cost you far more in capital losses than you ever saved in tax.

Do not let the tail wag the dog.

At the end of the day, the only return that matters is your after-tax, after-fee return.

If you earn:

10 per cent before tax

8 per cent after fees

and 6.5 per cent after tax

Your return is 6.5 per cent.

That's the number that compounds.

Everything else is noise.

The beauty of long-term investing is that it is naturally tax-efficient.

Low turnover. Long holding periods. Compounding unrealised gains. Collecting franked dividends.

You don't need clever tricks. You need discipline.

And why do I want to 'selfishly' pay more tax? Because it'll mean I'd made a lot of pre-tax money in the process!

It's kinda like the example before of being more than happy to pay higher fees if I get higher after-tax returns.

No, that doesn't mean I'm planning to pay more tax than I have to — just that if the amount of tax I have to pay is high... That is truly a first-class problem to have, and I've probably done very nicely in the process!

So let's go back to the plan.

Work hard. Save diligently. Invest regularly.

Keep costs low.

Let time do the heavy lifting.

Small leaks sink big ships. But small improvements compound, too.

You can't control markets. You can't control crashes. You can't control share prices.

But you can control:

Your costs.

Your turnover.

Your behaviour.

In investing, success rarely comes from brilliance.

It comes from respecting arithmetic.

And the percentage points are not optional.

Now, let's talk about you...

Beware the 'Helpers'

I absolutely think financial advice can be really helpful. I don't do my own plumbing, electrics or brakes. I get someone with skill, education and experience to help me or do it for me.

The same with financial advice.

But be careful on two fronts: One that's pretty short and one that needs some explanation.

First, keep your fees low, and make sure your adviser is earning those fees by generating more value than the advice costs.

Second, whether a licenced adviser or not, you'll have some people tell you that the strategies in this book are 'not complex enough'.

They'll tell you that they know some trading strategy, tax trick or investment idea that is better than what's in these pages. That your money 'won't be working hard enough' unless you take their advice.

In most cases, you should run—not walk—away from them as fast as you can. There is no shortage of greed, overconfidence and, frankly, shysterism in investing.

Now, in some cases, depending on your personal circumstances, adding some bespoke advice to the One-Page Investment Plan might improve your returns further. Maybe a tax strategy. Or specific guidance around superannuation contributions. Or coaching.

If so, excellent.

But my suggestion? Be wary, and don't take silly risks—you just don't need to.

If you think it might help, by all means see a personal financial adviser. Just be very careful to understand their incentives—you're their meal ticket. That doesn't mean they're all bad—there are some wonderful financial advisers.

Just...keep it simple. You're the tortoise, not the hare. Don't let them tell you otherwise.

What really matters

- Fees and taxes quietly erode investment returns over decades.
- Small differences in costs compound into enormous differences in wealth.
- Investors should focus on maximising after-tax, after-fee returns, not headline performance.

15

CONTROL YOUR MONEY, DON'T LET IT CONTROL YOU

> *The easiest way to feel wealthier is often simply to want less.*

There's a strange paradox at the heart of money: The more of it you have, the easier it is to lose control of it.

Or maybe the easier it is to lose control of *yourself*.

But that's kinda the same thing, at least in this context.

No, you don't lose control of your money physically (or even digitally), of course. It doesn't grow legs and wander off.

But psychologically? Emotionally? Subtly?

Money has a way of expanding to fill whatever space you give it. And if you're not careful, it stops being the tool and starts being the master.

This chapter isn't about asset allocation. It's not about ETFs or price/earnings ratios or dividends.

It's about something far more important.

It's about control.

Because the ultimate goal of investing isn't to be the richest man or woman in the cemetery. It's to build a life you value — and fund it sensibly.

If you lose sight of that, you can 'win' financially and lose personally.

And that's a terrible trade.

Wealth is a tool, not a destination.

Let's go back to first principles. Let's go back to the 'why'.

Why do you want to build wealth?

To feel secure.

To provide for your family.

To have options.

To retire comfortably.

To travel.

To give.

To reduce stress.

None of those goals are about the number itself. They're about what the number enables.

Money is the means. Not the meaning.

And yet, somewhere along the way, it can become very easy to confuse the two.

Now, I'm going to pause here for a bit. If you've grabbed this book as someone who hasn't invested yet, or who has started, but wanted a sense check, you might be thinking: 'Dude, come on. Are you saying having too much money is an issue? I'm worried about not having *enough*. Talk about a first-world problem!'

And I hear you. But this chapter is not (only) about how much you have the day before you shuffle off this mortal coil.

It's about your attitude to money today. And tomorrow. And every day between now and then.

And you're right. If your money stress is 'I'm worried I won't have enough', then worrying about the other stuff does feel like a luxury.

But this chapter isn't about how you'll feel at the end. It's about your relationship with money all the way along the journey.

I mean, I hope by this point in the book, your stress levels have dropped at least a tiny bit.

I hope I've been able to show you that the One-Page Investing Plan is a path that you can follow — financially, mentally and emotionally.

But I know that underlying stress is still there. And I hope that, as you follow the plan, that stress lessens, bit by bit, as you put it into practice.

As you automate your savings. As you regularly invest. As you ride the market's waves, and realise that, while it may never feel any better, you've come out the other side, and you know you can do it.

That's the first part of 'controlling your money'.

This chapter is essentially about not replacing one stress — one type of 'being controlled by money' — with another.

I have been flat broke. At one point in my 20s, I signed up to a rental lease I could only just afford, then had a couple of large bills arrive. I had the 'lying in bed staring at the ceiling' experience.

Now, this isn't a sob story. I was lucky. It was a short period, and I made it through. I was never in danger of being on the streets — I had family I could have moved back in with, if necessary.

I'm just saying that I know that stress.

I climbed out of that situation, and almost all of you can, too. Not everyone — I talked in Chapter 8 about the fact that some people just can't, based on their wage, living expenses and other obligations. But most of us can.

And I hope this book will play a part in that journey for you.

I hope you'll see the opportunity that investing can provide, and I hope the steps I've laid out give you a path.

What I don't want that path to be is simply swapping one level of stress for another.

I don't want the fear of not having enough to be replaced by the stress of trying to make the portfolio number go up.

Again, it might sound strange if you're just getting started, but if you're not careful, it starts to happen.

The number becomes the target.

The portfolio becomes the scoreboard.

The market becomes the judge.

It's subtle. Almost invisible.

Start with the end in mind

Another Buffettism, but this time a version of a centuries-old aphorism: 'The chains of habit are too light to be felt until they are too heavy to be broken.'[28]

I guess what I'm saying is that I don't want to turn awareness and interest into obsession and emotional slavery.

Maybe you start by checking your super balance a little more often. You compare your returns to someone else's. You feel quietly disappointed if your net worth doesn't grow as fast as you'd hoped — even if your life is perfectly fine.

The tool has started to become the destination.

That's when money begins to control you.

Wealth, properly understood, is freedom. But wealth pursued for its own sake can quietly become another obligation — another metric you feel compelled to improve.

It's worth pausing and asking yourself, occasionally and honestly:

How much do I need to feel secure?

How much would be enough to retire?

If your answer is 'more', then be careful. Because 'more' is like 'tomorrow' — it never comes.

Remember in Chapter 8, I talked about my first job, and how rich I felt when I got a tiny pay rise?

I'm sure you've had similar experiences.

Now, of course, inflation is real. And yes, I'm old, so my first job wasn't yesterday.

(And as I tell my 13-year-old, no, there were no dinosaurs, and yes, we had cars!)

But 'more' is a terrible master. It is never satisfied.

Here's the other thing: I absolutely want you to save and invest. Please.

But also — and I'm no psychologist or self-help guru — I want you to have a life.

Now, I'm not religious, but it's worth thinking about an exhortation from the Christian bible: 'Money is the root of all evil.'

That's a selective quote, used either as a criticism by those who think that we'd be better off without it (that would be a dystopian world, by the way), or, more often, by those who've simply heard that quote before, and don't realise it's selective.

The longer quote?

'*For the love of* money is the root of all evil'[29] (emphasis mine).

Now, I'll let others work out the religious implications, but for our purposes, the distinction is important when it comes to our relationship with our money.

There's no harm in wanting to be more comfortable, less stressed and less financially precarious. There's actually a lot that's *good* about it.

But you need a target that's more than, well, 'more'. Otherwise, you'll just replace one type of stress with another ... and might forget to really live your life to its fullest, because you never feel like you can spend as well as save.

We'll get to retirement in a bit, but here's the other stat: Many people die with more in super than they had when they actually stopped working.

Which ... is lovely for their kids, and others who might inherit that wealth. And if they lived a wonderfully full retirement ... brilliant!

But don't you reckon a non-trivial number of those people ended up in that position because they worried so much about not having enough that they forgot to enjoy their golden years?

Me too.

Bottom line? Both your investing and your spending should be *intentional.*

Lifestyle inflation: The 'hedonic treadmill'

Let's talk about a real enemy of financial control: lifestyle inflation.

You get a bonus. You renovate the kitchen.

You get a pay rise. You upgrade the car.

You get a promotion. You move to a more expensive suburb.

None of those things are inherently wrong. Life is to be lived, not hoarded.

But there's a psychological force at play here called 'hedonic adaptation' — sometimes called the hedonic treadmill.

And it's not just what you *do.* It's what your brain does... and we often don't even notice it.

It works like this: when something improves, you feel good.

Then you adjust. Very quickly.

The new car feels luxurious... for about three months. Then it just feels normal.

The renovated house feels wonderful... until you've walked past the new bench tops a few dozen times.

The bigger salary feels liberating... until your expenses quietly expand to match it.

And then you're back where you started.

That doesn't mean you can't rationally appreciate the quality of those things. Or that you don't realise you've upgraded.

You can, and you do.

But you stop feeling it to the same degree. You simply get used to it.

And so the treadmill doesn't stop. It just speeds up.

Here's the dangerous part: When your income rises but your expectations rise just as fast, you never actually feel wealthier.

You might earn more. You might spend more. But your sense of financial comfort remains oddly unchanged.

In fact, sometimes it gets worse.

Because now you have more to maintain. More fixed expenses. A larger mortgage. A higher standard of 'normal'.

You've increased your obligations without increasing your freedom.

And freedom is the point.

Not only that, but the higher income probably comes with more hours, more responsibility and probably more stress.

In which case, despite everything, your quality of life has actually gone ... backwards.

One of the most powerful financial moves you can make isn't finding the next big stock market winner.

It's preventing your lifestyle from inflating in lockstep with your income.

That gap — the difference between what you earn and what you spend — is where wealth is built.

But more importantly, that gap is where control lives.

The easiest way to be wealthier? Want less.

Did I just pull the rug out from under you? Sorry, not sorry.

As a finance bloke, there's an expectation that I should worship the ever-higher number.

That I should be some sort of hyper-capitalist. Frankly, some in my industry are precisely that.

But I have a sneaking suspicion I might be happier than they are.

Don't get me wrong: I like nice stuff. I like new stuff.

But I've learned to value experiences, and to try to keep things simple.

Oh, I'm woefully imperfect. I still *want* more. Because I'm human. But I'm consciously trying to take control of that impulse.

Yes, I'm still saving and investing. But I'm also (thoughtfully) spending. On the things that matter. Like *really* matter.

For me, now, that's family. Holidays and experiences. The memories of which will still be around when the new car, couch, computer or other thing has long since been consigned to the scrap heap.

So ... the simplest way to be wealthier is to want less.

Not to deny yourself joy. Not to become a miserable miser. (Yes, it turns out those words have the same origin!)

Not to avoid pleasure. Just to be deliberate.

How? I try to want less of the things that are unnecessary, temporary or of the keep up with the Jones' variety.

Because every dollar you don't need to spend is a dollar that can be invested. And every dollar invested buys you future flexibility.

Here's a quiet truth: Wealth is relative to expectations.

If your lifestyle requires an income of $200 000 a year to sustain, you need an enormous portfolio to feel secure.

If your lifestyle requires $80 000 a year and you're genuinely content, you need far less.

The second person is wealthier long before the first one reaches their number. If they ever do, because they're always chasing 'more'.

Here's the other thing: Wanting less isn't about living a smaller life. It's about clarifying it.

When you define what 'enough' looks like for you, something interesting happens. The anxiety eases. The comparison fades. The constant pressure to upgrade diminishes.

You stop running someone else's race: you start designing your own.

There's extraordinary power in saying, quietly and confidently, 'This is enough'.

That's not complacency. That's control.

Here's the more concrete benefit: When you know what your number is, you have something to aim for *and* a rough timeline.

Volatile markets might push or pull that timeline forwards or backwards by a few years, but you know what the finish line looks like.

You know when you're getting close. And that gives you options. You won't work forever 'just in case I don't have enough' — you'll get to that point and give yourself permission to keep working if it suits you, or stop if it doesn't.

And knowing what the finish line looks like means less stress along the way. It gives you a goal to work toward, and lets you feel the progress as you move closer to it.

Less stress. More freedom. Less 'more'. More 'less'.

Being a good steward

Okay, so this can get pretty moralistic, if you let it, but that's not how I mean it.

Stewardship is just another word for 'responsibility'. And that's kinda another word for what I mentioned earlier: 'intentionality'.

Money flows.

And if you don't direct it, like water it will find its own direction.

Being a good steward of your money doesn't require brilliance. It requires intention.

It means:

- knowing what you earn
- knowing what you spend
- understanding what you own
- choosing where surplus capital goes
- aligning spending with values.

Kinda old fashioned, really.

But then, isn't all good money advice old fashioned? Our living standards have increased markedly since our grandparents' time, but have our money habits improved? I doubt it.

Managing money in a way our grandparents would recognise might actually be a rule of thumb we can live by!

No, 'stewardship' isn't glamorous.

There are no television shows about disciplined budgeting.

But stewardship is what turns income into wealth and wealth into freedom.

It's also what prevents wealth from distorting your priorities.

You can earn a high income and still feel perpetually stretched. You can accumulate assets and still feel uneasy. You can hit financial milestones and still feel behind.

Without stewardship — without clarity — money becomes reactive. Emotional. Comparison-driven.

With stewardship, it becomes purposeful.

Please don't obsess over every transaction. But do be aware.

Where is your money going?

Does that align with what you say matters most?

Are you building options or just maintaining appearances?

A good steward doesn't worship money. Nor do they ignore it.

They manage it — calmly, consistently, deliberately.

That's control.

Having enough

I want to relay a story told by Jack Bogle about a billionaire's party attended by two literary greats. It goes:

> ... Kurt Vonnegut informs his pal, the author Joseph Heller, that their host, a hedge fund manager, had made more money in a single day than Heller had earned from his wildly popular novel Catch-22 over its whole history. Heller responds, 'Yes, but I have something he will never have ... Enough.'[30]

I hope that hits you right between the eyes.

But also, notice what it *doesn't* say.

It doesn't condemn the hedge fund manager.

It doesn't fetishise poverty.

It doesn't moralise about income.

It simply draws a distinction between accumulation and satisfaction.

'Enough' is not a number in a spreadsheet. It's a decision.

It's the moment you recognise that chasing more for its own sake has diminishing returns.

If you're constantly reaching for higher returns because someone else appears to be doing better, you're probably in for a rude shock at best ... and a world of pain at worst.

Because you're on the way to becoming Aesop's hare.

And at risk of chucking away a wonderful 'get rich slow' strategy, replacing it with the spin of a roulette wheel.

You might start taking on excessive risk, figuring it'll deliver much higher returns.

You might start trading too frequently, as you try to find 'the one'.

You'll start buying what everyone is buying, in the hope that the crowd will help you get rich.

But... if you understand what enough looks like — and the strategy to attain it — you're more likely to:

- stay disciplined
- keep costs low
- avoid unnecessary churn
- let compounding do its work.

'Enough' creates stability.

And stability is fertile ground for compounding.

And, of course, there is a suitable Warren Buffett quote for everything. This time, it's Buffett on the failure of hedge fund LTCM that I talked about in Chapter 3: 'To make money they didn't have and didn't need, they risked what they did have and did need. And that's foolish. It is just plain foolish.'[3]

Doesn't that kinda feel like the opposite of 'enough'?

The power of control

Control isn't dramatic.

It doesn't come with headlines or applause.

It looks like:

- Saying no to an unnecessary upgrade.
- Maintaining a sensible savings rate even after a raise.
- Ignoring the temptation to compare portfolios.
- Sticking to your investment plan during volatility.
- Choosing time over overtime when you already have enough.

Control is calm.

It's also rare. And let's be honest... it can be hard.

Because our culture encourages escalation. Bigger. Better. Faster. More.

Financial independence, properly understood, isn't about escaping work. It's about freedom and choice.

When you control your money, you're less likely to:

- stay in a job you hate purely for the money
- make investment decisions out of fear and panic
- feel inferior because the Jones' house is larger
- tie your identity to your net worth.

The difference is choice. And that's the real dividend of sensible investing.

Control your money — don't let it control you.

You've spent this book learning how to:

- think long-term
- ride out crashes
- understand risk properly
- avoid unnecessary costs
- harness the maths of compounding.

All of that builds financial capacity.

Now we're adding control to that capacity.

Money is powerful. It amplifies your choices.

If you're clear about your values, it amplifies purpose.

If you're unclear, it amplifies noise... and might rob you of the serenity that comes from 'enough'.

The goal isn't to accumulate endlessly. It's to build enough to support the life you actually want.

So:

- Define enough.
- Protect the gap between income and spending.
- Invest patiently.
- Keep costs low.
- Avoid comparison.
- Choose deliberately.

Control your money.

Don't let it control you.

Because in the end, the wealth that matters most isn't measured in dollars.

It's measured in freedom.

Now let's talk about the transition to that freedom.

The last double

We've talked about the value of compounding. Of the Rule of 72. The snowball that rolls down the hill, growing as it collects more snow on its descent.

And while I hope it's obvious, the larger the snowball becomes, the more snow it can collect with each revolution.

That's true with compounding, too.

The larger your portfolio becomes, the more each percentage point gain adds. When you have:

- $10, 10 per cent adds $1
- $100, it adds $10

- $50 000, it adds $5000
- $1 million, it adds $100 000.

That is, I hope, not a revelation to you.

But now let's invoke the Rule of 72 from Chapter 4, and think backwards.

The Rule of 72 allows you to roughly estimate how many years it'll take your money to double.

It works like this: Start with 72. Divide it by your rate of return as a percentage.

If you're earning 9 per cent, then 72 divided by 9 is 8—your money will double every eight years or so, on average.

If you're earning 6 per cent? About 12 years. Ten per cent? Around seven years.

Now, whether you spend 20, 30 or 50 years compiling it, here's the thing I want you to realise: Half of your final total portfolio value comes from just that last double.

Put another way, the last 'double' adds the same amount of money as everything you've done up to this point.

If you retire with $1 million at 67, and you've earned the market's average 9 per cent return, your last $500k has come since 59.

That is, you might have felt woefully short of your target before your 60th birthday, but your snowball did the rest!

The flip side? If you're 25, 35 or 45 and you don't feel like you have enough yet, don't despair. You absolutely should make sure you're on track, but the payoff is in 'the last double'—that's what you're working towards!

What really matters

- Wealth is a tool to support a good life, not an end in itself.
- Lifestyle inflation can quietly consume the benefits of rising income.
- True financial freedom often comes from wanting less rather than endlessly earning more.

16

RETIREMENT IS THE END ... OF THE BEGINNING

> *Retirement doesn't end your investing journey—it simply changes the mission.*

That finish line I mentioned last chapter? It's only the first of two.

No, don't worry—this isn't some dodgy bait and switch.

The first finish line is 'enough'—enough to retire or to work less or to change jobs.

That first finish line is where freedom starts.

The second finish line is... kinda more permanent.

Unless we discover the elixir of youth between now and then, our mortal demise is sadly inevitable.

But, if the actuaries are right, that could be two or three decades (or more!) after your last day at work. More again if your 'enough' number lets you retire early.

Indeed, let's say you achieve your 'enough' number at 55. You will have worked for maybe 30 to 40 years.

And if you live until 85 or 95, you might be retired for just as long as you worked!

Which, I hope, puts that first 'finish line' in perspective.

Even if you work until 65 (or even 70, if you're enjoying it), the average retiree will have decades ahead of them.

And it's what your 'enough' number is all about.

It's the point at which the referee blows half time. You hand in your lanyard or your tools and swiftly move from the first half to the second.

It's the time for 'enough' to become 'freedom'. But it's not the end of your investing journey.

Like work, it might be time for some changes, but the investing changes aren't as huge as they might seem.

Let's rewind a little.

The general view is something like 'When I retire, I can get my super'. Which is true enough (the actual rules are more complex than we'll cover here, but stick with me on the concept).

But what does that little word 'get' mean? Some people imagine the portfolio being handed over in cash. Others see a transition from investing to spending as two almost-unrelated concepts.

And sure, by all means, use some of your 'enough' money to do things like replace the car or remodel the kitchen, if that was your plan.

But after that? You're still an investor, and your money should still be working for you, giving you the best retirement possible.

True, it'll be working for you a little differently, but still working.

For two reasons:

1. To protect your purchasing power against inflation
2. To extend your ability to enjoy your retirement as long as possible.

And that doesn't mean playing it (too) safe.

The safest of all would seem to be cash. But there are two problems here.

First, the return on cash is ... pretty low. That means either your 'enough' number needs to be pretty high, or you'll have to spend down your capital more quickly than you'd like.

And second, that cash is being eaten away by inflation as surely as if moths were having their way with a woollen jumper in a closet.

The grocery bill doesn't freeze out of respect for your decades of service. Electricity prices don't plateau in honour of your long career. Health costs don't politely hold steady.

If inflation averages 3 per cent a year — which would hardly be a shock — prices double roughly every 24 years.

A 65-year-old who lives to 89 will see their purchasing power cut in half. And if everything costs twice as much, but their cash hasn't grown, they can only afford to buy half of the things they used to.

Now, I'm not suggesting retirees should necessarily be 100 per cent in shares.

Risk tolerance matters. Sleep at night matters. Cash flow certainty matters.

But eliminating growth altogether is often a greater risk than tolerating volatility.

The greatest retirement risk isn't market fluctuation. It's running out of money.

And, as strange as it might initially sound, one of the most reliable ways to increase the risk of running out of money is to abandon growth entirely in favour of capital stability.

We need to separate two ideas that often get bundled together:

1. Volatility
2. Longevity risk

Volatility is visible. It's noisy. It's emotionally uncomfortable.

Longevity risk is silent. It unfolds slowly. And it's far more dangerous, if you don't prepare for it.

A retiree who moves everything to cash may feel safe in the short term. The balance doesn't bounce around. They ignore the headlines about 20 per cent share market falls.

But if their inflation-adjusted returns are near zero and they're drawing 4 to 5 per cent a year to live on, the maths is unforgiving. Even modest inflation compounds against them.

This is why retirement portfolios still need to invest.

Not for speculative growth. Not 'swing for the fences' growth.

Just sensible, diversified exposure to productive assets — businesses that generate profits, reinvest, innovate and adapt. And, increasingly in retirement, pay dividends.

The same forces that drove compounding during accumulation don't stop working just because *you* stopped working.

In fact, retirement often increases the need for durable compounding.

Superannuation structures can make this transition feel technical. You move from the 'accumulation' phase to the 'pension' phase. Minimum withdrawal rates apply. The tax treatment changes. The statements look different.

But underneath the paperwork, the economic reality hasn't changed.

You are still a part owner of businesses.

You still benefit from earnings growth.

You still rely on dividends, reinvestment, innovation and economic expansion.

The difference is that you're now using up capital rather than adding to it.

Which means the conversation shifts.

During accumulation, the dominant question is: 'How big is the balance?'

In retirement, the question becomes: 'What can this portfolio sustainably provide?'

That's a subtle but important shift.

The goal isn't preserving the largest possible account balance. Indeed, if it's too big, maybe you're not really maximising your enjoyment in retirement.

The goal is funding your life.

And that includes flexibility.

One of the quiet strengths retirees have is adaptability. Spending isn't fixed. It can adjust in response to markets. A temporary pullback in discretionary spending during downturns can materially improve long-term sustainability.

But that only works if the portfolio has growth potential over the decades ahead.

Retirement isn't the end of investing.

It's the end of saving.

And those are not the same thing.

From accumulation to preservation and drawdown … for decades

Accumulation mode is psychologically straightforward (if still challenging, sometimes!).

You earn income. You save some of it. You invest it. You repeat the process. The flywheel builds momentum.

Market downturn? Annoying — but useful. Lower prices mean your next contribution buys more shares. Volatility is inconvenient, sometimes scary, but not existential.

Retirement changes the direction of cash flow.

Instead of money flowing into the portfolio, it flows out.

So how do we manage that without abandoning growth?

There are several practical approaches.

But here's my suggestion.

First, make sure your 'enough' number has been chosen well.

I can't choose it for you, but it might be something like 'the portfolio size that allows me to earn 75 per cent of my pre-retirement income'.

Why 75 per cent? Generally because you're no longer investing a portion of your income, so you don't need that portion in retirement. And your costs in retirement tend to be lower than when you're working.

But if you want to use a different percentage, go for it.

Second, think about how your 'enough' number provides that income.

Are you going to slowly draw it down to zero in retirement?

Or are you hoping to live off the returns that your investments will earn, so you don't have to touch the capital, letting it compound to fight inflation?

Why that matters is that it determines how your retirement income is generated.

And here's the simple rule of thumb: The more of your portfolio income that's generated by dividends, the less of a cash buffer you need. The more of your portfolio income that's generated by capital gains, the larger your cash buffer needs to be.

Why?

Well, if you're funding your lifestyle with dividends, you'll be getting regular payments from your companies, and you don't need to worry about share prices fluctuating. Sure, you should still have a cash buffer in case one or more of those companies reduces its dividend, but the buffer needn't be particularly large.

On the other hand, if you're intending to slowly sell shares to pay the bills, you don't want to be selling the very month the COVID crash wiped one-third off the ASX! As we've learned, shares have always gone back up to, then surpassed, previous highs, but it can take a while. And you don't want to be a forced seller, so it makes sense to hold more cash, allowing you more control over when you sell and when you don't.

(It's also possible to combine either strategy with some lifestyle choices — making the timing of things like holidays dependent on when you're being offered a particularly good price to sell some of your shares. It's not how I'd design my retirement — I'd like some steady income — but it's an option if you prefer it.)

Whichever you choose, what matters is that the structure acknowledges variability.

Because, like accumulating during your working life, retirement is not a straight line.

And here's something underappreciated: many retirees do not spend in a straight line either.

Research shows spending tends to follow a curve. Early retirement — the 'go-go' years — often involves higher travel and lifestyle spending. Later years often see a natural reduction in discretionary outlays.

Yes, healthcare costs may rise later. But the idea that spending steadily increases forever isn't borne out by most real-world data.

That's important because it challenges the instinct to clamp down hard at retirement.

You may never be healthier or more capable than you are in your first decade of retirement.

As Mal Leyland, one half of the famous Aussie explorers the Leyland Brothers, is fond of saying, 'You'll never be as young as you are today'.

Delaying experiences out of fear can mean missing the window entirely. That would really be a shame.

So, from an investment standpoint, the core philosophy remains unchanged.

You still want ownership of productive assets.

You still want diversification across sectors and geographies.

You still want low costs.

You still want to avoid concentrated bets.

But we'll add one more, here: Don't just chase the highest dividends you can find.

For two reasons (there seem to be a lot of two reasons in this chapter!).

The first one is that the highest dividend yields (a percentage that just compares the dividend to the share price) are often unsustainable. Why? Well if the dividend was sustainable, the market would bid up the price of the shares, driving the yield lower. You might also find the highest yielding companies clustered in one or two sectors or industries. Which seems fine—the income is lovely—unless and until something befalls that sector and you ask yourself whether you might have let short-term income override the importance of diversification.

Second, you likely want the dividend for income, but some growth in the portfolio itself to offset the inflation we mentioned earlier. So you might trade a little income for a little more growth, just to keep things rolling smoothly.

Remember, dividends are simply part of the total return. A company that reinvests profit wisely may create more sustainable long-term wealth than one that pays out *everything* today.

So, again, the principles don't change.

- Own quality.
- Diversify broadly.
- Keep costs low.
- Manage withdrawals thoughtfully.

Retirement doesn't require a new investing religion. It requires a structural adjustment—not a strategic one.

The long game still applies. You're just turning the dial from accumulation to spending.

Managing volatility in retirement

Volatility feels different when you're no longer earning a salary.

That sounds obvious. It is obvious.

But you need to confront what that means.

When you're 45 and markets fall 20 per cent, you can intellectually reframe it. You're still earning. You're still saving. You're still adding capital. Lower prices may even help you.

When you're 70 and markets fall 20 per cent, the emotional response is amplified. You're not replenishing your portfolio with wages. You're drawing from it. The decline feels permanent. The recovery feels uncertain. The stakes feel higher.

Totally reasonable, and totally real.

And it's why volatility management in retirement is less about mathematics and more about psychology.

Let's start with a simple truth: Volatility does not begin at retirement.

It was always there.

As we've talked about, the Australian and US share markets have experienced meaningful falls roughly once a decade. The 1987 crash. The early 1990s recession. The dot.com bust. The GFC. The COVID crash. Each felt different. Each felt unprecedented. Each felt terrifying in the moment.

And yet, diversified quality portfolios recovered from all of them.

Not immediately. Not painlessly. But consistently.

The key difference in retirement is that volatility interacts with withdrawals.

Remember, a retiree who abandons equities after a 25 per cent fall and moves permanently to cash locks in the damage and forfeits the recovery. History shows that by the time markets 'feel safe' again, much of the rebound has already occurred.

We've seen this pattern repeatedly. During the GFC, many investors capitulated in early 2009 — near the lows — because it felt like the financial system might collapse. Those who stayed invested recovered. Those who sold often missed one of the strongest rebounds in decades.

The lesson isn't that markets always bounce instantly. It's that abandoning productive assets after a decline has historically been far more destructive than tolerating volatility.

We've already talked about that, but it's important to do it in the context of retirement, to make sure we don't think the rules have changed.

So what should retirees actually do?

First, *calibrate asset allocation to temperament* — not bravado.

There's no prize for having the riskiest portfolio in the retirement village. If a 30 per cent decline would cause sleepless nights or trigger rash decisions, maybe your portfolio needs reviewing.

It's the sleep-at-night test, again, but turbocharged by the two factors we mentioned earlier: you're not adding anything more, and you're worried that it might not last.

Second, *build structural shock absorbers.*

Cash buffers can be enormously helpful—not because they boost returns, but because they reduce forced selling. Having one to three years of spending in cash or short-term defensive assets allows you to ride out downturns without immediately liquidating growth assets.

Diversification matters, too. Exposure across industries, geographies and asset classes reduces the likelihood that a single shock derails the entire portfolio.

Third—and perhaps most importantly—*maintain perspective.*

Every crash feels permanent when you're living through it.

The dot.com collapse felt like the broken promise of technology. The GFC felt like the end of banking. COVID felt like the end of civilisation. Inflation spikes feel like the end of monetary stability.

Yet businesses adapt. Economies adjust. Innovation continues. Profits recover.

That doesn't mean markets rise in a straight line. It means that productive assets have historically trended upward over time because human enterprise creates value.

Retirement portfolios must be built with that long-term reality in mind.

The objective is not to avoid volatility entirely.

It's to survive it.

Because survival allows compounding to resume its quiet work.

Prepare, don't predict.

That mantra applies doubly in retirement.

You prepare by building a portfolio that'll serve your needs. You prepare by deciding how you'll fund your spending. You prepare by building buffers.

You do not prepare by trying to forecast the next downturn. Or freaking out when it happens.

Volatility in retirement is inevitable.

Permanent loss is not.

Knowing when to stop: Having enough, but enjoying your retirement

There is a strange irony in retirement planning.

The very traits that helped you accumulate wealth — discipline, caution, delayed gratification — can become obstacles when it's time to spend.

You've spent decades training yourself to defer consumption. To save first. To invest regularly. To resist lifestyle inflation. To prioritise long-term security over short-term indulgence.

Then retirement arrives and the instruction manual flips.

Now you're *meant* to spend.

That transition is not trivial.

I've met retirees with more than enough who still spend too little, scared they'll run out. They scrutinise every expense. They experience guilt over discretionary purchases.

That is not a criticism. The habits are hard to break. The fear is understandable: Running out of money in advanced age is a deeply unsettling prospect.

But it would be an enormous shame to waste the healthiest years of retirement through excessive caution.

This is where the concept of 'enough' becomes more than philosophical.

It becomes practical.

You do not need infinite wealth to fund a finite life.

At some point, the marginal value of an additional dollar sitting in your portfolio is lower than the marginal value of an experience.

And that point is far, far earlier than most of us might imagine, once you have enough.

That overseas trip you've dreamed about for decades.

That extended visit with grandchildren.

That home renovation that makes daily life more comfortable.

That charitable contribution aligned with your values.

Money is a tool.

If it's not used to improve your life or the lives of others, its purpose is incomplete. Wasted, frankly.

Safe withdrawal rates are helpful guidelines, not commandments. The well-known '4 per cent rule' (where you withdraw 4 per cent of your portfolio every year to live on) emerged from historical modelling—and even then, it assumed fixed withdrawals that didn't change with age.

Also, if you're Australian, it didn't include the franking credits we discussed earlier that could add 1 per cent or so to that number, depending on your circumstances.

The objective isn't to hit a textbook percentage.

It's to sustain your desired lifestyle with high probability.

And, remember what I said earlier? Most retirees do not spend in a straight line.

Spending tends to be higher in the early, active years—travel, hobbies, social engagement. It often tapers in later years as activity levels decline. Healthcare costs may rise eventually, but discretionary spending frequently falls.

That pattern means the early years of retirement are the most valuable.

You are likely the healthiest you'll be. The most mobile. And the most capable of pursuing experiences.

Excessive frugality during these years can lead to regret.

Please don't waste them!

There's also an emotional burden attached to hoarding wealth unnecessarily. Children and grandchildren may benefit more from modest support earlier in life—education, housing deposits, life experiences—than from a larger inheritance decades later.

This doesn't mean recklessness.

It means intentionality.

And I'm not telling you what to do with a future inheritance. But if the kids can use the money, maybe now is better than later. And, as a bonus, you get to see them benefit from it!

One useful exercise in, and as you get close to, retirement is to articulate what a 'good retirement' looks like in *non-financial* terms.

Is it travel? Community involvement? Time with family? Creative pursuits? Volunteering?

Only then can you look at how you can fund that 'good retirement'.

You can work out how you can maximise the value you get from those things ... rather than maximising your portfolio.

The fear of overspending is real.

But so is the risk of *under living*.

The goal of retirement should not be to die with the largest possible portfolio.

The goal should be to convert the financial capital you worked so hard to build into life satisfaction — sustainably, thoughtfully, joyfully.

Does that sound strange coming from a finance guy? Probably — because most finance types are fixated on making a number bigger. It's an occupational hazard.

But I'm convinced that 'enough' is far, far better.

And 'enough' is about reaching a point where additional accumulation no longer materially improves your security — and recognising that.

That recognition can be surprisingly difficult, thanks to the habits of a working lifetime.

But it is liberating.

A quick word on advice in retirement

Our tax system is stupidly, unnecessarily complex. But I'll save you that rant.

And maybe the most complex part of it is retirement, with rules upon rules relating to superannuation structures, asset- and means-testing for benefits, preservation ages, minimum drawdowns ... it's a mess, but that mess can work for or against you.

So a good adviser can add value here.

But, I would suggest, the value probably isn't through stock-picking brilliance, but rather through planning, structure, tax optimisation, behavioural coaching and maybe even estate planning.

For many retirees, the behavioural component alone is worth the fee. Having a calm, experienced voice during market downturns can prevent costly mistakes.

But it's important not to over-mystify retirement *investing*.

There is no secret retirement portfolio that overrides the fundamental laws of investing.

The principles that built wealth remain the principles that sustain it.

You still want productive assets.

You still want diversification across sectors and geographies.

You still want low costs.

You still want to avoid concentrated bets driven by emotion.

You still want to align your portfolio structure with your temperament.

Retirement does not require abandoning the philosophy that carried you through accumulation.

It requires applying it in a slightly different cash flow context.

Instead of 'Invest. Add. Wait.'

It becomes:

'Invest. Withdraw thoughtfully. Wait.'

Instead of focusing on growth, you focus on sustainability.

Instead of maximising contributions, you optimise withdrawals.

But you do not suddenly start predicting markets.

You do not suddenly trade aggressively — or go to cash.

You do not abandon diversification.

Prepare, don't predict.

That principle has served investors for decades. It serves retirees just as well.

Remember: Retirement is not a different game.

It's the same game, just the second half.

And if you've internalised the lessons of the long game — discipline, patience, diversification, behavioural control — then retirement is not something to fear.

You've spent decades building productive assets.

Now they work for you.

Not perfectly. Not without volatility. Not without adjustment.

But reliably, if handled with respect for the principles that built them.

Retirement isn't the end.

It's the end of earning wages.

The investing journey continues.

And if you've played the long game well, the second half can be just as rewarding as the first.

Perhaps even more so. And you've earned it.

Let's check in on what that future might look like.

What really matters

- Retirement is not the end of investing—portfolios may need to last decades.
- The focus gradually shifts from accumulation to preservation and income.
- Managing volatility and withdrawals becomes crucial for long-term security.

17

WHAT FUTURE 'YOU' LOOKS LIKE

> *The best investors build systems today that their future selves will thank them for.*

You are on the precipice of greatness.

Too grandiose and just a little ... saccharine?

Fair enough.

But you are most definitely at a turning point.

You now know enough—and have the tools—to build towards 'enough' and to turn 'enough' into a richly fulfilling post-work life.

The choice is now yours. If you follow the plan, I'm going to take a stab at what your future might look like. What future 'you' might look like.

I hope, in a decade's time, you're quietly grateful for present-day you.

Not because you nailed the perfect time to buy.

Not because you predicted the next recession.

Not because your investments did better than your brother-in-law's.

But because you built habits that started that snowball rolling down the hill, while protecting you from yourself.

The thing about investing is that it rarely feels particularly great while it's happening. There are no medals for sticking to a strategy. No applause for ignoring a headline. No awards for reinvesting dividends quietly for decades.

But when you look back—in ten, 20 or 30 years—the gap between someone who built disciplined habits and someone who chased emotion is extraordinary.

This chapter isn't about tactics. You've got the strategy now.

It's about identity.

Because over time, investing stops being something you do occasionally.

It becomes part of who you are.

Air Force pilots talk about not flying the plane but *being* the plane. I'm not going to tell you that investing will feel like that, but I will tell you that it gets easier over time, to the point it feels… natural.

The habits of good investors

If you study investors who compound wealth quietly over decades (and I have)—not the loudest voices on finance TV, not the traders bragging about last month's win—but the steady accumulators… you notice something consistent.

They don't operate on adrenaline.

They operate on routine.

Good investors build systems that reduce the number of decisions they need to make.

They automate contributions.

They diversify early and constantly.

They increase investments when income rises.

They review periodically — not daily.

And they avoid environments designed to trigger emotion.

This last one is underappreciated.

Warren Buffett famously left the hustle and bustle of Wall Street and returned to his mid-Western United States hometown of Omaha, Nebraska, where he could sit and think without the pressure and hype of New York.

Financial media exists to generate engagement, not serenity. Brokerage apps are built for activity, not restraint. Social media amplifies extremes — either euphoria or panic — and specialises in personal echo chambers.

Future you understands that your environment shapes behaviour.

So future you engineers your environment carefully.

You might still read widely. You might still follow markets. But you don't place yourself in a constant state of reactivity.

Early in your investing life, outcomes feel personal.

A stock falls 15 per cent and it feels like a verdict on your intelligence.

A stock rises 30 per cent and it feels like validation.

Totally natural.

But the longer you do it, the more you realise that's your emotions talking.

And that sometimes, you can be right for the wrong reasons, and wrong for the right reasons.

And so you learn to separate process from outcome.

A well-chosen investment can decline in the short term and still be sound. It can even decline permanently because of fraud, competition, technological change ... or just because you got your analysis wrong. It happens.

A speculative bet can rise temporarily and still be reckless. Even if the speculation plays out, you might owe that result to dumb luck ... and luck isn't a repeatable process.

Future you judges decisions based on reasoning, not just results.

This is subtle — and powerful.

It protects you from overconfidence during good runs and self-doubt during rough patches.

Author and former poker player, Annie Duke calls it 'resulting'. She says:

> A decision can be good, even if the outcome is bad.
>
> A common line of thinking: 'If something worked, it must have been a good call. If it failed, it must have been a mistake.'
>
> This is called 'resulting,' or confusing the quality of a decision with the luck of the outcome.
>
> Think of a CEO deciding to enter a new market. They might run the numbers, talk to customers, and carefully size the risks. If the expansion fails, it's tempting to call it a 'bad

decision.' But that's outcome bias. The CEO could've done everything right and still lost, because chance plays a role.

The flip side is also true. Sometimes leaders make hasty, sloppy choices that happen to work out. That doesn't mean the decision process was good — it just means luck was on their side.

So how do you know if you're actually improving as a decision-maker?

- Focus on your process: write down the criteria you used
- Imagine a pre-mortem: what could go wrong?
- Set exit rules in advance, so you know when to quit

You can't control luck. But you can control the process that stacks the odds in your favor.

When you look back on a choice, ask yourself if you decided well, not if it worked out or not.[31]

Good investors also build a series of pre-commitments.

When markets fall sharply, they don't have to decide whether to invest. The direct debit is already scheduled.

When dividends arrive, they don't debate whether to reinvest. It happens automatically.

When income increases, they don't wonder if they 'should' invest more. They have a percentage rule.

- Work hard.
- Save diligently.
- Invest regularly.
- Repeat.

That's not inspirational.

It's kinda boring, actually.

But you bet it's effective.

Because here's another thing about compounding: Habits compound just like capital.

The difference between someone who invests 10 per cent of income automatically and someone who invests 'when it feels right' becomes enormous over decades.

Future you also becomes less interested in being right.

Does that sound strange? Why wouldn't you want to be right?

New investors tend to crave validation. They want to prove they can beat the market. They want to spot the next big winner. They want to be 'good' at this investing thing.

Later, you realise that consistent, diversified exposure to productive assets does most of the heavy lifting.

You don't need genius.

You need endurance.

And perhaps the most underrated habit of all: humility.

The longer you invest, the more you realise how much randomness shapes short-term outcomes. That humility reduces leverage. It reduces concentration. It reduces the temptation to swing for the fences.

Future you doesn't need to look clever.

Future you needs to stay in the game.

Your investing calendar: Daily, weekly, yearly

And what does future you do? Well, only you will know, but here's what I think is something to aim for.

One really simple thing you can do is to create an investing calendar.

Not a trading calendar. An investing calendar.

Because investing is not an always-on activity. In fact, it's a mostly-off one.

It's cyclical. It has rhythm.

And when you set that rhythm in advance, you reduce the chance that emotion, boredom or ill-discipline fills the gaps.

Let's start with daily behaviour.

Daily

Almost nothing.

This sounds counterintuitive in a world of 24-hour markets and real-time updates.

But daily price movements are mostly noise.

If you're investing for decades, a 1 per cent move today is irrelevant. Even a 5 per cent move this week is rarely thesis- or outcome-changing.

Future you doesn't check markets compulsively.

Not because you don't care — but because you understand that constant checking invites emotional volatility to match market volatility.

There's a reason long-term investors often outperform active traders.

They simply interfere less.

Daily investing activity should be close to zero. So close that it's almost imperceptible!

Weekly

Learn, don't act.

If you want a weekly ritual, make it educational.

Read an annual report from an ASX company.

Study how a business earns money.

Listen to a podcast interview with a founder.

Review long-term economic trends.

But resist the urge to trade.

Most good investing decisions don't expire within days. When you remove urgency, you remove pressure.

Quarterly

Light review. Very light.

Every few months, have a look at your portfolio.

Not to react — but to confirm.

Has a position become uncomfortably large?

Has a core thesis fundamentally changed?

Quarterly reviews are about calibration, not excitement.

Future you approaches them calmly.

Yearly

Strategic check-in.

This is where the real work happens.

Once a year, step back.

Review your portfolio. Consider what you own and what risks and opportunities have changed.

Make changes if necessary. Not 'possible', necessary.

Increase contributions if income has risen.

Double check your fees.

Revisit long-term goals.

This annual cadence allows thoughtful adjustments without constant tinkering.

It also forces you to think long-term.

Markets shout daily. Compounding whispers annually.

An investing calendar protects you from yourself. It creates guardrails against boredom trading, panic selling and impulsive speculation.

But it also gives you real actions to take to make sure you're on the right track—mentally, emotionally and financially.

Future you doesn't operate on reaction.

Future you operates on rhythm.

How your investing mindset will evolve over time

Early on, investing feels urgent. You want confirmation it's working.

You compare returns. You check balances. You watch benchmarks.

There's an impatience to it. Natural, but generally unhelpful.

But over time, that urgency fades.

Not because you stop caring. But because investing loses its novelty. And because you begin to understand the shape and nature of compounding.

Wealth creation is not linear.

Five strong years may drive most of a decade's returns. A single bear market may erase three years of gains before recovering.

Future you isn't surprised by this anymore.

You've lived through downturns.

You've seen markets fall 20 per cent, 30 per cent, maybe even 50 per cent.

And you've seen them recover. That experience changes you.

You become less reactive to headlines. Less impressed by forecasts. More comfortable with uncertainty.

You also realise how frequently 'experts' get it wrong.

Recessions are predicted annually. Crashes are forecast constantly. Booms are declared permanent. Frankly, your response is to yawn. You've seen and heard it all before.

Future you internalises something liberating.

Nobody knows what markets will do next year. But over long periods, ownership of productive assets has historically created wealth.

Once you really 'get' that, your stress and anxiety levels fall. You stop trying to 'win' each year—not because it wouldn't be a lofty goal, but because you realise it's almost impossible.

And you're only setting yourself up to fail if you try.

Instead, you start thinking in decades. And you fix your gaze on the horizon, not the ground in front of you.

That also brings us to the humility we mentioned earlier. Your ego takes a back seat.

That humility protects you from overconfidence during bull markets. It also protects you from despair during bear markets.

Future you becomes comfortable saying, 'I don't know'.

And, paradoxically, that makes you stronger.

Because investing is not about knowing what happens when. It's about believing that the patient, sensible, diversified investor is rewarded over the long-term.

Paying it forward—helping others invest

At some point, investing stops being just personal.

No, I don't mean you turn into an evangelist for the cause (though you may!).

It's often the small things.

You begin to notice how uneven financial literacy is.

Some people are paralysed by fear. Others can't help but speculate. Many avoid investing entirely because it feels overwhelming and they don't know where to start.

Future you can help.

By buying them a copy of this book. (I'm kidding... mostly!)

In all seriousness, this is how you can do it: Not by boasting about returns. But by modelling calm.

When markets fall and others panic, you can say, 'This is normal'.

When someone thinks investing requires brilliance, you can explain it requires discipline.

When a young colleague or family member is too overwhelmed to start, you can show them the power of small, regular contributions over decades.

There is enormous leverage in helping someone begin early.

A 25-year-old who invests modestly and consistently can accumulate more than a 45-year-old who starts aggressively but inconsistently.

Time matters more than intensity.

Teaching reinforces your own discipline.

I have had many listeners of *Motley Fool Money*, a podcast I co-host, tell me that they've been able to share some of what they've learned, and were stunned when they realised how much they had to share.

Explaining diversification deepens your own understanding.

Helping someone through a downturn strengthens your own resolve.

And perhaps most importantly, you normalise long-term thinking.

In a culture that celebrates immediacy, modelling patience is powerful.

Future you doesn't just build wealth.

Future you builds capability — in others.

Leaving a legacy

Legacy is often framed in dollar terms.

But money is only one part of the story. True legacy is influence. Values. Behaviour modelled consistently over time.

Yes, financial capital can amplify impact.

An inheritance thoughtfully structured can provide opportunity — education, housing, business ventures — for the next generation.

Charitable giving can support causes aligned with your beliefs.

Foundations, scholarships, community initiatives — all can extend your impact beyond your lifetime.

But there is also a quieter legacy.

Children and grandchildren who grow up watching steady investing, thoughtful spending and calm reactions to volatility absorb those norms.

They learn that wealth is built patiently.

They learn that markets fluctuate.

They learn that discipline matters more than excitement.

That mindset may be more valuable than the inheritance itself.

There's also an important question to consider: What do you want your money to do when you're no longer here?

Preserve? Enable? Empower? Transform?

Legacy planning isn't about maximising numbers.

It's about aligning capital with values. And magnifying outcomes, financially and otherwise.

Future you is not defined by a final portfolio balance.

Future you is defined by how that capital was used — during life and after it.

You worked hard.

You saved diligently.

You invested regularly.

You waited patiently.

And then you deployed that capital with intention.

That is what future you looks like.

Not a financial fortune teller. Not a brilliant tactician.

Just a disciplined steward of capital — for decades.

And future you starts today.

Are you ready to hear a secret?

What really matters

- Successful investors build habits that support long-term discipline.
- Investing works best when it becomes routine rather than reactive.
- Wealth accumulated over decades can ultimately benefit others, not just ourselves.

18

THE SECRET OF INVESTING WELL

> *The secret of investing well is simple: do the right things, consistently, for a very long time.*

Let me disappoint you properly this time.

The secret is ... there is no secret.

There is no secret stock.

No magic trading strategy.

No undiscovered clue hiding in the back pages of an annual report.

No mystical pattern in a share price chart that, once decoded, unlocks guaranteed wealth.

There isn't a quiet corner of the internet where the rules don't apply.

There isn't a club you haven't been invited to.

And if that sounds anticlimactic, good.

You kinda knew it anyway, didn't you?

Because it's also incredibly reassuring.

Markets are competitive. Incredibly so.

Millions of participants. Trillions of dollars. Superannuation funds, sovereign wealth funds, hedge funds, high-frequency traders, AI-driven systems.

If there was a reliable, repeatable shortcut to outsized returns without risk, once it was found by more than one person, the opportunity would disappear almost instantly.

That's the nature of markets.

Which means the idea that investing success comes from secret knowledge—or so-called 'smart money'—is comforting... but wrong.

The truth is both more ordinary and more powerful.

Successful investors don't know something magical. They simply behave differently.

They accept uncertainty.

They resist emotional impulses.

They stick to a plan when it feels uncomfortable.

They let time compound quietly in the background.

That's not glamorous. They won't make a movie about it.

But it is effective.

And the absence of a secret is, paradoxically, the greatest secret of all.

Because if you think there is a secret, you spend time, effort and money trying to find it. Trying to find the process that turns ordinary metals into gold.

But there's not.

That's incredibly freeing.

Now let's unpack that a bit.

See, if there is no hidden trick, then there is no missing piece.

You won't be behind because you haven't discovered 'the thing'.

You won't underperform because someone else has a better spreadsheet.

You won't be at a permanent disadvantage because you didn't study finance at university.

You already have what you need.

If you understand that:

- shares represent ownership in real businesses
- markets fluctuate but businesses create value over time
- time magnifies behaviour
- costs matter and discipline matters more…

Then you are equipped.

I hope that feels liberating. Because that means investing well isn't a puzzle to be 'solved', but rather a habit to be fostered and maintained.

But if the game isn't about discovering something new — it's about consistently applying what works — then your focus changes.

You stop chasing novelty.

You start prioritising durability.

And that changes everything.

It removes the anxiety of missing out. It reduces the need to constantly adjust. It lowers the emotional temperature.

You don't need to outsmart the market. You need to outlast your impulses.

And that's a far more achievable goal.

Simplicity. Patience. Discipline.

If I had to reduce decades of investing history and behavioural finance into three words, it would be those: Simplicity. Patience. Discipline.

Not because it'd look good on a bumper sticker, but because almost every investing failure—failure, not temporary mistake—can be traced to abandoning one of them.

Simplicity

Simplicity feels unsophisticated. It doesn't make for exciting conversation over dinner or a beer.

It feels almost negligent. Like not trying hard enough. And it almost implies that if you tried harder—if you made things more complex—you could somehow get a better result.

'I bought a broad market ETF and held it for 20 years' doesn't exactly light up the group chat. It doesn't make you a stock-picking superstar.

But simple systems are robust systems.

A portfolio built on:

- high-quality businesses with durable economics
- low-cost diversified index-based ETFs

... is not flashy.

But it *is* resilient. And powerful.

Complexity sounds smart. It takes a lot of thought and planning and that mental work is real. But *better*?

We're tempted to think so. Wired to think so.

There's an apocryphal story about the US and Russian space programs. The US, goes the story, spent millions of dollars trying to invent a pen that worked in space. The Russians... just used a pencil.

It's a cute story, and makes a nice point. It's also not true.

Still, the idea is useful, I think.

Einstein (paraphrased, apparently) this time: 'Everything should be made as simple as possible, but not simpler.'

Simple portfolios don't d6 epend on forecasts. Or timing. They don't require constant intervention and tinkering. They don't hinge on one theme or idea or trading strategy, playing out exactly as expected.

They rely on a broad truth: Productive businesses, over time, tend to grow.

The simpler your framework, the easier it is to stick with when volatility arrives.

And that matters more than theoretical optimisation (which rarely survives contact with reality!).

Because the best strategy on paper is useless if you abandon it under pressure... or if it just doesn't work.

Simplicity is not about laziness. Or a lack of intelligence or ability.

It's about understanding the true source of long-term returns.

Patience

Patience is where most investors struggle.

I've routinely challenged my social media followers to engage in the #5DayInvestorChallenge, which simply asks them not to check their portfolio for a whole trading week.

Most ignore it. Some engage with it, but can't make it. Some make it through.

And that's just five days.

And here's the other thing: I have no evidence for this, but I am 100 per cent sure that there's a correlation between regularly checking share prices and the temptation to react or respond to changes. And a correlation between that temptation and action.

If you just don't check... you'll carry on, blissfully unaware *and* untempted.

See, we live in a culture of 'now'. Same-day delivery. Instant notifications. Real-time updates. Minute-by-minute share price movements.

The market tempts you to believe progress should be visible daily. It gives you constant information that our brains instinctively treat as 'feedback'. And then prompts us to recalibrate, based on that feedback. The roar of a lion... the crack of a branch overhead... the smell of smoke. We've evolved — for our survival — to be 'reaction machines'.

But compounding doesn't work like that.

It works quietly.

In the early years, your portfolio growth feels almost disappointing. You contribute more than it earns. Gains feel modest. Sometimes, your portfolio goes backwards. Progress seems slow.

Then, gradually, something shifts.

Your contributions matter less. The compounding matters more.

Returns begin to generate returns. Dividends generate dividends.

Your money is making money, and the rolling snowball becomes noticeable.

And then the amount of snow it picks up with each roll is noticeable.

But that only happens if you allow it to roll long enough.

Patience is uncomfortable because it feels inactive. It feels passive. It feels like you're not 'doing' enough.

But in investing, inaction is often a strategic choice. *The* strategic choice.

Holding through noise. Holding through fear. Holding through boredom. Holding through booms and busts.

Patience is not waiting aimlessly.

It is waiting with conviction.

And the longer your horizon, the more powerful it becomes.

Discipline

Discipline is the bridge between simplicity and patience.

Without discipline, simplicity becomes tinkering. Without discipline, patience becomes panic.

Discipline means sticking to your plan in both directions:

Not selling everything when markets fall. Not getting carried away when markets soar.

It means accepting that volatility is normal.

It means tolerating underperformance relative to someone else's bragging.

It means resisting the urge to constantly adjust your portfolio.

(You'll rationalise that 'adjusting' as 'finding better investment ideas'. It'll probably just be conscious or unconscious rationalisation for the need to 'do something'.)

Discipline is emotional fitness. Forbearance.

It is the ability to experience discomfort without reacting impulsively.

And make no mistake — investing will test you.

There *will* be crashes. There *will* be bubbles. There *will* be headlines predicting disaster. There *will* be friends bragging about speculative wins.

Please internalise that now so that you can start inoculating yourself against the temptation to act that'll accompany those things.

Discipline doesn't eliminate those experiences. It simply prevents them from dictating your decisions. And that, more than IQ or technical skill, separates long-term success from costly regret. Let time do the work... and stay out of its way.

Time is the most powerful force in investing. But it only works if you allow it to.

Imagine hiring the best employee you've ever had — brilliant, consistent, quietly productive — and then interrupting them every five minutes to change direction.

That's what overmanaging your portfolio looks like. When you invest in productive assets, your job gradually shifts.

At first, it's about learning. Then it's about allocating. Eventually, it's about restraint.

Most long-term underperformance doesn't come from owning terrible businesses.

It comes from behaviour.

There is some great research out of the US that highlights two things.

The first, as we discussed on page 158, is that the average managed fund (Americans call them 'mutual funds') has a lower after-fee return than the overall market.

The second: The average mutual fund investor has a lower return than the average mutual fund. Which sounds strange at first.

The reason? They keep chopping and changing. Tinkering. Chasing last year's winners. Not leaving well enough alone.

That's impatience and ill-discipline. And it's not a criticism ... just an observation.

Time cannot compound if you constantly reset the clock.

Compounding requires continuity.

It requires that gains remain invested long enough to generate further gains.

Your role is not to accelerate the process.
Your role is to avoid interrupting it.

Charlie Munger once said: 'The first rule of compounding is to never interrupt it unnecessarily.'

Invest. Add. Wait.

That's not a slogan. It's a mantra.

Focus on the doing. Trust the process. The results will come.

Here's what you can't control:

- The market's return next year.
- Macroeconomic surprises.
- Interest rate decisions.
- Geopolitical events.
- The sentiment of other investors (and traders).

But you can control:

- How much you save.
- How regularly you invest.
- How diversified you are.
- How low your costs remain.
- Whether you panic.
- Whether you stay the course.

Those inputs matter more than most people realise.

It's why the One-Page Investing Plan focuses not on the other stuff, but the things you can control.

Returns are an outcome. Process is a choice.

If you measure success by short-term results, you will feel like you're constantly failing. Some assets will always outperform yours. Some themes will always look smarter in hindsight.

Worse, sometimes you'll feel like you're winning. Huh? How is that worse? Because, it'll almost certainly be hubris. The feeling that your last 'trade' validates your tactics. That action is required for success. And that now you've 'cracked the code' you can double-down.

You risk being the lotto winner who, convinced they're lucky, ploughs all of the winnings back into more tickets, sure they'll win even bigger next time.

But if you measure success by whether you executed your plan responsibly and consistently, you win far more often. But more importantly than how 'often' you win, is whether you win in the long-term.

Good football teams tend to win because they get the process right. It doesn't mean they don't miss tackles, drop the ball or even occasionally lose games.

They hate it when those things go wrong, but they recognise that the real goal is long-term success, despite those things.

Because good process compounds. And a strong process eventually produces strong outcomes.

The market is unpredictable in the short term. Even in the medium term. But disciplined behaviour is surprisingly predictable over decades.

Focus on what you can do.

Trust that *repeated, sensible actions accumulate.*

Here's the thing: Deep down, I think we all know that's true. What stops us isn't that we don't know, it's that we find it hard to focus on them when there are short-term 'outcomes' all around us, begging for our attention.

It's easy to get distracted. Doubly so when we're not sure if the long-term outcomes will actually work in our favour.

Again, I can give you no guarantees. And I make you no promises. But I can point to history.

Results rarely arrive dramatically.

They accumulate quietly... until suddenly they look extraordinary.

The thief of joy... and returns

You probably know by now that I'm a fan of quotes. To quote a quote, this time from Sir Isaac Newton. 'If I have seen further, it is by standing on the shoulders of giants'.

In other words, we all owe an enormous debt to those who came before us, for creating the building blocks that we use in our own lives.

One other favourite of mine is 'comparison is the thief of joy'.

It is a more succinct way of mashing the ideas that 'the grass is greener on the other side of the fence' with 'keeping up with the Jones'.

And I'm maxing out the quotes quota to make an important point at this point of the book, and this point of your investing journey.

Because there'll always be someone with more money, better returns, or, well, greener grass than you.

And you know what? That's okay. More than okay, it's great.

Because you or I could devote time, energy and effort to trying to be 'the best' or 'better than the other person', but where would that leave us?

Probably disappointed, dispirited (there can only be one winner) and disengaged.

For what?

Ego? Bragging rights? To be the richest guy in the cemetery?

Yeah, nah.

The One-Page Investing Plan isn't about any of that rubbish. If you need to be the best, can I humbly suggest it's time for a reality check?

If that sounds harsh, I'm sorry. But, well, also not sorry.

Wasting a life trying to win a competition that no-one else cares about is about as futile as it gets.

Let's go back to your 'why'.

Was it really to 'be the richest person in the cemetery'? No, I didn't think so.

Remember Charlie Munger's quote about envy on page 33? It's been a few pages, so let me repeat it:

> Envy is a really stupid sin because it's the only one you could never possibly have any fun at. There's a lot of pain and no fun. Why would you want to get on that trolley?

It reminds me of the marathon runner. Yes, a very small few are competing to win. But most runners are there for the sheer enjoyment of the accomplishment, and to be the best version of themselves: to set a personal best.

That is a far, far more useful aim for investors, too. And really captures the spirit of the One-Page Investing Plan beautifully.

Yes, it requires effort. Yes, it is long-term. And yes, the only benchmark that truly matters is how close you get to your 'enough' number. (And by the way, even if you don't end up with as much as you'd like, it is very likely that you'll end up with more—perhaps much more—than you would have if you'd never tried in the first place!)

It is a reminder not to let 'perfect' be the enemy of 'great'.

Let's torture the metaphor: Investing is not a sprint. It is more like a marathon. But even then, you're the only runner.

And the concept breaks down further: A marathon comes at the end of a long, consistent and dedicated effort to prepare yourself for a single race.

Maybe investing is closer to the training itself. Just far, far less gruelling!

There will be times when investing feels easy. When the market is going up, and it feels like shooting fish in a barrel.

There will be times when the market goes backwards. When everything you own is falling, and every new investment goes backwards after you buy it.

Both happen regularly. But the market is up — a lot — despite both.

Over the long-term, your greatest obstacle will not be market volatility. It will be your own reactions.

Impatience when progress feels slow.

Fear when prices fall.

Greed when prices rise.

Comparison to others.

The investor you are competing against is not your neighbour or your colleague.

It is your emotional self.

So let's go back to the idea that comparison is the thief of joy.

If you can slowly become calmer ... more patient ... more disciplined ...

If you can become incrementally calmer ... incrementally more patient ... incrementally more disciplined ...

You tilt the odds dramatically in your favour.

Because the market rewards endurance. And endurance is internal.

So what's the secret?

What really matters

- There is no hidden formula or secret strategy to investing success.
- Long-term wealth comes from simplicity, patience and discipline.
- Investors succeed by trusting the process and letting time do the heavy lifting.

THE ONE-PAGE INVESTING PLAN

INVEST. ADD. WAIT.

Know your why

Be clear about what you're investing for — security, freedom, generosity — and write it down so you have a north star when markets wobble.

Earn more over time

Grow your income through skills, effort and opportunity — you can only invest what you don't spend.

Pay yourself first

Automatically invest around 10 per cent of your take-home pay every single payday, before your lifestyle expands to consume it.

Spend intentionally

Focus on what truly matters, avoid lifestyle creep and protect the surplus that funds your future.

Build your 'oh, shit' fund

Hold three to six months of expenses in cash so emergencies never force you to sell.

Invest regularly

Add money on a schedule — no matter what.

Own diversified, productive assets

Buy diversified, broad, low-cost ETFs and/or quality shares representing real businesses earning real profits.

Reinvest and minimise costs

Reinvest dividends, avoid unnecessary trading, and keep fees and taxes as low as possible.

Stay the course — even in retirement

Expect volatility, shift gradually from growth to income when needed, but let compounding start (and keep) working for decades.

That's it. That's the whole thing. Everything else is details.

ACKNOWLEDGEMENTS

Like investing itself, this book is the result of a long chain of contributions, influences, encouragement, mistakes and a fair bit of luck.

First, to the countless investors I've had the privilege of speaking with over the years — members, listeners, readers, followers and the occasional person who's stopped me in the street or at the pub to talk shares (yes, that happens more than you'd think). Your questions, your doubts, your wins and your frustrations have shaped the way I talk about investing.

To my colleagues — past and present — thank you for the conversations, debates and occasional disagreements that sharpened my thinking. Investing is an exercise in humility, and I've been lucky to work with people who remind me of that regularly.

To the great investors and thinkers whose work has influenced me — directly or indirectly — thank you for being generous with your ideas. I've borrowed more than I can possibly cite, and hopefully added something of my own along the way. Isaac Newton talked about 'standing on the shoulders of giants', and that's what I'm doing-too.

To the team at Wiley who gave me encouragement, a sounding board and guidance along the way, thank you. I want to specifically thank commissioning editor Jordon Lott for her endless enthusiasm, positivity and counsel, project editor Chris Shorten for his calm, thoughtful and masterful stewardship of the manuscript, and copy editor Melanie Dankel for her empathetic, supportive approach, mixed with a razor sharp literary scalpel for excising stuff that, well, just didn't work, even when I thought it did! And, to the rest of the Wiley team: I had no idea just how complex and time-consuming the process of publishing a book would be, or how many people would be involved, in large and small ways. Thank you, all.

And to my family. To my wife, Ruth, thank you for having my back, and being my biggest supporter. And for giving me the time and space to turn this obsession into the finished product. To my sons, Peter and Ian, and my daughter-in-law, Ailis, you were the people I continually thought of when picturing the reader of this book. I am immensely proud of you, and I hope I've done you proud. To my Mum, Wendy, and my late Dad, Ian: you gave me the most wonderful gifts — unconditional love and unwavering belief. To my sister, Nicole, who got me my first job and has never let me forget it, look where that first opportunity ended up taking me! Thanks for being proud of your big brother. And to my nephews Caleb and Jayden and niece Mackenzie, thanks for letting me be the crazy uncle who continues to badger you to keep investing, even when you'd really rather I stop.

And finally, to you — the reader.

You're the one doing the hard part. Reading is easy (though apologies for my strange turns of phrase and idiosyncratic writing style!). Acting is not. If this book helps you make even one better decision, avoid one costly mistake or stay the course when it matters most, then it has been worth writing.

Because, in the end, investing well isn't about intelligence or access or even information. It's about behaviour. And that part is entirely up to you. You've got this!

REFERENCES

1. de Saint-Exupéry A. 1948, *Citadelle*, Gallimard.
2. Buffett W. 2011, 'Morning session – 2011 meeting,' Warren Buffet Archive, https://buffett.cnbc.com/video/2011/04/30/morning-session-2011-berkshire-hathaway-annual-meeting.html.
3. Housel M. 2021, *The Psychology of Money*, Harriman House.
4. Miro n.d., 'What is the 5 Whys framework,' Miro, https://miro.com/root-cause-analysis/what-is-5-whys-framework/.
5. Vanguard 2025, '2025 Vanguard index chart: Market returns 1 July 1995 to 30 June 2025,' Vanguard, fund-docs.vanguard.com/AU-Vanguard_2025_Index_Chart_poster.pdf.
6. Wilson E.O. 2021, 'Humanity is paleolithic emotions, medieval institutions and God-like technology,' YouTube, https://www.youtube.com/watch?v=1DLW4TUb6Fg.
7. National Archives n.d., 'FDR's fireside chat on the Recovery Program,' National Archives, https://www.archives.gov/education/lessons/fdr-fireside.
8. Buffett W. 1986, 'To the shareholders of Berkshire Hathaway Inc.', Berkshire Hathaway, https://www.berkshirehathaway.com/letters/1986.html.
9. Munger C. 2003, 'Morning sessions – 2003 meeting,' Warren Buffett Archive, https://buffett.cnbc.com/video/2003/05/03/morning-session-2003-berkshire-hathaway-annual-meeting.html.
10. Zweig J. 2024, *The Intelligent Investor,* HarperCollins.
11. Zweig J. 2016, 'What fund investors really need to know,' Jason Zweig, https://jasonzweig.com/what-fund-investors-really-need-to-know/.
12. Lowenstein R. 2002, 'When genius failed: How one small bank created a trillion-dollar hole,' 4th Estate GB.

13. Einstein A. (attrib.) n.d., 'Quote origin: Compound interest is man's greatest invention,' Quote Investigator, https://quoteinvestigator.com/2011/10/31/compound-interest/.
14. Dire Straits 1985, 'Money for nothing,' Vertigo Records.
15. Drucker P. (attrib.) 2017, Quote origin: Culture eats strategy for breakfast, Quote Investigator, https://quoteinvestigator.com/2017/05/23/culture-eats/.
16. Buffett W. 1987, 'To the shareholders of Berkshire Hathaway Inc.', Berkshire Hathaway, https://www.berkshirehathaway.com/letters/1987.html.
17. The Motley Fool 2023, 'A bull market is coming: 4 Warren Buffett investing quotes to live by,' https://www.fool.com/investing/2023/02/19/a-bull-market-is-coming-4-warren-buffett-investing/.
18. Graham B. 1949, *The Intelligent Investor*, HarperCollins.
19. Bezos J. 2017, 'Jeff Bezos is the world's richest man – and he divulged 4 of the secrets to his incredible fame and fortune,' Business Insider, https://www.businessinsider.com/amazon-ceo-jeff-bezos-secrets-for-success-2017-11.
20. Vanguard 2025, 'The enduring wisdom of John C. Bogle in five quotes,' Vanguard, https://www.vanguard.com.au/personal/learn/smart-investing/understand-the-basics/enduring-wisdom-of-john-bogle-in-five-quotes.
21. Buffett W. 2016, 'To the shareholders of Berkshire Hathaway Inc.', Berkshire Hathaway, https://www.berkshirehathaway.com/letters/2016ltr.pdf.
22. Buffett W. 2007, 'To the shareholders of Berkshire Hathaway Inc.', Berkshire Hathaway, https://www.berkshirehathaway.com/letters/2007ltr.pdf.
23. Buffett W. 2001, 'Memo to Berkshire Hathaway Managers,' Berkshire Hathaway, https://www.berkshirehathaway.com/letters/letters.html.
24. Buffett W. 1989, 'To the shareholders of Berkshire Hathaway Inc.', Berkshire Hathaway, https://www.berkshirehathaway.com/letters/1989.html.
25. Buffett W. 2004, 'To the shareholders of Berkshire Hathaway Inc.', Berkshire Hathaway, https://www.berkshirehathaway.com/letters/2004.html.

26. Buffett W. 2025, 'To the shareholders of Berkshire Hathaway Inc.', Berkshire Hathaway, https://www.berkshirehathaway.com/letters/2025ltr.pdf.
27. Buffett W. 2005, 'To the shareholders of Berkshire Hathaway Inc.', Berkshire Hathaway, https://www.berkshirehathaway.com/letters/2005ltr.pdf.
28. Carricaburu L. 1996, 'Wizard of Wall Street holds audience spellbound in rare appearance at WSU,' *Salt Lake Tribune*, p.D5.
29. King James Bible, 1 Timothy 6:10.
30. Bogle J.C. 2007, 'Enough,' James Clear, https://jamesclear.com/great-speeches/enough-by-john-c-bogle.
31. Duke A. 2018, *Thinking in Bets: Making smarter decisions when you don't have all the facts*, Portfolio.

INDEX

ABC Learning 194
accumulation mode 286–290
accumulation phase 285
active investing 162
active investors 161
Afterpay 135–137
airline industry 164
All Cafe Index 173
Amazon 121, 178
Amazon.bomb 211
Amazon shares 71–74
Amazon Web Services (AWS) 72
ANZ 176
Apple 178
asset classes 100
ASX *see* Australian Securities Exchange (ASX)
ASX 300, 162
Australian economic risks 96
Australian psyche 24
Australian Securities Exchange (ASX) 3, 78, 81, 96, 103, 149, 157, 165, 171, 191, 194, 208, 218
Australian share market 9, 46
Australian shares ETF 160
Australian Stock Exchange 161
Australia's dividend imputation system 113
automation 111
AWS *see* Amazon Web Services (AWS)

bad debt 135–137
bank account 146–148
bankruptcy 79
behavioural finance 172
behavioural mistakes 83
behavioural risk 93
Berkshire Hathaway 196–198, 201
Bezos, Jeff 121
BHP 176
Big Four banks 96
Bitcoin 106
Blockbuster 181, 182, 186, 201
Bogle, Jack 158, 159, 165–166, 275
Bogle's invention 162
bonds and cash 104–105
—collectables 107
—cryptocurrency 106
—pros and cons 107–108
borrowing capacity 109
Broken Hill 171
brokerage 253–254
brokerage account 147–149
budget 118–123
budget management tools 136
Buffettism 266
Buffett, Warren 2, 32, 36, 37, 52, 64, 81, 114–115, 159, 164, 177, 181, 196–197, 210, 239, 251, 252, 276, 303
business
—cafe 173–175
—capitalism 171–172

business (*cont'd*)
— derivative instruments 169
— growth and value 181–183
— investment 61–62
— management 179–180
— margins 179
— moats 177–178
— shareholder 175–177
— stock market 170
— Woolworths 172
buy and hold 186–187
'buying things on special' mindset 85
buy to hold 187–188, 201

CAGR *see* compound annual growth rate (CAGR)
capital gains tax (CGT) 255–256
capitalism, democratic 170–172
Carsales. com. au 178
cash, bonds and 104–105
— collectables 107
— cryptocurrency 106
— pros and cons 107–108
cash flow 118, 119
cash reserves 91
CBA 193
CGT *see* capital gains tax (CGT)
Chicken Littles 222
Churchill, Winston 170
churn 253–254
Clarkson, Jeremy 4
Coke 178
Coles 178
Coles shares 203
collectables 107
CommSec 147, 157
compound annual growth rate (CAGR) 72, 73
compounding 135
compounding cost 246–248
compounding growth 244
compounding value 278–279
compound interest 43, 135
— account balance 50
— exponential growth for 48
— magic source of 54–56
— simple interest 45–46
conscious decisions 127
consumer debt 135
costs
— brokerage and churn 253–254
— compounding 246–248
— managed funds and ETFs 250–252
— percentage point 243–245
— superannuation 249–250
COVID 51, 68–69, 80, 165, 208, 210, 211, 227, 287, 291, 292
— ASX 81
— GFC 79
crash
— cause 222–226
— dot. com 209
— emotional timeline of
— disbelief 216–217
— exhaustion 215–216
— fear 214
— just make it stop 215
— rationalisation 213–214
— shock 213
— market (*see* market crash)
— matters 237–240
— mistakes investors
— consuming fear 229–231
— selling to 'stop the bleeding' 227–228
— stopping contributions 228–229
— opportunity 218–222
— rule 235–236
— subtle shift 236–237
credit card 137
credit conditions 109
Credit Suisse 46
cryptocurrency 106

'crypto' ETFs 165
culture trading 70
current savings rate 3

daily investment 307-308
#5DayInvestorChallenge 321
DCF analysis *see* discounted cash flow (DCF) analysis
debit card 137
debt 113–114
decentralised systems 106
defensive assets *see* bonds and cash
democratic capitalism 170–172
demographic shifts 109, 110
derivative instruments 169
Dick Smith 194
digital scarcity 106
digitisation 111
discounted cash flow (DCF) analysis 182
discretionary spending 128, 139
diversification 82, 85, 91, 104, 108, 112, 193–198
dividend franking 256–257
dividend yields 289
dollar-cost averaging 82, 91, 108, 151–154, 191–193, 225
dollar investment 272
dot. com 209, 210
Drucker, Peter 59
dud stock 188
Duke, Annie 304

economic calendar 307-309
economic forecasts 85
economic opportunities and constraints, wealth 109–112
EFTPOS card 145, 148
emergency fund 85
emotional durability 92
emotional tolerance 87
enduring competitive advantage 178
envy 33, 329
ETFs *see* exchange traded funds (ETFs)
excessive leverage avoidance 85
exchange traded funds (ETFs) 35, 112, 320
— active *vs.* passive investing 162
— Bogle 165–166
— definition 160
— double-leveraged 'bear' 163
— finance industry 158
— index 161
— investment services 160
— managed funds 158, 250–252
— selling 165
— Vanguard's index-based 160

Facebook Marketplace 202
fear 31–32
fees and taxes
— costs 246–248
— brokerage and churn 253–254
— managed funds and ETFs 250–252
— superannuation 249–250
— for investors
— CGT 255–256
— dividend franking 256–257
— minimise tax 257-259
— percentage point 243–245
financial choice 121, 139
financial confession 123
financial decisions 121
financial fitness 137–139
financial freedom 139
financial independence 119
financial institutions 208
financial instruments 100
financial life preparation 87
financial management 136
financial media 303
Ford Foundation 34
'4 per cent rule,' retirement 295

franked dividends 113
franking credit 256, 257
franking credit balance 256
fund 132–134, 158
funding risks 96
fund managers 251

gambling 18
#getabetterrate 127–132
'get-rich-quick' scheme 32
Global Financial Crisis (GFC) 51, 78, 79, 208, 210, 211, 218, 227, 291, 292
good investors 36
 —habits of 302–306
'good retirement' 296
Google 130
'Gotrocks' 251, 252
government policies 125
Graham, Ben 114
greed 32–33

health check 249
hedge fund 276
hedonic treadmill 269–273
Heller, Joseph 275
'Helpers' 252, 260–261
high-quality bonds 105
HIH Insurance 194
Housel, Morgan 2, 80, 218
housing market risks 96

IGA 179
inaction, risk 83
income-protection insurance 91
index-based ETFs 161–163
index fund 159, 160
inflation 83, 110, 121
inflation-adjusted returns 284
infrastructure development 110
infrastructure spending 109
initial public offering (IPO) 72
innovation stack 11–12
Instagram 129
insurance 90–92
insurance companies 131
insurance premiums 91
investing calendar 307–309
invest in retirement 87
investment
 —boredom 33–34
 —boredom virtue 69–70
 —business 61–62
 —of control 67–68
 —culture strategy 70–71
 —daily 307–308
 —discipline 323–328
 —dollar 272
 —envy 33
 —evolution 310–311
 —fear 31–32
 —greed 32–33
 —ideas 324
 —importance 2
 —long-term mindset 62–63
 —overconfidence 34–36
 —patience 321–323
 —profit 1, 71–74
 —quarterly 308
 —regular 265
 —secret 317
 —shares 60–61
 —simplicity 320–321
 —smart, rich or early to 19–20
 —speculation 64–65
 —support 311–313
 —temperament IQ 36–40
 —trading 63–64
 —under-confidence 34–36
 —weekly 308
 —works 6–10
 —yearly 309
investment account 145, 146, 148, 149
investor 190, 191, 194
IPO *see* initial public offering (IPO)

Jobs, Steve 59

Keep Investing Simple, Stupid (KISS)
—Aesop fables 149–151
—bank account 148
—brokerage account 147–149
—dollar-cost averaging 151–154
—how long you invest for 142
—how much you invest 142
—investment account 145, 146, 148, 149
—'Oh, shit' account 145, 146, 148
—Pareto Principle 154–155
—pre-commitment 145, 146, 154
—work, save, invest 143–145
—your return rate 142
KISS *see* Keep Investing Simple, Stupid (KISS)
Kodak 181, 186

labour market dynamics 110
legacy 313–314
lending capital 105
leverage 101
Leyland, Mal 288
lifestyle inflation 127, 269–273
lifetime rule 22
liquidation 83
literal (and metaphorical) insurance 90–92
local supply dynamics 109
longevity risk 284
long-term accumulators 88
Long-Term Capital Management (LTCM) 38–39
long-term compound returns 43
long-term goals 119
long-term investment 62–63
long-term investors 23, 68
long-term returns 88
long-term stock market returns 94
long-term sustainability 87
long-term wealth creation 99
loyalty tax 132
LTCM *see* Long-Term Capital Management (LTCM)

managed funds 158, 250–252
Mann, Bill 172
market crash 31–32
—market falls 10 per cent 232
—market falls 20 per cent 232–233
—market falls 30 per cent 233–234
—market falls 40 to 50 per cent 234–235
market downturn 286
Mastercard 165
media's role, money 22–23
Microsoft 178
moats 177–178
money beliefs 16–17
money control 263, 265, 277
—Buffettism 266
—hedonic treadmill 269–273
—power of control 276–278
—stewardship 273–274
money myths
—Australian psyche 24
—discomfort 23–24
—gambling 18
—lifetime rule 22
—media's role in 22–23
—money beliefs 16–17
—property safety, shares 18–19
—share market 15
—smart, rich or early to invest 19–20
—story 25
money stress 265
mortgage debt 136
mortgage interest 44
Motley Fool Money 312

Munger, Charlie 33, 325, 329
mutual fund 158

NASDAQ 209
negative compounding 246
Netflix 182
network effects 111
non-negotiable expense 119

'oh, shit' fund 132–134
One.Tel 194
opportunity 218–222
opportunity cost 120, 123
overconfidence investors 34–36

Pareto Principle 154–155
passive investing 161
PayPal 137
Pearler 147
pension phase 285
percentage point 243–245
permanent loss of capital 83
portfolio at retirement 89
portfolio income 287, 292
power of money control 276–278
preparation, risk 85–87
price discovery 161
productive asset 60
productivity gains 110
product manufacturers 162
profit, investment 1, 61, 71–74
property 100–102
— safety and shares 18–19
public markets 111

quality businesses 91
quality of life, retirement 83, 84
quarterly investment 308

reasonable price 202
regret minimisation framework 121, 128
regular investment 265
reinvesting dividends 54
rental income 101
residential property ecosystem 109
resilience 93, 118
resilient investors 91
retirement
— accumulation mode 286–290
— advice in 297–299
— '4 per cent rule' 295
— goal of 296
— income 287
— planning 293–296
— risk 284
— saving 15
— volatility management 290–293
return of principal 105
returns on property 101
risk
— Australian market 79
— bankruptcy 79
— banks 79
— behavioural mistakes 83
— COVID 79–81
— diversification 82, 95–96
— dollar-cost averaging 82
— erosion 83, 84
— governments 79
— inaction 83
— literal (and metaphorical) insurance 90–92
— pattern recognition 84
— permanent loss of capital 83
— planning 92–93
— poor decisions 78
— portfolios 79
— pre-COVID 81
— preparation 85–87
— risk tolerance *vs.* risk capacity 87–88
— slow cost of inaction 88–89
— volatility 80–88, 91, 93–95
risk capacity 87
risk-management system 92, 93

risk mitigation 93
risk of permanent capital loss 93
risk tolerance 87
Roberts, Julia 257
Rule of 72, 51–52, 278, 279

scalability and consistency, 112–113
secret retirement portfolio 297
self control, money 263
self-defence mechanism 124
selling
— company's future 201
— reasonable price 202
— shares 203
sensible position sizing 85
sequence risk 88
shareholders 104, 175–177
share market 15, 109
share prices 190–191, 199, 200
shares 102–104, 108–109
Sharesies 147
shares, investment 60–61
— in Amazon 71–74
Siegel, Laurence 34
simple interest 44–46
skilled property investor 109
slow cost of inaction 88–89
small amount investment 85
smart investors 83
smart money 318
social media 29, 321
software scalability 111
S&P 500, 161, 162, 218
speculation 64–65, 69
speculative momentum 109
Star Trek 189
stewardship money 273–274
stock market 10, 169, 170
— returns 7
stock market long-term average return 124
stock market predictions 85
stock split 71
structural undersupply 110
structural weakness, risk 83
successful investors 318
superannuation 125, 249–250, 284, 297
superannuation funds 318
sustainability, long-term 87

tax 68
— CGT 255–256
— dividend franking 256–257
— implications 203
— minimise tax 257–259
tax efficiency 113
technological innovation 106
Telstra 193
temperament IQ 36–40
temperament test 2
term deposits 105
Tesla's shares 200
threat management 93
Toyoda, Sakichi 5
Toyota 4–5
trading investment 63–64, 70
transaction costs 102
Tyson, Mike 208

Uber 193
unavoidable expenses 134
under-confidence investors 34–36
university debt 136
urban concentration 110
US stock market 11

Vanguard 159, 160
Vanguard Index chart 7–8, 51
Vanguard's 30-year index chart 188–189
Vanguard U.S. Total Market Shares Index ETF 160

Visa 165
volatility 104, 105, 117, 284
volatility management,
  retirement 290–293
volatility, risk 80–88, 91, 93–95
Vonnegut, Kurt 275

Wall Street 303
ways to find money to invest
  127–132
wealth
  —bonds and cash 104–105
    —collectables 107
    —cryptocurrency 106
    —pros and cons 107–108
  —debt 113–114
  —diversification 112
  —economic opportunities and
    constraints 109–112
  —property 100–102
  —scalability and consistency
    112–113
  —shares 102–104, 108–109
  —tax efficiency 113
wealth-building strategy 106
weekly investment 308
Welch, Jack 59
Westpac 203
Wilson, EO 30
Woolies 176, 178, 179, 193
Woolworths 73, 171, 172
work hard 143, 144
work-life balance 3

yearly investment 309

zoning changes 109
Zweig, Jason 34